RELIGION AND SOCIAL CONFLICT

RELIGION AND SOCIAL CONFLICT

Based upon Lectures given at
the Institute of Ethics and Society
at San Francisco Theological Seminary

Edited by
ROBERT LEE
MARTIN E. MARTY

NEW YORK OXFORD UNIVERSITY PRESS 1964

Library of Congress Catalogue Card Number: 64-11231
Printed in the United States of America

About the Contributors

ROBERT LEE

Robert Lee is Margaret S. Dollar Professor of Christian Social Ethics and Director of the Institute of Ethics and Society at San Francisco Theological Seminary. He is the author of several works, including *The Social Sources of Church Unity, Protestant Churches in the Brooklyn Heights, Religion and Leisure in America,* editor of *Cities and Churches,* and has contributed chapters to the following volumes: *Ethics and Bigness, The Church and the Changing Ministry, Masterpieces of Christian Literature, The Challenge to Reunion,* and *Evangelism and Social Issues.*

MARTIN E. MARTY

Martin E. Marty is Associate Editor of *The Christian Century* and is currently teaching Church History at the University of Chicago Divinity School. He has written *The New Shape of American Religion, A Short History of Christianity, The Improper Opinion, The Infidel: Freethought and American Religion, Second Chance for American Protestants,* and has edited *The Place of Bonhoeffer.*

ROBERT A. NISBET

Robert A. Nisbet is Vice Chancellor and Professor of Sociology at the University of California (Riverside). He is author of *The Quest for Community* and *Human Relations in Administration,* co-editor with Robert K. Merton of *Contemporary Social Problems,* and contributor to *Studies in Leadership.*

CHARLES Y. GLOCK

Charles Y. Glock is Director of the Survey Research Center and Professor of Sociology at the University of California (Berkeley). Among his writings are chapters contributed to *Sociology Today, Sociology in the U.S.A., Religion and the Face of America,* and *The City Church: Death or Renewal.*

CHARLES MC COY

Charles McCoy is Professor of Religion in Higher Education at Pacific School of Religion. He has co-authored *Gospel on Campus* and has contributed to *Perspectives on a College Church.*

RALPH LORD ROY

Ralph Lord Roy is Lecturer in Philosophy and Religion at Mills College of Education and Pastor of Grace Methodist Church in New York City. He has written *Apostles of Discord* and *Communism and the Churches.*

SEYMOUR M. LIPSET

Seymour M. Lipset is Professor of Sociology and Director of the Institute of International Studies at the University of California (Berkeley). He is the author of *Agrarian Socialism, Union Democracy, Political Man,* and *The First New Nation,* co-author of *Social Mobility in Industrial Society,* co-editor of *Class, Status, and Power, Decade of Sociology,* and *Culture and Social Character: The Work of David Riesman Reviewed,* and contributor to *Handbook of Social Psychology, Sociology Today,* and *The New American Right.*

BENJAMIN A. REIST

Benjamin A. Reist is Professor of Systematic Theology at San Francisco Theological Seminary. He is a member of the Special Committee on Relations Between Church and State of the General Assembly of the United Presbyterian Church, U.S.A. and has contributed to the Committee's report on *Church and State.*

WILL HERBERG

Will Herberg is Professor of Social Philosophy at Drew University. He is the author of *Judaism and Modern Man* and *Protestant, Catholic and Jew,* editor of *Four Existentialist Theologians* and *The Writings of Martin Buber,* and has contributed to *Religious Perspectives in American Culture.*

JOHN R. BODO

John R. Bodo is Professor of Practical Theology and Chairman of the Department of Practical Theology at San Francisco Theological Seminary. He is author of *The Protestant Clergy and Public Issues.*

Contents

ROBERT LEE
Introduction: Religion and Social Conflict 3

ROBERT A. NISBET
The Impact of Technology on Ethical Decision-Making 9

CHARLES Y. GLOCK
The Role of Deprivation in the Origin and Evolution of Religious Groups 24

CHARLES S. MC COY
The Churches and Protest Movements for Racial Justice 37

RALPH LORD ROY
Conflict from the Communist Left and the Radical Right 55

SEYMOUR M. LIPSET
Religion and Politics in the American Past and Present 69

BENJAMIN A. REIST
Church and State in America: A Theological Inquiry 127

WILL HERBERG
Religious Group Conflict in America 143

JOHN R. BODO
The Pastor and Social Conflict 159

MARTIN E. MARTY
Epilogue: The Nature and Consequences of Social Conflict for Religious Groups 173

RELIGION AND SOCIAL CONFLICT

ROBERT LEE

Introduction: Religion and Social Conflict

Social conflict is a likely guest whenever human beings set up forms of social organization. It would be difficult to conceive of an on-going society in which social conflict is absent. The society without conflict is a dead society. Hence the most peaceful place in the world, in terms of the absence of conflict, is a graveyard. Like it or not, conflict is a reality of human existence and therefore a means of understanding social behavior.

Although social conflict is an ancient and recurring tale in the saga of mankind, it is nonetheless appropriate to think of our own time as an "age of conflict." Daily events remind us vividly that we live in a world wrought by upheaval and revolution. How often we hear it said sagely, if a bit platitudinously, that "these are times of turmoil." Hardly a person exists who is not in some way profoundly influenced by the consequences or the threat of conflict at one or another level: international, national, community, party, inter-group, inner self. Contemporary events have disabused us of such irenic notions as harmony, stability, security. Instead the key ethical words of our day are crisis, tension, dilemma, power struggle, conflict.

Who has not played the children's game "King of the Royal Mountain" during childhood days? Recall that one player sets himself up on a high place and announces his kingship over the territory. The game moves forward as the other players attempt to invade his "mountain," displace the "King," and thereby take over command themselves. If one player is stronger than his competitors or rivals, he usually remains on top enjoying his reign for a long time. Others may scheme and band together to remove him by force. Or some may strive to win the

King's favor, or try to get on his good side, or seek to manipulate power.

While not to be taken too literally, children's games frequently bear close resemblance to adult social situations. In a sense the world is a stage where a grandiose game of "King of the Royal Mountain" is being played — for keeps! And who can help but shudder when he thinks of the cosmic "King of the Royal Mountain" game being acted out by modern statesmen of the world? The game is all the more awesome because we know that we cannot stand on the sidelines or refuse to participate in it. We are both participants and spectators. Social conflict is indeed universal.

By "conflict" we simply mean a struggle for power by contending forces, a clash of views, or a difference of opinion. This inevitable social process frequently involves competition, conquest, or coercion, but it does not always imply violence or revolution. Social strain and stress may induce change in an accommodative manner without recourse to battle or tumult. In dealing with "social conflict" we mean to consider those situations of conflict which emerge from man's group or corporate existence. Obviously the variety of social conflicts is legion. This volume is limited to a discussion of issues that relate to technology, church organization, race, extremist religio-political groups, politics, inter-religious, and inter-institutional sources of conflict. Thus our concern is not with the pecking order of the henhouse or the conquest of man over nature, but with human conflict in the social arena.

When the Swedish social scientist Gunnar Myrdal entitled his monumental study of Negro-white relations *An American Dilemma,* he was pointing to the irrepressible conflict between valuations and goals of a people and their actual practices on the plane of daily existence. Racial tensions, like most other types of social conflict, are ignored or obscured at our own peril.

All too many people, however, court this peril. To many, social conflict is a sign of trouble, something to avoid, to run away from, or to conceal because it is freighted with controversy. The tendency to "pass by on the other side" of social conflict goes hand in hand with a frame of mind that fundamentally distrusts power. Of course, a healthy distrust of power that recognizes its potential abuse is desirable; but when it results in "handwashing" and retreat from political realities, it is simply illusory, a vain flying in the face of the hard facts of life. A flight from power is usually a flight from responsibility.

Of course, as a fundamental social process, conflict may contain the seeds of disruption and disorder; but conflict need not be destructive. Yet seldom is it viewed as a sign of health, as the context for the inbreaking of newness, as the process for initiating and gaining a greater measure of social justice.

Although universal, conflict is not universally bad. There are positive functions served by it. Conflict may be a stimulus for social change. Progressive legislation and struggles for social justice, such as the struggle for women's rights and the right to bargain collectively, are achieved at the price of considerable conflict. It is in keeping with democracy as a dynamic process that social conflict may lead to orderly social change. Without the stimulus of conflict, without pressures for innovation and creativity, social organizations run the risk of ossifying and becoming rigid forms ill-adapted to changing circumstances.

Many areas of our common life, especially inter-racial and inter-religious group relations, provide ample evidence of the fact that social injustice cannot be easily resolved by moral and rational suasion alone, since reason is always to some degree a servant of interest. Hence conflict is an inevitable prerequisite of social solidarity and cannot be erased from the human situation regardless of purity of heart or religious purity.

Conflict, then, is not merely to be feared, but also something to welcome. Surely the cutting edges of a democratic society are at the points of conflict and tension, rather than in those areas where the issues are settled or dormant, where growth is curtailed and social stagnation sets in.

The chapters in this volume grow directly out of the 1962 lectures of the Institute of Ethics and Society at San Francisco Theological Seminary. This series of lectures dealt with the theme "Religion and Social Conflict." Each of the distinguished lecturers was invited to explore a different facet of the theme, and then to revise his remarks for publication.

One of the major purposes of the Institute is to stimulate interdisciplinary dialogue. The contributors to this symposium represent a variety of viewpoints and approaches. Some of the chapters are more empirically-minded or data-oriented than others. Similarly, some of the chapters have a theoretical interest, while others display a practical bent. Although the reader is called upon to shift intellectual gears as he journeys through the book, his discovery of important vignettes along the way in each of the chapters should justify the effort. No attempt is here made to create a false uniformity among the lecturers.

Nevertheless, each of the essays illumines our common theme:

Robert A. Nisbet deals with the increased technological complexity of modern society which has induced a proliferation of value conflicts and has left the individual with a lack of focus in discharging his ethical decision-making responsibilities.

Charles Y. Glock discusses the dynamics of religious organizational development and shows how a theory of deprivation accounts for the formation of religious groups.

Charles S. McCoy considers the ambiguous role of the churches in recent protest movements for human dignity and racial justice wherein conflict precipitates social change and produces a greater measure of justice in American society.

Ralph Lord Roy examines the resurgence of radical right and left-wing groups as they impinge upon religious institutions and foment discord and conflict.

Seymour Martin Lipset explores the inter-relation of religion and politics in American history and shows how religious groups and values have played an important role in shaping conflict and consensus in American political life.

Benjamin A. Reist presents a theological essay which provides background considerations for relating Christian faith to contemporary issues of conflict between church and state.

Will Herberg analyzes the sources of conflict and tension in the tripartite system of Protestant-Catholic-Jew, which is viewed in the context of American pluralism.

John R. Bodo draws out implications for clergymen as he points out the pastor's responsibility in the presence of social conflict, the strictures which inhibit his functioning as a prophetic leader, and guidelines by which a pastor can equip himself for active leadership in social conflict.

Martin E. Marty weaves together the various threads of our discussion in a concluding Epilogue which points up the significance of social conflict for religious groups.

It is true that the age-old concern of social conflict has been studied from many perspectives. The distinctiveness of this volume, however, is its treatment of conflict in relation to religious institutions. Contrary to popular misconceptions, conflict is no stranger in the household of faith. Although there is a tendency to idealize the church as a "Divine Community," one cannot overlook the fact that Jesus said, "I came to bring not peace but a sword" (Mt. 10:34), or that the Pauline Epistles are replete with situations fraught with actual or potential conflict. Conflict and controversy were a normal part of the life of the early church. Indeed, the apostle Paul seemed to have thrived on conflict and was a trouble shooter par excellence. Those who rally around the doctrinal creeds of the church often forget that many of these creeds were forged at the cost of considerable bloodshed and dissension.

This book makes no attempt to exhaust the subject, although the chapters touch upon many of the contemporary concerns and persistent problems of social conflict. There is here no extended discussion of conflict between gangs, families in conflict, labor-management disputes, nations warring against nations. Nor are these pages written with the intention of resolving social conflicts. It is too easy and even perhaps dishonest to think that the church is the solvent of social conflict. In a mood of confession we know that the church is often part of the problem and not merely the cure. Too often when the church is confronted by conflicting communities of interest, it is embarrassed by the differences of opinion and beats a hasty retreat to the lofty places where eternal verities may be proclaimed. The church as an institution lends itself to the divisions of class, race, political, and inter-group strife. It is itself the source of considerable social conflict. We are not concerned with any easy resolution of conflict through this or that panacea.

Our task in these chapters is to ask the goading questions and to seek clarity and understanding of the ways in which social conflict as a pervasive phenomenon of human existence impinges upon the institutional life of religion. We seek to take the measure of the problem by examining various arenas of religion and social conflict. We acknowledge only that we cannot shun human conflict, that it is part of the life of decision-making and of faith-bearing, and that conflict may be the matrix in which God's grace is expressed.

The quest for clarity and understanding about the role of religion in relation to social conflict is essential if we are to break through the old roadblocks of resistance to pursue new avenues of thought. It is high time we pay heed to the alarm sounded so clearly by the late C. Wright Mills: "If you do not specify and confront real issues, what you do will surely obscure them. If you do not alarm anyone morally, you will yourself remain morally asleep. If you do not embody controversy, what you say will be an acceptance of the drift to the coming human hell." We trust that the discussion begun on these pages will open the way to greater moral sensitivity and social responsibility on the part of those who find themselves confronted by conflict situations. For those not so confronted, we trust that they will be shaken from their moral drowsiness.

The editors wish to express deep gratitude to the Board of Christian Education and its Office of Church and Society of the United Presbyterian Church, U.S.A., whose initial grant made possible the establishment of the Institute of Ethics and Society at San Francisco Theological Seminary; to the contributors to this volume who graciously agreed to deliver papers in stimulating seminar sessions and then willingly rewrote their presentations; to William G. Doty and Dieter Hessel, research assistants of the Institute, for their helpful services; and to members of the Seminary faculty committee for the Institute: Roy Fairchild (chairman), John Bodo, Benjamin Reist, and Theodore A. Gill.

ROBERT A. NISBET

The Impact of Technology on Ethical Decision-Making

Technology, like any other force, has moral consequences only when it becomes a part of the effective normative environment. Considered solely in its mechanical aspects, technology is no more capable than the raw, physical environment of directly affecting cultural and moral consciousness. It may have a broadening or limiting effect on economic and social possibilities — and therewith on ethical alternatives — but it will not become a significant ethical force until it is involved in a pattern of social meanings central to society.

This is, I think, the basic and lasting point that Max Weber made in his critique of Marx's account of the origins of capitalism in the West. Despite certain inadequacies in Weber's application of the point to the causal relation between puritanism and capitalism, the essence of his value theory, applied to historical change, can scarcely be challenged. Only when technology becomes institutionalized, only when technology becomes itself a social system, subject to processes common to all social systems, can we discover its impact on ethical decisions.

I THE PLACE OF TECHNOLOGY IN CONTEMPORARY LIFE

There has never been a time since man emerged from the higher primates when he has not been in possession of at least a minimal degree of technology, and so were created the first earthen pot, the spear, and the mortar. Behind the appearance of each of these lay some extraordinary mind, restless and dissatisfied, working in terms of its own and other observations, striving to bring environment within control, to facilitate the business of living. In our own overwhelmingly technological age there is often a danger that we will underestimate the role of technology in other ages. We must not, for it has always been present in one degree or another in human history.

So much is true, yet it must be emphasized that in no other age of history has technology held the central and determining role that it does in our own. Never have so many persons been involved so directly in technological pursuits. At no time in the human past has the technologist-scientist held the crucial role that he does today. Marvel though we may at the ingenious accomplishments of Hellenistic Greece, Imperial Rome, the late Middle Ages, and the Renaissance, they are small indeed by comparison with the works of the modern age.

What philosophy, theology, and art have been in other periods — the major contexts of human creativity — technology is today. Each age produces its own type of hero: soldier, diplomat, theologian, scholar, statesman, or businessman. Today, who would deny that the technologist occupies the hero's niche? Nobel laureates, National Academy members, scientist-administrators, all possess a prestige that makes front page news and carries them to the highest councils of government and society. The time has passed when technology needs to justify itself by its contributions to other spheres of society. Today the ends of technology are sufficient and autonomous.

More important is the fact that in the modern West, for the first time in history, technology has become institutionalized. An institution is a way of behavior, common to a large number of persons in a society. Handed down from generation to generation, it is a generally recognized solution to a recognized problem. In every relevant respect, technology today is as fully and distinguishably an institution as law, religion, or kinship. It is neither more nor less "material" than other institutions. There is no more reason for limiting technology, as a concept, to the machines and tools it employs than there is for limiting the family to housing, law to court rooms, or religion to church buildings.

What is central to technology is the application of rational principles to the control or re-ordering of space, matter, and human beings. We are prone to think of technology in its physical manifestations — skyscrapers, lawn mowers, nuclear bombs — but technology represents social things as well — organizations and processes concerned with human ends. There is as much technology in a school of business administration or education as there is in a school of engineering. The one is as concerned as the other with the rational and calculated achievement of ends which, more and more in our society, are autonomous and self-justifying ends.

This last point may require brief justification. Surely, it will be said, the ends of technology are subordinate to those of economy, religion, politics, and war — all older and more accepted areas of human purpose. This was true, once, but it is no longer true. The conquest of space, the control of physical environment, the mastery of organization, are objectives today fully as distinct as any to be found in the classic areas of statecraft, war, and business.

Innumerable foundations, institutes, vast research and development laboratories, not to mention huge budgets for technological development, all attest to the autonomy as well as prestige of technology. Admittedly, military defense is the context of a great deal of present-day technology, but I would argue that technological imperatives have attained a degree of primacy not likely to be offset by any changes in the international scene.

Modern technology has its own characteristic structures, its built-in drives, its moral codes, its dedicated servants (as hierarchically ordered and motivated as any to be found in church or state), even its own mystique. Because technology serves an autonomous set of values in our society, and because it is itself a clear pattern of functions and authorities, it inevitably comes into moral conflict with other institutions in society. The tension that Thorstein Veblen was able to discern a half-century ago between the engineer and the price system has become a not uncommon tension between technology and other areas of society — political, esthetic, religious, as well as economic.

Until perhaps a century ago, technology was only an instrumental value. Its significance came from the institution it served. Throughout much of the modern era, especially in the nineteenth century, this significance was economic. Hence the still almost synonymous use of the words "industrial" and "technological."

But before industry, technology served the needs of war. The word engineer was indeed so closely identified with military activities from the fifteenth century on that it became necessary in the late eighteenth century to prefix it by the word "civil" in order to specify a non-military orientation. But quite apart from its earlier ancillary function in society, technology is today an autonomous pattern of ends, functions, authorities, and allegiances.

From the point of view of the history of social institutions, there is nothing extraordinary in this process of "autonomization." We can see it in the histories of religion, politics, and education. In the early Roman Republic, religion, far from being a separate institution, was simply one function of the family. The chief end of religion under the *patria potestas* was that of welding the family into a unity, not merely in space but in time. But as we know, religion became, at a later period in Rome, a separate and autonomous institution; and in its Christian form, a powerful rival to both family and state.

The same transition may be seen in economic processes. In many cultures, economics is subordinate to some other institution: family, religion, or community. It is ethnocentric to assume, as did the classical economists in the nineteenth century, that economic ends and processes are everywhere sovereign and independent. In the West, since approximately the Enlightenment, economic institutions have been autonomous, though this situation shows signs in our own age of undergoing significant change.

As an institution, technology has today, then, its own function: the rational control of man, space, and matter — and its own governing values. It is no stretch of meaning, I suggest, to hold that technology has sacred overtones in the minds of many. To contravene the values of technology in favor of, say, nationalism or economic profits can seem as impious to a scientist today as contravention or religious ends, in the name of economic gain, seemed to a medieval theologian.

II ETHICS AND SOCIAL CONFLICT

Because technology in our society is an institution and because ethical decisions are closely related to what happens to institutions, it is important at this point to examine briefly the character of institutional change. It is my contention that conflict is the essence of such change. And it is in circumstances of institutional change that ethical values become most luminous.

Too often institutions are conceived as structures endowed with imminent tendencies toward change. They are regarded much as the biologist regards organic life — as something inherent in growth and development, with new phases arising directly and inexorably out of the old. For a long time this organic analogy has plagued Western social thought and confused the study of change in society.

Institutions are complexes of functions, authorities, and values, and apart from their interaction with other institutions — competitive and conflicting interaction — there is no reason to suppose that significant change in any one of them takes place.

In all institutional behavior there is a powerful tendency toward integration and conformity, resulting from the implicit striving of each institution for the total allegiance of its members. What Frank Tannenbaum has written along this line is instructive:

Each institution in its own inner logic tends to be all-embracing, laying claim to the entire man, and showing an impelling tendency to assume all responsibility in society . . . Institutional friction and instability are, therefore, the normal state of society, and the hope of peace and quietude is an idle dream. Completion, imbalance, and friction are not merely continuous phenomena in society, but in fact, are evidences of vitality and "normality." [1]

Conflict and competition in the institutional scene are inevitably reflected in the minds and moral aspirations of the persons concerned. Institutional conflict is matched by the conflict of human loyalties. Conflict of this type can sometimes be drastic and difficult, as we know from the frequently agonizing experiences of immigrants involved in the transplanting of mores and life-patterns from one culture to another. Much of American social history is made up of this transplanting and with it there has been frequent conflict of institutional and moral loyalties. Out of such conflicts, to be sure, have come some of the great intellectual and moral achievements of American civilization, but out of them have also come some of our bitterest social and moral problems.

In the orthodox, rationalist tradition, little attention was paid to change considered as crisis and to the persisting conflicts of values among institutions of the same society. The gospel of homogeneity and adjustment held the field. That a plurality of institutions could exert powerful and possibly irreconcilable conflicts of allegiance upon individuals was not often envisaged by those who saw change as a smooth and orderly process.

Nevertheless the conflict is there, and it is a fact of the highest significance in history. Sometimes this conflict is passive, awakening only vague sensations of tension. Elements of persistence and conformity in the individual may reduce the effects of conflict on his allegiances. At other times it may be fierce and overt, reflected in widespread mass upheaval and in the central problems of moral philosophies.

Such conflicts, small and large, do not, as the progressive rationalist has thought, resolve themselves inevitably into systems of new coherence and order — either in the individual consciousness or in the overt relationships of major institutions. Where they are matters of crucial allegiance — as with respect to family, church, ethnic group, and state — they may remain for centuries, now relatively passive, now evocative and fiercely antagonistic.[2]

Ethical history is fundamentally a history of the conflict of social loyalties. How else do we account for the history of moral values in ancient Athens except in terms of the struggle between the ancient kinship group and the new city-state? The fifth century B.C. was a time of the breaking up of ancient kinship structures and the gradual emergence of the individual as ethical man, as political man. The reforms of Cleisthenes a century earlier had led to the reduced political position of tribe and clan, but the moral appeal of these groups and their implicit and ancient norms remained binding for the Athenian.

It was in the gradual diminution of kinship norms and the simultaneous rise of the free individual and the popular state that the great moral issues of the age found their setting. Of all ethical problems the greatest was individual responsibility. This is the recurrent theme of the dramas of Aeschylus, Sophocles, and Euripedes. How is guilt to be assigned? To the individual, as the new legal polity suggested? Or collectively — to family and clan — as ancient tradition had it? This was the great conflict in the fifth century, and it would be difficult to understand either the moral philosophers or the dramatists apart from it.[3]

In Roman civilization we see the conflict between the family and the military power, between *patria potestas* and *imperium*. In political terms it is a conflict for power over individuals and property. In social terms it is a conflict of statuses — the status of the son under kinship authority and the status of the son as soldier under the *imperium*.

Ethically, the conflict is to be seen in the problem of both where guilt lies — in family or in the individual — and where the sanctions for violation of norms lie — in the family or in the state. The conflict reached its zenith in the final century of the Republic, a period of pandemic disorganization, and was resolved, legally at least, by Augustus' far-reaching decrees on morals which for once and all, put moral sanctions in the hands of the state.

But the diminution of the moral authority of the family was one of the factors leading to the attractiveness of Christianity to Roman masses. By the second century, the struggle between church and state characterized the ethical history of Rome, which was not moderated until Constantine's conversion.[4]

In various ways the conflict of institutions continued in the periods that followed in the West. In the early Middle Ages, at a time when the church sought to Christianize the Teutons, the struggle was between church and clan. It was a conflict between two inner ethical orders — the moral order of the family and the moral order of the church.

Expressed most concretely in such matters as rights over baptism, marriage, and disposition of the dead, the struggle manifested itself in a host of ways, all related to functions and authority within each institution, and to the loyalties which these two institutions were able to attract. In the process of its eventual victory over kinship, the church took on many of the attributes of an enlarged family.[5]

The triumph of the church in matters of individual conduct was short-lived, for, as we know, by the thirteenth century political power began to challenge religious power. Here was perhaps the most fundamental and implicative conflict in the whole history of the West. At first it looked as though the church would win — consider the monumental significance of Canossa. In the long run, however, the centralizing, nationalizing tendencies of the state could not be stayed. Again we see, as we did in Athens, the simultaneous emergence of the individual and the state, each freed, increasingly, from the legal and moral bonds of medieval traditionalism.

In the twentieth century such conflicts continue, and are to be seen in court cases involving the competing claims of church or family against state in such matters as flag observances in the schools, released time for worship, military service, and other matters. On a vaster and profounder scale they are to be seen in countries where totalitarianism has taken command; here the old conflict between the state and social groups is converted from something latent or intermittent to something that is at the very heart of freedom and morality. The struggle between family and state, between church and state, between trade union and state was vivid in the early days of National Socialism in Germany. It was only when the Nazi state destroyed or completely fettered these competing groups that its own power could be called totalitarian.

So, too, in the non-Western societies throughout the twentieth century, do we see institutional conflict that is deeply moral and spiritual in result. Sidney Nettleton Fisher has concretely expressed this conflict as it appears in the Near East:

> At the heart of the tension is the clash of family and national loyalties. The family or the clan has been the basic unit of Near Eastern society for millennia: The ecumenical context in which these units have been more or less loosely welded together has been the religious commune to which they gave allegiance and in which they cooperated for larger ends. Yet today the nation state and militant nationalism are thrust between these two, claiming to overarch, if not indeed to supersede them. There emerge tensions and fears, hesitation and irresolution on the part of individuals and groups who suspect, generally unconsciously, their ancient values are threatened, and therefore they draw back from wholehearted allegiance to the nation, at least to the nation's claimant representative. Just when the state or government wishes and needs to prevent a strong front against some opposition or threat, so often a politician's or statesman's family and communal ties will interfere and hopelessly tangle the web of decision.[6]

The conflict between Western and non-Western cultures is, as A. J. Toynbee has written, the single most important fact of the twentieth century. In whatever form it first expresses itself, political, economic, or technological, it becomes inevitably moral and spiritual: it becomes a tension of ethical norms and judgments.

Normative loyalties tend to become directed toward the spheres which have the greatest significance in maintaining life and integrative social meanings. Although never a crude relationship, there is a close relationship between the spiritual appeal of symbols and the extent to which symbols are rooted in the effective social community.

As Susanne Langer has written:

> The mind, like other organs, can draw its sustenance only from the surrounding world; our metaphysical symbols must spring from reality. Such adaptation always requires time, habit, tradition, and an intimate knowledge of a way of life. If now the field of our unconscious symbolic orientation is suddenly plowed up by tremendous changes in the external world and in the social order, we lose our hold, our convictions, and therewith our effectual purposes.[7]

This plainly is what is happening to large parts of the non-Western world at the present time, and the results are frequently to be seen in cultural disorganization and moral confusion. The wresting of economic significance from clans or social classes; the withdrawal of political power from the tribe; the introduction of a new administrative or technological system in a native area; all of this can have deep moral consequences.

III TECHNOLOGICAL PROCESSES AND ETHICAL DECISION-MAKING

Let us return to technology and to some of the specific forms of its impact on society and ethics. In the foregoing pages I have emphasized two major points: 1. Technology will significantly affect human behavior only as it ceases to be something external and becomes internalized in a culture, a recognized part of norms and institutions. 2. Conflict, in one degree or another, is the essence of social change, and ethical conflicts are themselves manifestations of institutional struggle for functional dominance and superiority.

There is an abundant literature in history, anthropology, and sociology documenting the impact of technology on culture and social institutions. As one surveys this literature, there are four distinguishable processes, it seems to me, which represent the common and even predictable effects of technology. Naturally, they do not work alone. Technology never enters a culture, or makes its rise within a culture, apart from political and economic currents which provide contexts. Nevertheless, the technological processes are distinguishable and important. They are: abstraction, generalization, individuation, and rationalization.

1. The first of these I choose to call *abstraction*. I mean by this the separation of moral values from the contexts of immediacy and concreteness that they tend to have in traditional, pre-technological society. The norms of science and technology are abstract and impersonal, and their net effect, over a period of time, can be to make other values seem less urgent, less sacred in character, and more like propositions of utility. Moral behavior is concrete and personal; it is tied to sharply defined symbols in the community which draw their own efficacy from essentially non-rational sources. The more abstract and remote, the more impersonal and utilitarian these symbols become, the less urgency they have to individuals.

There is also the key role in traditional society of *social membership*. Norms arise from and are inseparable from the close groups in which individuals have membership. It is never man as man, but man as member of clan, tribe, guild, or class that is important. The ethical values are properties of these close and influential groups.

In the kind of society that technology helps create, however, human identity does not rest exclusively on the small and personal type of association. It tends increasingly to come from qualities which the individual holds in common with large numbers of other persons whom he never sees or knows, persons who fall into abstract categories.

Ostrogorski has described this vividly in his treatment of the impact of technology on modern Europe.

> In proportion as the new conditions of existence enlarged the social horizon in the sphere of life, just as it expanded by means of thought, the process of abstraction extended to all social relations The rapid growth of large towns destroyed the old neighborly intercourse, or at all events, its intimate character. The extension of markets stripped buyers and sellers of their concrete individuality, and resolved them into the general categories of *tradesmen* and *customers*. Railways, by bringing together for half an hour men who saw each other for the first and perhaps the last time, reduced them to the general notion of *travelers,* all placed on an equal footing by uniform tickets, a piece of pasteboard printed wholesale for all present and future travelers. In great industrial enterprises creative energy and active will associated in the form of *shares,* negotiable securities, transferable to an infinite series of potential entities existing only as *shareholders*. Even the feelings which take their rise in the depths of the soul, such as the love of one's neighbor and pity, were obliged, when projected over a larger area to conform to abstract notions; the familiar picture of the wretched Jim or Tom who had been the regular recipient of relief, gave place to the idea of the poor man, the poorer classes.[8]

The Hammonds, writing with particular reference to the impact of technology on England in the nineteenth century, could see the machine in the guise of a new rhythm and tempo of life. Gone was the rhythm of the rural countryside, based upon the direct experience of the passing of the seasons, the rising and setting of the sun, the planting and harvesting of the crops. In its place now was the rhythm of the machine, the never-ending turning of the wheels and gears. Behind the rhythm represented by the factory bell and the overseer, the precise division of the day into units of wages-time, and the machine itself, there lay, as the Hammonds emphasized, the great, impersonal system within which human beings congregated not as members of a moral community but as so many abstract units of energy and production, rationally organized for specific, mechanical purposes.[9]

2. Closely related to abstraction is a second process, *generalization.* Again it is illuminating to quote Ostrogorski.

Confined hitherto to the narrow range of his social circle, it (the moral sentiment) now spread further and further beyond these limits; the tribunal of public opinion sat in judgment wherever cognizance could be taken of the individual's conduct; at the bar of his conscience man became responsible not only to his own society in the restricted sense of the word, but to society in general, to his country, to the nation, even to humanity. Thus a readjustment of forces took place in man's social existence between the particular which constituted nearly all his being and the general which occupied but a small portion of it. Destined as he is by his finite and limited frame to cling to the concrete and the particular as his starting point and strongest support, man nevertheless launched on all sides into the general, with the result that henceforth his social relations were bound to be guided not so much by sentiment, which expresses the perception of the particular, as by general principles, less intense in their nature perhaps, but sufficiently comprehensive to take in the shifting multitudes of which the abstract social groups were henceforth composed, groups continually subject to expansion by reason of their continual motion.[10]

In one of the most illuminating chapters of his *Democracy in America,* Tocqueville has shown how the concept of honor, beginning as a fundamental value of one class alone, the nobility, and drawing its sustenance from feudal contexts of authority, becomes steadily more general in modern times. Tocqueville concludes:

When ranks are comingled and privileges abolished, the men of whom a nation is composed being once more equal and alike, their interests and wants become identical, and all the peculiar notions which each caste styled honor successively disappear. The notion of honor no longer proceeds from any other source than the wants peculiar to the nation at large, and it denotes the individual character of that nation to the world . . . As honor among democratic nations is imperfectly defined, its influence is of course less powerful; for it is difficult to apply with certainty and firmness a law that is not distinctly known.[11]

What Tocqueville writes of honor is not less true of a large number of other values — loyalty, integrity, guilt and innocence, patriotism, piety. In each instance we are dealing with a norm that arose in the first instance within clear and decisive contexts. Generally, they were the contexts of small association. Morality, as we have noted, was indistinguishable from the inner order of clan, village, or class. It was as concrete as it was associative, and because it was concrete it had meaning in the daily lives of individuals.

In the same way that the development of the political community has meant the generalization and abstraction of all the local and particularized authorities which traditional society abounded in, so the spread of technology has meant the generalization and abstraction of the various norms which, in earlier times, had been limited to small communities. The same technology which made possible mass society made possible mass norms — another way of referring to generalization and abstraction.

3. A third process to be noted is *individuation.* Technology is one of the modern forces that have had a frequently fragmenting and dissolving effect upon traditional communities. Because technology is itself a social system, with a place in it for the individual conceived in a new status, it has an individualizing effect upon the older communities. By virtue of the abstract and impersonal character of the technological system, the individual is able to perceive himself more vividly as a separate being rather than as an organic member of a community. The late G. P. Adams wrote:

It is not strange that the self discovery and self consciousness of the individual should have steadily mounted higher as the environment of the individuals more and more takes on the form of an impersonal, causal, and mechanical structure. For the mobility and freedom of the individual can be won only as he becomes detached from his world; his world becomes separated from him only when organized and defined in objective and impersonal terms.[12]

Such sociologists as Tönnies, Simmel, Durkheim, and Weber have all emphasized the processes of modern history that have led to a mechanization and atomization of the primary social relationships. No doubt it is easy to exaggerate this, and we cannot forget that technology has synthesized even as it has fragmented, but it remains true that the very impersonality and abstractness of technology formed a background against which the individual could seem more real than the primary and communal ties from which he was being separated.

The rationalist image of society in this age powerfully supported the individualizing tendencies of the new technology. In man alone were now placed virtues and stabilities that had earlier developed within associations. How else, rationalists asked, could the moral imperatives of emancipation be fulfilled except by the premise of man's separateness and his autonomy? The demands of freedom appeared to be in the direction of the release of large numbers of individuals from the statuses and identities that had been created for them by history. A free society would be one in which individuals were morally and socially as well as politically free, free from ancient traditions and corporate groups. Order in society would be the product of a natural equilibrium of economic and political forces, just as order in technology itself is the result of an equilibrium of levers and gears.

4. To these three processes I would add one more that seems to me deeply embedded in the impact of technology on society: *rationalization.*[13] Here I am referring to the widespread tendency throughout modern society to bring under the formal rules of hierarchical administration areas of thought and behavior which have been traditionally areas of informal and individual decision-making. Rationalization of decision-making is plainly a deep tendency in education and religion as well as in industry and the state.

The very progress of modern administrative techniques has created a problem in the maintenance and nurture of individual thought and action. In the same way that the technological revolution reduced man's significance through the transfer of, first, strength, then skill, and finally thought itself, to the machine, it now appears to have a fourth phase: one in which individual decision is being transferred to the machine — conceived as scientific and channeled organization. By its very triumph of rationality, scientific administration has reduced much of the elbow room, much of the intellectual and moral friction which ethical individuality must have if it is to flourish.

In one of his essays, the distinguished physicist, P. W. Bridgmen, now retired, tells us that it becomes steadily more difficult for him to conceive the emergence of great *individual* physicists in our age of science, simply because of the increasing involvement of so much scientific research in the costly and elaborate machinery of administrative organization. Such administration, and all that it implies, can too often take away the informal and challenging atmosphere that creative people need.

Ethical decision-making is, from one point of view, a form of creativity, and it is no exaggeration to suggest that it may suffer in related ways. Quite apart from the time-consuming complexity of much administration, it can contain a kind of tyranny. The tyranny consists of tiny rules governing action and decision; of innumerable channels and levels; of committees and all the other types of rational administration which, however effective they may be from a purely technical point of view, powerfully affect the ethical role of the individual. Ethical decision-making, like leadership, requires a certain degree of autonomy from the rules, an opportunity for occasional error and an understanding that the individual himself, not the organization, bears responsibility.

Decision-making, as Robert Presthus has recently written, becomes vague and impersonal in the big organization, the instrument of an anonymous, fragmented intelligence.

> Each decision is the result of various technical and personal considerations, the sum of the contributions of the sum of everyone involved in the deciding process. This diffusion means that "everyone" (i.e., no one) is responsible. In extreme cases the condition may lead to arbitrary and immoral behavior, particularly when compounded by intense personal identification with the state, the party, the church, or the "organization." In every case, the probabilities that the organization may act unjustly are increased by the weakening of individual responsibility. Only "the system" is responsible.[14]

In a brilliant article, Harold Rosenberg has recently dealt with the Eichmann trial in these terms. Mr. Rosenberg points out that Eichmann's defense was based almost entirely on a proposition that he knew could not help but have appeal to large numbers of persons in our society. Basically, this defense rested on his transference of guilt from himself, as an individual, to a soulless, impersonal organization within which he was but a simple cog. Guilt, as we have known the concept throughout most of history, is individual, and thereby requires a sense of the self. But if the self is obliterated, if the organization takes command, reducing individuals to roles without responsibility, how can there be guilt? The very essence of the Nazi system was the blurring and extinguishing of the sense of the self. And as Eichmann shrewdly realized, this has become a pervading characteristic of the modern technological world.

> Eichmann's defense was designed to appeal to the universal appreciation of the plight of the organization man. Who cannot grasp that one in the middle of a chain of command — a link in the sausage — simply passes down orders he receives from above, without having the power to alter their content or to influence their ultimate effect? Everyone in an organization is in a sense

nothing but a traffic officer while the directors at the top reach decisions that reflect a collective mind separate from that of each . . . It is not thinkable to be the dispatcher of human shipments to death factories but by analogy with the clean hands of the office man in charge of shipping fertilizer or veal carcasses, it *is* thinkable.[15]

IV CONCLUSION

We conclude where we began. Technology viewed simply as the machine is powerless to affect human culture or ethics. Only as it becomes institutionalized, only as its ends conflict with and override established norms, does technology become a dislocating and moulding force in society. Technology need not weaken individuality in society — not any more than physical landscape need weaken it. But when its institutionalization reaches the point of reducing the normal conflict of institutions through techniques of abstraction, generalization, and rationalization, it may be regarded as posing a threat to individuality and to ethical decision-making. Technology becomes one of the forces in society whereby the individuality and concreteness of ethical norms — such norms as honor, guilt, loyalty — become tenuous and indistinct.

The making of ethical decisions is always related to conflict of one kind or another: there is a conflict of *institutions* in society or a conflict of *ends* in the individual consciousness. It is unlikely that without the large institutional conflict, any significant inner conflict of ends and meanings could occur. Within the very circumstances which helped liberate individuality from the older traditional types of community, the key problem of the present age, I believe, is that of maintaining individuality of ethical decision-making.

NOTES

1. Frank Tannenbaum, "The Balance of Power in Society," *Political Science Quarterly* (December 1946).
2. See my *The Quest for Community* (New York: Oxford University Press, 1953), Chapter 4.
3. The best treatments of this are Gustave Glotz, *La Solidarité de la famille dans le droit criminel en Grèce* (Paris: A. Fontemoing, 1904) and Louis Gernet, *Droit et société dans la Grèce ancienne* (Paris: Sirey, 1955).
4. I have dealt with this at greater length in an article, "Kinship and Political Power in 1st Century Rome," to appear in 1963 in a volume, *History and Sociology,* edited by Werner Cahnman and Alvin Boskoff [to be published].
5. The best of all treatments of medieval institutions and the conflicts among

them is Edward Jenks, *Law and Politics in the Middle Ages* (New York: Henry Holt, 1898).

6. S. N. Fisher, *Social Forces in the Middle East* (Ithaca: Cornell University Press, 1955), p. 258.
7. Susanne Langer, *Philosophy in a New Key, A Study in the Symbolism of Reason, Rite, and Art* (New York: New American Library, 1948), p. 237.
8. M. Ostrogorski, *Democracy and the Organization of Political Parties* (New York: Macmillan, 1902), Vol. 1, pp. 45ff.
9. J. L. and Barbara Hammond. See esp. *The Town Laborer* (London: Longmans, Green, 1917), *passim.*
10. Ostrogorski, op. cit.
11. Alexis de Tocqueville, *Democracy in America* (New York: Knopf, 1945), Vol. 2, bk. 3, ch. 18.
12. G. P. Adams, *Idealism and the Modern Age* (New Haven: Yale University Press, 1919), p. 35.
13. It was, of course, Max Weber whose writings first identified and documented this process in modern European history.
14. Robert Presthus, *The Organizational Society* (New York: Knopf, 1962), pp. 53–4.
15. Harold Rosenberg, "The Eichmann Trial," *Commentary* (November 1961).

CHARLES Y. GLOCK

The Role of Deprivation in the Origin and Evolution of Religious Groups *

This essay [1] discusses an old problem in the sociology of religion: what accounts for the rise and evolution of religious groups in society? Three aims may be listed:

1. To review briefly what sociologists have previously said concerning the conditions which give rise to new religious groups, with particular attention to that part of existing theory which attributes such formations to class differences in society.
2. To propose a more general theory, based on the concept of *deprivation,* to help explain the origin of religious groups.
3. To suggest how this broader theory can help to account for the directions in which religious groups evolve.

I THE FORMATION OF RELIGIOUS GROUPS: THE "SECT-CHURCH" THEORY

Current thinking about the origin and development of religious groups in Western society has been largely informed by so-called "sect-church" theory. The distinction between church and sect, as formulated in the work of Max Weber [2] and his contemporary, Ernst Troeltsch,[3] was initially an attempt to distinguish types of religious groups and not an effort to discover the conditions under which religious groups originate. Sects were characterized, for example, as being in tension with the world, as having a converted rather than an inherited membership, and as being highly emotional in character. Churches, in contrast, were seen as com-

* This is Publication Number A-15 in the series of the Survey Research Center, University of California, Berkeley.

promising with the world, as having a predominantly inherited membership, and as restrained and ritualistic in their services.

The sect-church distinction was later refined by H. Richard Niebuhr, who postulated a *dynamic inter-relationship* between the two types. In this inter-relationship he saw a way to understand the development of new religious groups.[4] Briefly, the compromising tendencies of the church lead some of its members to feel that the church is no longer faithful to its religious traditions. These dissenting members then break away to form new religious groups. At the outset, these new groups take on a highly sect-like character, eschewing the dominant characteristics of the church they have rejected. They assume an uncompromising posture toward the world, they gainsay a professional clergy, they insist on a conversion experience as a condition for membership, and they adopt a strict and literalistic theology.

Over a period of time, however, the conditions which gave rise to the sect change, and the sect slowly takes on the church-like qualities which it had originally repudiated. Once it has made the transition from sect to church, the religious group then becomes the breeding ground for new sects which proceed anew through the same process.

New sects, according to sect-church theory, recruit their membership primarily from the economically deprived, or as Niebuhr calls them, "the disinherited" classes of society. Their emergence is therefore to be understood as a result not only of religious dissent but of social unrest as well. The theological dissent masks an underlying social protest. The new sect functions, however, to contain the incipient social protest, and then to help eliminate the conditions which produced it.

The containment is accomplished through a process of *derailment.* Sects provide a channel through which their members come to transcend their feelings of deprivation by replacing them with feelings of religious privilege. Sect members no longer compare themselves to others in terms of their relatively lower economic position but in terms of their superior religious status.

Built into the sect ideology is a puritanical ethic which stresses self-discipline. Thrift, frugality, and industry are highly valued. Over time, the ideology helps to elevate sect members to middle-class status which in turn socializes them to middle-class values. Because the economic deprivation itself has been eliminated, feelings of economic deprivation no longer need to be assuaged. As the sect members become accommodated to the larger society, their religious movement proceeds to accommodate itself too. In so doing, it makes the transition from sect to church.

This is an admittedly brief and simplified account of sect-church theory and omits the many refinements that have been made in it over the last decades.[5] However, for our purposes, it conveys the essential points of traditional theory: (1) new religious movements begin by being sect-like in character, (2) they arise by breaking off from church-type bodies, (3) they are rooted in economic deprivation, (4) they gradually transform themselves into churches.

While valid in many cases, this theory falls short of being a general theory of the origin and evolution of religious groups. It overlooks the fact that not all religious groups emerge as sects. Some are churches in their original form. This was true of Reform Judaism in Europe and of Conservative Judaism in America. Most Protestant groups were from their beginnings more like churches than like sects.

Not only may new religious groups emerge in other than sect form, they need not, contrary to the theory, draw their membership primarily from the lower class. The American Ethical Union was clearly a middle-class movement from its inception, as was Unity and probably Christian Science.

The theory also does not take into account religious movements which draw their inspiration from other than the primary religion of the culture, and which are consequently not schismatic movements in the same sense as sects — concerned to preserve the traditional faith in purer form. Thus, while the theory may be adequate to explain the Pentecostal movement or the evolution of such religious groups as the Disciples of Christ (The Christian Church) and the Church of God in Jesus Christ, it does not provide a way to account for Theosophy, or the I Am movement, or the Black Muslims. Nor does the theory account for religious movements which show no signs of evolving toward the church form. Finally, the theory ignores the question of the conditions which produce a religious rather than a secular response to economic deprivation.

II THE DEPRIVATION THEORY AND RELIGIOUS ORGANIZATION

The theory of religious organization that will now be outlined is not so much an alternative to existing theory as a generalization of it. In this revised formulation, deprivation is still seen as a necessary condition for the rise of new religious movements. However, the concept of deprivation is broadened and generalized beyond its customary usage in sect-church theory.[6]

Sect-church theory conceives of deprivation almost entirely in economic terms. To be sure, in every society there are individuals and groups which are economically underprivileged relative to others; there are some whose deprivation places them at the very bottom of the economic scale. However, there are forms of deprivation other than economic ones, and these too have implications for the development of religious and secular movements as well.

Deprivation, as we conceive it, refers to any and all of the ways that an individual or group may be, or feel, disadvantaged in comparison either to other individuals or groups or to an internalized set of standards. The experience of deprivation may be conscious, in which case the individual or group may be aware of its causes. Or it may be experienced as something other than deprivation, in which case its causes will be unknown to the individual or the group. But whether directly or indirectly experienced, whether its causes are known or unknown, deprivation tends to be accompanied by a desire to overcome it.[7] Efforts to deal with deprivation will differ, however, according to the degree to which its nature is correctly perceived and individuals and groups are in a position to eliminate its cause. It is primarily the attempt, then, to overcome some of the deprivation, that leads to social conflict and may ultimately lead to the formation of a new social or religious group. We must now examine the major types of deprivation in order to understand the relationship of the deprivation to the reaction of the person who perceives the deprivation.

There are five kinds of deprivation to which individuals or groups may be subject relative to others in society. We shall call these five, economic, social, organismic, ethical, and psychic. The types are not pure; any one individual or group may experience more than one kind of deprivation. However, we can distinguish among them not only analytically but empirically since one type of deprivation is likely to be dominant for particular individuals and groups in particular situations.

Economic deprivation has its source in the differential distribution ot income in societies and in the limited access of some individuals to the necessities and luxuries of life. Economic deprivation may be judged on objective or on subjective criteria. The person who appears economically privileged on objective criteria might nevertheless perceive himself as economically deprived. For our purposes the subjective assessment is likely to be the more important.

Social deprivation is a derivative of the social propensity to value some attributes of individuals and groups more highly than others and to distribute societal rewards such as prestige, power, status, and opportunity for social participation. Social deprivation, then, arises out of the differential distribution of highly regarded attributes. The grounds for such differentiation are virtually endless. In our society, for example, we regard youth more highly than old age. The greater rewards tend to go to men rather than to women. The "gifted" person is given privileges denied to the mediocre.

Social deprivation is additive in the sense that the fewer the number of desirable attributes the individual possesses, the lower his relative status, and vice versa. In our society, it is in general "better" to be educated than uneducated. But one's status is further enhanced if one is white rather than Negro, Protestant rather than Catholic, and youthful rather than old.

The distinction between economic and social deprivation is akin to the distinction sociologists make between social class and social status. Designations of social class tend to be made on economic criteria. Social status distinctions, on the other hand, give greater attention to considerations of prestige and acceptance. While the two tend to go together, the correlation is not perfect. For our present purposes, we will consider social deprivation to be limited to situations in which it exists independently of economic deprivation.

Organismic deprivation refers to the fact that some individuals are deprived, relative to others, of good mental or physical health. It would include persons suffering from neuroses and psychoses, the blind, the deaf, the crippled, and the chronically ill.

Economic, social, and organismic deprivation share the characteristic that the individual does not measure up to society's standards. In ethical and psychological deprivation, on the other hand, the individual feels that he is not living up to his own standards. *Ethical deprivation* exists when the individual comes to feel that the dominant values of the society no longer provide him with a meaningful way of organizing his life, and that it is necessary for him to find an alternative. The deprivation is, in part, a philosophical one, but the philosophy sought is one which will provide ethical prescriptions as to how the individual should organize his everyday life.

Ethical deprivation is relatively independent of other forms of deprivation; in fact, it is more likely to arise when other forms of deprivation are not present. It would be exemplified by the person who becomes satiated with the economic and social rewards of life and with the efforts necessary to obtain them, and who seeks some alternative system of values which will inform him as to how he should act.

Psychic deprivation is somewhat akin to ethical deprivation. Here, too, there is a concern with philosophical meaning, but in this case philosophy is sought for its own sake rather than as a source of ethical prescriptions as to how one is to behave in relation to others. Psychic deprivation is primarily a consequence of severe and unresolved social deprivation. The individual is not missing the material advantages of life but has been denied its psychic rewards.

We suggest that a necessary pre-condition for the rise of any organized social movement, whether it be religious or secular, is a situation of felt deprivation. However, while a necessary condition, deprivation is not in itself a sufficient condition. Also required are the additional conditions that the deprivation be shared, that no alternative institutional arrangements for its resolution are perceived, and that a leadership emerge with an innovating idea for building a movement out of the existing deprivation.

Where these conditions exist, the organizational effort to overcome deprivation may be religious or it may be secular. In the case of economic, social, and organismic deprivation — the three characterized by deprivation relative to others — *religious* resolutions are more likely to occur where the nature of the deprivation is inaccurately perceived or where those experiencing the deprivation are not in a position to work directly at eliminating the causes. The resolution is likely to be *secular* under the opposite conditions — where the nature of the deprivation is correctly assessed by those experiencing it and they have the power, or feel they have the power, to deal with it directly.

Religious resolutions, then, are likely to compensate for feelings of deprivation rather than to eliminate its causes. Secular resolutions, where they are successful, are more likely to eliminate the causes, and therefore also the feelings.

These tendencies do not hold for ethical and psychic deprivation. In the case of ethical and psychic deprivation, as we shall see, a religious resolution may be as efficacious as a secular one in overcoming the deprivation directly. Resolutions to psychic deprivation tend in practice to be always religious, defined in the broad sense of invoking some transcendental authority. However, secular solutions are conceivable.

Both religious and secular resolutions may follow from each kind of deprivation. However, whether religious or secular, the resolution will be different in character according to which type stimulates it.

Economic deprivation, once it becomes intense, has in it the seed of revolution. When the movements which it stimulates are secular, they are likely to be revolutionary. However, to be successful, revolutions require a degree of power which the deprived group is unlikely to be able to muster. Consequently, even when it is intense, economic deprivation seldom leads to revolution.

Religious resolutions to economic deprivation, while not literally revolutionary, are symbolically so. The latent resentment against society tends to be expressed in an ideology which rejects and radically devalues the society. Thus, for those in the movement, the society is symbolically transformed; actually it is left relatively untouched.

This is characteristically what sects do, and it is this form of religious organization which is likely to arise out of economic deprivation. This is in accord with what we have said earlier in our discussion of sect-church theory, and we need not further elaborate on the way that sect members compensate for economic disadvantage by substituting religious privilege in its place. We would add, however, that the religious movement which grows out of economic deprivation need not have its theological base in the traditional religion of the society. The Black Muslim movement, for example, borrows heavily from an "alien" religious doctrine. Yet in its strong tone of social protest and its doctrine of Negro superiority it exemplifies the kind of religious movement which grows out of economic deprivation (with its accompanying social deprivation).

Social deprivation, where it exists without a strong economic component, ordinarily does not require a complete transformation of society, either literally or symbolically, to produce relief. What is at fault is not the basic organization of society but one or several of its parts. Consequently, efforts at resolution are likely to be directed at the parts without questioning the whole. As with economic deprivation, however, resolutions are not always possible. Once again, responses to the deprivation are most likely to be secular where its cause can be attacked more or less directly.

Many secular movements with roots in one or another kind of social deprivation have arisen in America over the last century. The women's suffrage movement, the Townsend movement, the many hyphenated American societies, the NAACP, all represent movements whose purpose was to eliminate the social deprivation of a particular group.

Social deprivation may be experienced as religious deprivation and, where this is the case, efforts at resolution will take a religious form. Such religious groups as the African Methodist Episcopal Church, the ethnic sub-denominations of Lutheranism, and Conservative Judaism were organized because the existing religious structure was incapable of meeting the religious needs of the groups involved. While overtly a means to overcome religious disadvantage, these organizations also served to overcome social deprivation. For example, the organization of the Augustana Lutheran Church did not immediately produce an increase in the status of the Swedish immigrants who founded it, but it did help to ease their accommodation to American society and hence to relieve incipient feelings of social deprivation. This is generally characteristic, as we have said before, of religious resolutions to deprivation.

The organizational form of religious groups that emerge out of social deprivation tends to be church-like rather than sect-like. This is because the basic interest of the socially deprived is to accommodate themselves to the larger society rather than to escape from it or alternatively to completely transform it. Consequently, they tend to adopt those institutional arrangements with which the larger society is most comfortable.

The psychoanalytic movement, group dynamics, and Alcoholics Anonymous are examples of a secular response to organismic deprivation where the mental component of this form of deprivation is dominant. In turn, the Society for the Blind, the Society for Crippled Children, and the American Cancer Society would exemplify secular efforts toward resolution where the physiological element is primary. However successful or unsuccessful these movements, they all represent attempts to deal with a problem directly. They are revolutionary in that they seek to transform the individual either mentally or physiologically. However, they do not question the value system of the society *per se.*

There have been religious movements — healing cults, for example — which are organized primarily as resolutions to organismic deprivation. More often, however, we find that religious responses to this form of deprivation are not the entire *raison d'être* of a religious movement, but are included as one aspect of it. We note that a faith healing movement has been organized within the Episcopal Church. Many sects — such as that of Father Divine, for example — include a healing element, as do cults such as Christian Science and Unity. Thus, religious responses seem not to be identified with any particular organizational form. We suspect, however, that where healing is the exclusive concern of the religious movement, as with the snake charming movement, it is more likely to be cult-like in character than to be a sect or a church.

As we have already suggested, religious resolutions to ethical deprivation may be as efficacious as secular ones in overcoming the deprivation. However, while alike in providing a direct means of overcoming ethical deprivation, secular responses do differ from religious ones in their source. Secular responses — for example, the existentialist movement and the beatniks — reflect a rejection of the general value system around which the society is organized. Religious responses, on the other hand, represent an alienation from the dominant religious system.

The religious movements which grow out of ethical deprivation cannot be as easily classified as those which emerge out of economic, social, and psychic deprivation. They tend to be more church-like than sect-like; at the same time, they might be more appropriately classified as societies than churches. Thus, the Ethical Culture Union might be loosely considered a church. Or, it may be thought of as having an organizational form which is distinct from the familiar ways in which religious groups tend to be organized. Unitarianism, too, has the quality of being an association, particularly in the way that the Unitarian Fellowships are now organized.

These organizational deviations are to be explained, we would suggest, by the fact that religious responses to intellectual deprivation tend to be deistic rather than theistic. Consequently, some of the accoutrements of more traditional religious groups are no longer relevant.

Responses to psychic deprivation often have religious overtones in that they invoke some form of transcendental authority. However, this authority may or may not derive from the predominant religion of the culture and indeed, as in the case of the flying saucer movement, may not even borrow from an existing religion. However, whether they are offshoots of the dominant religion — Christian Science or Unity, for example — or borrow from alien religions — Theosophy, Vedanta, or the I Am movement — or are essentially new inventions, these movements almost invariably assume a cult-like rather than a sect-like or church-like form. They tend to draw their membership from the severely socially deprived middle class, they require a certain amount of intellectual facility on the part of their adherents and function to relieve the deprivation by stimulating an attitude of mind over matter. At the same time, they avoid the ritualistic trappings of the church and gainsay a professional clergy.

Deprivation need not be immediately present to stimulate an organizational response. The prospect of deprivation may produce a similar effect. The White Citizens' Councils in the South, for example, can be conceived of as organizations growing out of anticipated economic and social deprivation. The John Birch Society is a response to anticipated social deprivation. Protestants and Other Americans United is an example of a religious movement organized around anticipated ethical and social deprivation.

In sum, present or anticipated deprivation would appear to be a central factor in the rise of new movements. The organizational response to deprivation may be either religious or secular. In the case of economic, social, and organismic deprivation, religious responses tend to function as compensations for the deprivation, secular ones as means to overcome it. The type of deprivation around which a movement arises is influential in shaping its character in all cases except organismic deprivation. Generally speaking, religious movements emerge as sects where they are stimulated by economic deprivation, as churches where the deprivation is social, and as cults where it is psychic. Religious movements arising out of ethical deprivation tend to develop an organizational form which is distinct from that of traditional religions.

III DEPRIVATION AND THE DEVELOPMENT OF RELIGIOUS GROUPS

Deprivation is important not only to the rise of new movements but to the path of their development and their potentiality for survival. Movements may evolve in a myriad of ways, and we have no intention of trying to cope with all of their variety. We would suggest, however, that movements tend to follow one of three basic patterns. (1) They may flower briefly and then die. (2) They may survive indefinitely in substantially their original form. (3) They may survive but in a form radically different from their original one

How movements develop, and whether or not they survive, is influenced by the type of deprivation which stimulated them, how they deal with this deprivation, and the degree to which the deprivation persists in the society and, therefore, provides a continuing source of new recruits.

Movements arising out of economic deprivation tend to follow a pattern of either disappearing relatively quickly or of having to change their organizational form to survive. They seldom survive indefinitely in their original form. This is because the deprivation they respond to may itself be short-lived or because they themselves help to overcome the deprivation of their adherents.

Few sects survive as sects. They either disappear or evolve from a sect to a church. Where they follow the former course, it is likely that their source of recruitment suddenly withers because of conditions over which they have no control. Thus, depression-born sects tend to have a low survival rate, lasting only as long as the depression itself. Sects also have the tendency, noted earlier, to socialize their members to higher economic status. In the process, their organizational form is transformed to conform to the changing status of their membership.

Secular responses to economic deprivation follow a similar pattern. Depression-born movements — technocracy, for example — tend to flower briefly and then die. More fundamental movements, such as revolutions, tend, where they are successful, to lose their revolutionary character and to survive as movements functioning to maintain the advantages which have been gained.

Organizational responses to social deprivation may also follow a pattern of disappearing quickly, but where they survive, they are likely to do so without radical alteration of their original form. Which of these paths is followed is largely dependent on the persistence of the deprivation which gave rise to the movement. Successful elimination of the experienced deprivation — for example, the successful attempt of women to gain the right to vote — is likely to produce an early end to the movement.

It is characteristic of many kinds of social deprivation to persist over extended periods of time and to continue from generation to generation. This is because the value systems of societies tend to change slowly, and the differential social rewards and punishments of one era are not likely, in the natural course of events, to be radically altered in the next.

The ability of churches to survive in basically unchanged form is, in substantial part, a consequence of the persistence of social deprivation. Participation in a church, we would suggest, functions to provide individuals with a source of gratification which they cannot find in the society-at-large. Since there are always individuals who are socially deprived in this sense, there exists a continuing source of new recruits to the church. Furthermore, church participation only compensates for the deprivation; it does not eliminate it. Thus, the condition does not arise, as with the sect, that a primary reason for the existence of the church is dissipated over time.

The contention that a major function of church participation is to relieve members' feelings of social deprivation is made here primarily on theoretical grounds. What little empirical evidence there is, however, suggests that churches tend to gain their greatest commitment from individuals who are most deprived of the rewards of the larger society. Thus, it is the less gifted intellectually, the aged, women, and those without normal family lives who are most often actively involved in the church.[8]

Organismic deprivation produces movements whose evolution is likely to be influenced by the development of new knowledge about the causes and treatment of mental and physical disorders. Existing movements can expect to thrive only so long as the therapies they provide are subjectively perceived as efficacious and superior to prevailing alternatives. However, the survival of these movements is constantly threatened by innovations in therapy or treatment which eliminate their *raison d'être*.

Under such conditions, they may simply disband — like the Sister Kenny Foundation, for example — or they may elect to chart their course along a different path, like the National Foundation.

Religious movements or sub-movements which are sustained by organismic deprivation may survive for a very long time and recruit new members from those who cannot find relief through secular sources. In the long run they too may become victims of innovations coming from increments in secular knowledge.

Movements which originate in ethical deprivation have a great propensity, we would suggest, to be short-lived. This is not because ethical deprivation is not a persistent element in society; there are always likely to be some individuals who feel that the dominant value system provides an inadequate answer to this concern. However, resolutions which seem appropriate at one time are not likely to be so at another. In effect, ethical deprivation tends to be subject to fads. Consequently, organizational responses to ethical deprivation tend to capture attention for the moment and to be quickly replaced by alternative and new solutions. The beatnik movement exemplifies this propensity.

The exceptions — the movements of this kind which survive — do so because they provide solutions which have relevance to long-term trends in society. These trends function to provide these movements with a continuing source of new recruits. For example, the long-term trend toward secularization in American life is, we suspect, a major factor in the survival and recent acceleration in growth of the Unitarian movement. In general, ethical deprivation characterizes only a small minority of a population at a given time and movements which respond to such deprivation are likely — whether they survive or not — always to be minority movements.

For much the same reasons movements which arise out of psychic deprivation share this tendency to be short-lived. Theosophy and the I Am society were short-lived movements, and we suspect that this will be true of the flying saucer movement also. Christian Science seems clearly to be more than a fad and so would be an exception to our generalization. The success of this movement to relieve not only psychic deprivation but also the social deprivation which almost invariably accompanies it may account for its survival. Other movements, like Theosophy and I Am may be less capable of relieving psychic and social deprivation because of their reliance on alien religious ideas.

Our aim in this essay has been to assess theoretically the general role of deprivation in the origin and evolution of social movements and to specify its special significance for religious organization. The essay has been informed by the view that religion functions to compensate for deprivations for which direct means of resolution either do not exist or are not possible of employment. By reducing the propensities toward self-destructive behavior which are loosed whenever feelings of deprivation are not resolved, religion, we are asserting, plays an important role in the maintenance of personal and social integration.

It may seem to some readers that we have reduced religion to a sociological variable. This is definitely not our intention. To say that religion relieves deprivation in no sense comprehends all that religion is or does. It merely confirms one claim which religions make: that those who accept the faith will be relieved of the cares of the world. However, religion cannot be understood only in terms of what its adherents receive from it; the question of what they give to it — of what consequences follow from being religious — needs also to be considered. Our essay has been concerned exclusively with the first of these questions. The task of studying the consequences of religion for the individual and the society has, in our judgment, still to be done effectively.

NOTES

1. The author is indebted to his colleagues, Gertrude Jaeger Selznick and Robert E. Mitchell, for constructive criticism and editorial advice.
2. Max Weber, "The Social Psychology of the World's Religions" in Gerth and Mills, eds., *From Max Weber: Essays in Sociology* (New York: Oxford University Press, 1940).
3. Ernst Troeltsch, *Social Teachings of the Christian Churches* (New York: Macmillan, 1949), esp. Vol. I, pp. 331–43.
4. H. Richard Niebuhr, *The Social Sources of Denominationalism* (New York: Henry Holt and Co., 1929).
5. See, for example, J. M. Yinger, *Religion in the Struggle for Power* (Durham, N.C.: Duke University Press, 1946); Bryan Wilson, "An Analysis of Sect Development," *American Sociological Review,* 22 (Feb. 1957); and Leopold Von Wiese and Howard Becker, *Systematic Sociology* (New York: John Wiley and Sons, 1932).
6. This paper has also been informed by Robert K. Merton, "Social Structure and Anomie" in *Social Theory and Social Structure* (Glencoe, Ill.: The Free Press, 1957).
7. This is not the case, however, where the value system of the society warrants deprivation, for example, the Hindu caste system.
8. See Charles Y. Glock, "A Sociologist Looks at the Parish Church," Afterword in Walter Kloetzli, *The City Church: Death or Renewal* (Philadelphia: The Muhlenberg Press, 1961).

CHARLES S. MC COY

The Churches and Protest Movements for Racial Justice

In mid-May 1961, headlines across the nation told a story of raw and ugly violence in Alabama. A Greyhound bus carrying an interracial group had been burned. Mobs in Anniston and Birmingham had threatened the passengers and intimidated the drivers. Several persons had been badly beaten. Public order was seriously threatened, yet the police seemed indifferent, either standing by doing little or failing to arrive in time to prevent disorders. Federal marshals at last were sent in to cope with a situation which local police and state officials refused to handle.

What caught the eye of the public through the mass media was not an isolated phenomenon, but formed part of a movement for racial justice which had a long past and would not be ended with the litigation surrounding the Alabama episodes. It is this movement especially in its recent manifestations but also in its broader context and significance that we shall examine here.

Organized religion has had close relationships with the various forms of social conflict arising from racial injustice. Every discussion of attempts to end slavery, discrimination, and segregation must take account of the assistance and opposition of churches. And a discussion of the churches and social conflict in this country cannot avoid dealing with the explosive and rapidly changing racial situation. What I shall suggest here is that organized religion has played and continues to play an important part in the movement toward racial justice. We must not, however, expect organized religion to exercise determinative force in situations of social conflict, and we certainly cannot expect churches to exercise the functions of courts or government or law enforcement agencies.

Central to our analysis is our understanding of religion and its relation to society.

On the one hand, if we understand religion in the Freudian or Ritschlian sense of a defense for man against the encroachments of nature, we shall be at a loss to comprehend the prophetic fervor of Western religion. On the other hand, if we accept a notion of religion which views it only as a social phenomenon, we shall be unable to grasp its inner depth and force.

Instead, religion can best be understood as referring primarily to that center of ultimate commitment and loyalty from which men derive their understanding of reality, of themselves and their companions, and of what is truly of value. Only in a secondary sense does religion refer to the social organizations and phenomena which form around this commitment and interpretation.[1]

Religion in its initial moment operates integratively and cohesively, providing common loyalties and purposes which bind humanity into communities. As a result of this integrative power, religion may in other moments be devisive or socially revolutionary. Viewed in this way, the churches will always be related to conflicts and tensions around them, but this relation will be primarily with reference to inclusive interpretations and meanings. Only secondarily and less decisively will it provide concrete solutions for social problems

We may therefore expect that religious organizations will tend to play ambiguous rather than unequivocal roles in social conflict. And this will be especially true insofar as these organizations tend to be "churches" rather than "sects," in Troeltsch's terms. A church, precisely because it is inclusive of various social groupings, will tend toward ambiguity on important social issues. A sect, on the other hand, has the possibility of embracing persons with sufficiently similar social techniques and goals to be relatively unambiguous in situations of social conflict. Only when the church is understood as a remnant in the Biblical sense rather than as an inclusive social organization will it appear less ambiguous in situations of tension and conflict.

To the extent, therefore, that religious organizations are understood in terms of the primary function of religion, the less we may expect churches to play unambiguous roles in social conflict or to provide solutions which are significantly and immediately decisive. Only secondarily and in particular circumstances will we find churches able to take relatively decisive roles in society.

The relation of the churches to the protest movements for racial justice illustrates this view. For our purposes here we focus on four specific segments of this over-all movement: the Montgomery bus boycott of 1955–6, the student "sit-ins" of 1960, the Freedom Rides of 1961, and the Black Muslims. But first, we must place these movements in their wider context.

I A NATIONAL AND WORLD PERSPECTIVE

The situation of political power on the international and national scene does at least as much to explain the emergence and success of the protest movements at this particular time as the teaching of the churches on race relations.

Certainly the churches and churchmen have long taken a significant part in the attempts to secure a greater measure of justice for Negroes in American society. Those Rhode Island ministers of the eighteenth century who denounced the slave trade while some of their wealthiest members derived their incomes from that source were early links in a long chain of courageous protest on this issue. John Woolman, going about laying the concern for freeing slaves upon the Quakers, the abolitionists during the era before the Civil War, and many Christians of this century have dared to go against the prevailing patterns of discrimination and segregation. By 1920, the churches had widened their social vision so that the Social Creed of the Federal Council of Churches included "supporting equal and adequate opportunities for Negroes" and favored "voting-rights for all without regard to race." Church school literature and teachings began more and more to reflect these views. By 1946 the Federal Council had come out flatly for "an integrated church in an integrated society." This did not mean that all members agreed, but it did mean that a firm consensus had been reached by the leadership of the churches, clergy and laity alike, and that the weight of education and persuasion in the churches would be in this direction. Many groups within the churches — youth groups, women's organizations, voluntary fellowships, etc. — were well ahead of this emerging consensus.

Yet for all the agitation and education going on within the churches, important as these were in producing a general climate of readiness, forces of a different sort created the specific conditions for the success of the protest movements. Factors of international and national politics produced the immediately favorable situation of the past decade.

Though the events which make headlines in connection with protests on behalf of racial justice most often occur in the South, we must be clear that race is a national problem with particular facets in each region of the country and with important bearing on the national political scene. Beyond its national scope, the problem of race is a world problem and a factor in the struggle between the communist and free-world blocs, especially in relation to the uncommitted nations of Asia and Africa. Neither the world-wide interest in our racial violence nor the shape of particular events in themselves would be comprehensible apart from the national and world perspective.

Most anthropologists and biologists deny that race is a useful concept for designating human groups. Liston Pope writes:

> At the present moment, most serious students of the question agree that "race" is almost a meaningless term as far as scientific knowledge is concerned. . . . Perhaps "common stock" would be a better term than race. . . .[2]

It remains starkly clear in the realm of international politics, however, that race is a symbol loaded with explosive significance for large segments of the world's population. This circumstance cannot be overlooked in assessing the impact of movements in this country seeking to end segregation and racial discrimination. In most of Africa, "colored" peoples have come to dominance. The new nations of that continent have native African leaders.

As these nations shape their political and economic affairs, all are plagued by the problem of achieving industrial development without compromising their independence. As they vacillate in allegiance toward communism, or toward Western democracy, or toward neutralism, not only does the memory of Western colonialism make them suspicious of the white man, but also the present reality of segregation and violence keeps their suspicions of Europe and America alive and strong. With all of these newer nations, racial attitudes emerge as a powerful factor in their relations with the United States. The communists, of course, exploit our racial violence to the utmost. In connection with the Freedom Rides of 1961, for example, Moscow Radio had this to say:

> Scenes of bloodshed in Montgomery are . . . the worst examples of savagery . . . taking place in a country which has the boldness to declare that its way of life is an example for other people. . . . The brutal attacks on people in antisegregation demonstrations have aroused indignation throughout the world. They are particularly enlightening for . . . those countries where people of the Negro races and other colored people live.

But Soviet statements are appealing to feelings that exist apart from communist propaganda and are often voiced by non-communists. The official *Ethiopian Herald* commented also on the racial conditions in the

United States: "Africans feel that any segregation against the Negro is simultaneously segregation against [Africans]" which makes it "difficult for [the United States] to sell to the outside world, especially the non-white world, that she stands for . . . equality of all men." The government-controlled paper of Angola, *Diario de Buanda,* drew an even worse conclusion. It deplored the "tragedy of Negro life in America" where there is no respected American scientist, politician, or religious leader "who does not consider the Negro inferior to the white." When, *Diario* continued, "an Adlai Stevenson . . . is obliged to shake hands with some Nkrumah he does it only under the strict political necessity of the disturbed world. . . . He is hypocritical and sells his soul to the devil . . . The Nkrumahs, the Tubmans and the Tourés know it well." [3]

Whether or not we find it palatable, the attitudes of these new nations and the pressure of expansionist communism are important aspects of the racial scene in America. Without the urgent demands of international politics upon us, it is doubtful that we would have made such rapid and significant strides in this area over the past fifteen years.

Just as we cannot ignore the international facets of our domestic problems, so also we must note the aspects of our national life which bear upon our racial difficulties. Obviously not all segregation exists in the South. Indeed, nowhere in the continental United States have we overcome discriminatory practices and the tensions which accompany feelings of injustice. Residential segregation and the consequent tendency toward segregation in schools is noticeable in New York or Chicago, in Philadelphia or San Francisco. We cannot exonerate North or West at the expense of the South, though in the South discriminatory practices have deeper roots in custom and law. Racial injustice is a national problem in terms of discrimination.

It is also a national problem because of the strong drive toward justice heritage — what Gunnar Myrdal in *An American Dilemma* calls the "American dream." Whatever violates this tradition is of concern to all of us.

But there is still another aspect of the national scene which has special bearing on the protest movements for racial justice. It is the growing political importance of the Negro in American life.

Since World War II the Negro has come of age as a social and political force in the United States. On the one hand, he has been moving out of the South. As recently as 1910, of the Negroes in this country 90 per cent lived in the eleven states that formed the Confederacy — the real "South." By 1960 only 52 per cent still lived in these southern states; around half now live in the North and West. On the other hand, the

Negro has become much better educated. No group in the nation has made greater strides educationally in recent years. Today only 7 per cent of American Negroes are illiterate. And between 1940 and 1959, the proportion of college graduates among Negro young adults increased threefold.[4] In this brief period the Negro community acquired greatly increased leadership, not only devoted and filled with zeal, but also well trained for the struggle to acquire civil rights. Both these factors have important bearing on the recent protest movements.

The movement from South to North and West means that the Negro has acquired a political power he did not possess before World War II, a political power significant not primarily on the local scene North or South but of national scope. Moving out of the South has meant the right to vote and wider freedom of the ballot for more Negroes. Increasingly the Negro vote has had to be reckoned with by politicians of both major parties. By 1960 the population of Newark was 35 per cent Negro, Detroit 29 per cent, Philadelphia 26 per cent, while New York City, Chicago, Los Angeles, Cleveland, and the San Francisco–Oakland area each had a substantial Negro vote. The great influx of Negroes has been into big cities in states with large electoral votes. This has meant that Negroes now occupy a strategic position in Presidential elections. The big-city states have a total electoral vote of 197, around three-fourths of the number needed for election.

The importance of the Negro vote became clear to the politicians in the presidential election of 1948. Truman squeaked past Dewey by 33,612 in Illinois, by 17,865 in California, and by 7,107 in Ohio. Truman's strong stand for civil rights seemed undoubtedly sufficient to explain his margin in these crucial states. Since that time politicians of both parties have cultivated the Negro vote carefully, and parallel to this development, there has been a growing confidence among Negro leaders.

Perhaps the most dramatic illustration of the importance of the Negro vote was provided in the 1960 presidential election. In late October Martin Luther King, Jr., was jailed in Georgia, refused bail, and was whisked away to a state prison. Many Negroes feared for his life. With the campaign for the Presidency drawing to a climax, the two major candidates were faced with a difficult decision. Each one was forced to decide whether to aid King and gain northern Negro votes or to keep quiet and gain southern white votes. Richard Nixon said nothing. John F. Kennedy phoned Mrs. King, expressing sympathy and offering assistance. Word of Kennedy's action spread quickly among Negroes throughout the nation. The press reported it. Martin Luther King, Jr., was released on bail rather than being held. The following Sunday Martin

Luther King, Sr., proclaimed publicly from his pulpit in Atlanta that he was switching from Nixon to Kennedy and taking a "suitcase full of votes" with him for the Democratic candidates. Kennedy's staff was not slow to make capital of this break. A million leaflets reporting the incident and giving quotes from prominent Negro leaders were distributed at Negro churches the Sunday before the election. It is likely that this provided the margin of victory for Kennedy in Illinois, Michigan, South Carolina, and Texas and thus the margin of victory in a very close election.[5]

This rise in political power has direct bearing on the entire protest movement. Now no national administration can ignore these movements. They receive increasing attention from the press, the public, and the government. The pressure of the federal government on the southern states, in turn, has produced wider voting rights for the Negroes there and greater political leverage to secure increased economic and educational opportunities. This new political situation in the nation makes clear one of the central reasons for the rising tide of success that the protest movements are having.

The role of the churches, while not in the foreground, remains. Once the pressure of contemporary events has forced the problem of race to public attention, the view which has been officially formulated and vigorously inculcated by the churches becomes the framework in which the problem is viewed and solutions sought. The guilty conscience of America about segregation, the basis for our international vulnerability on the issue, is in no small measure due to the teaching of the churches at home and abroad.

Despite segregationist customs, white Americans of prominence have tended to see the solution in terms of integration. Negro Americans have also tended to understand the solution in these terms, despite the segregationist teachings of the Black Muslim sect, a view which might seem attractive to Negroes embittered by centuries of injustice. The church has played an important role, but not the one that the more ardent social activists outside and inside the church expect and demand.

II FOUR RECENT PROTEST MOVEMENTS

Once various social forces have produced an eruption of social conflict, the churches may provide a focal point of loyalty around which to organize and a framework of interpretation and guidance for the resulting movement. Because religion refers primarily to a center of commitment from which derive inclusive understandings of reality, man, and value, such a role is essentially what we may expect from the churches. Only in a secondary sense and as they tend to represent limited segments of society, will religious organizations precipitate conflict or offer solutions to situations of tension. This point may be illustrated in a discussion of the churches and four of the recent protest movements for racial justice.

1. *The Montgomery Bus Boycott.* The Montgomery bus boycott began as an unplanned protest against segregation and arbitrary treatment of Negroes in the city buses of Montgomery, Alabama. On Thursday afternoon, December 1, 1955, Mrs. Rosa Parks boarded a city bus to return home after a tiring day on the job in a downtown department store. She sat down in the first seat behind the section reserved exclusively for whites. More white passengers got on. The bus driver ordered Mrs. Parks to relinquish her seat to a white man. This would have meant standing, as the seats farther back were all taken. Mrs. Parks, apparently without plan or forethought, refused and was arrested. E. D. Nixon, a Pullman car porter active in the labor movement and the NAACP, signed the bond for Mrs. Parks. But he also proposed a one-day boycott of the buses.

A meeting Friday night was attended by leaders from all important sectors of Negro life — lawyers, businessmen, union leaders, teachers, physicians, and a substantial group of clergymen. The boycott was set for Monday with a mass meeting to follow in the evening at a large Baptist church to discuss further action. Leaflets were distributed on Saturday. Ministers announced the protest from their pulpits on Sunday, emphasizing its importance. Negro taxi drivers agreed to transport Negroes to work on Monday for bus fare alone. To the surprise of many, the boycott on Monday was almost 100 per cent successful, with empty buses traveling the Montgomery streets.

The meeting that night at the church was packed, with several thousand listening outside via loud speaker. The opening hymn was "Onward Christian Soldiers," followed by a prayer, Scripture, and an address by Martin Luther King, Jr., a young Baptist minister who had been elected chairman of the protest organization, just that afternoon named the Montgomery Improvement Association. In his address he called for a continuation of the protest, but in a spirit of love rather than hate. "If you will protest courageously, and yet with dignity and Christian love, when the history books are written in future generations, the historians will have to pause and say, 'There lived a great people — a black people — who injected new meaning and dignity into the veins of civilization.' This is our challenge and our overwhelming responsibility."

The meeting enthusiastically responded to this call to action by approving a resolution calling upon all Negroes of Montgomery "not to resume riding the buses until (1) courteous treatment by the bus operators was guaranteed; (2) passengers were seated on a first-come, first-served basis . . . ; (3) Negro bus operators were employed on predominantly Negro routes." [6]

This was the beginning of a difficult, protracted movement of protest in Montgomery. A volunteer transport system was placed in operation with morning pickup points mainly at Negro churches and afternoon return arrangements. Automobiles were purchased and sponsored by churches to form a transportation pool. Even so, many Negroes had to walk the many miles to work and back again through the long months of the protest.

White opposition attempted to break the boycott by economic and political pressures, but did not succeed. Violence was threatened by segregationists. Homes of some of the leaders were bombed. Martin Luther King set a course for the Montgomery movement by drawing on the teachings of Jesus and Gandhi about non-violence.

Meantime, the matter of segregation in Montgomery buses was being fought through the courts. On November 13, 1956, the U.S. Supreme Court affirmed a District Court ruling that Alabama's state and local laws requiring segregation were unconstitutional. Preparation of Negro citizens for integration was begun immediately with the assistance of Glenn Smiley, a southern-born white minister and member of the Fellowship of Reconciliation. On December 21, 1956, more than twelve months after the boycott began, the city buses of Montgomery were integrated. More violence was to come, but the battle had been won.

Out of the Montgomery protest emerged the Southern Christian Leadership Conference. Established in January 1957 and headed by Martin Luther King, Jr., it has become one of the most influential national movements in the struggle for racial justice.

Although an incident on a city bus started it and the course of developments was influenced by diverse factors, the Montgomery protest and the organizations to which it gave rise were formed within the churches, nurtured and guided by churchmen, clergy and laity, and remain a channel of Christian impact on this arena of social conflict.

2. *The "Sit-in" Movement.* Though different in many ways from the Montgomery bus protest, the "sit-in" movement illustrates a similar

point about the relationship of the church to social conflict. Only in a very indirect sense can it be said that the churches helped initiate the protest movement. Yet churches served in many instances as rallying points once the "sit-ins" were under way, and the faith of the church provided interpretation and guidance.

On February 1, 1960, four Negro college students sat down at a segregated lunch counter in Greensboro, North Carolina, and requested service. They entered at 4:30 p.m. They left at 5:30, when the lunch-counter closed, still unserved. Word of the episode spread rapidly. The action in Greensboro set off a series of similar "sit-in" movements which in the brief span of two months had spread to sixty-five cities [7] and during the subsequent two years embraced parks, swimming pools, theaters, restaurants, churches, interstate transportation, voter registration, libraries, museums, art galleries, laundromats, employment, housing, real estate offices, beaches, and courtrooms.

Centered primarily in southern cities, "sit-ins" protested various forms of segregation in all parts of the country. A sympathy movement among students in the North and West did much to add pressure on national chain stores with southern branches practicing segregation.

The movement was begun by students, and it was carried out in its early stages without the consent or even the knowledge of the established Negro leadership. Advice was soon sought and given, but the students maintained direction and control.

Following the example of Martin Luther King and the Montgomery protest movement, non-violent techniques were carefully adhered to, with training sessions usually provided for those participating in order to ensure success in not retaliating.

Though not as intimately related to the churches as the Montgomery movement, the connection remains strong. Meetings and training sessions were frequently held in churches. Campus religious groups often provided the rallying point for organizing "sit-ins" as well as leadership for them. The Christian tradition formed the dominant mode for interpreting and guiding the movements. One of the students writes:

> The greatest deterrents to the propagation of segregation have been the black man's exposure to education and his exposure to Christianity—and the greatest of these is the latter. In the struggle for the abrogation of his servile position, the strong belief in a God who is both Messiah and Suffering Servant has enabled the Negro to evaluate his dilemma beyond the stage of hatred. This by no means implies that only ministers are interested in erasing the signs of segregation from the blackboards of America. This, of course, would be misleading. What I am saying though, is that the fact that

ministers have been in the vanguard seems to show that Christianity has played an important role in the development of the movement.

That the students are aware of the Christian influence in the movement is borne out by the Statement of Purpose adopted at an Atlanta meeting of the Student Nonviolent Coordinating Committee. The Statement, drawn up in October, 1960, says in part:

> "We affirm the philosophy or religious ideal of nonviolence as the fundamental of our purpose. The presupposition of our faith and the manner of our action, nonviolence as it grows from the Judaeo-Christian traditions, seeks a social order of justice permeated by love."

Thus, the part played by religion has been a strong and important one. The movement, of course, could have started on secular grounds and probably could have gone far. I believe, however, that the fact that it has its underpinning in the roots of Christianity is the reason the movement has thus far succeeded. . . .[8]

Again we see the religion of the churches providing a framework of meaning for what is being done, pointing to deep factors of motivation, and providing guidance as to goal and method. Yet this meaning, motivation, and guidance are brought to bear on a movement not begun by the churches and about which organized religion, viewed generally, was and remains decidedly ambivalent.

3. *The Freedom Rides.* To carry our analysis further, the Freedom Rides may be used to exemplify one aspect of this ambivalence, the Black Muslims another aspect.

In May 1961 another phase of the protest movement for racial justice was inaugurated. The Freedom Ride, which was planned by the Congress of Racial Equality, began when an integrated group set out across the South to discover how well federal rulings requiring desegregation of interstate travel facilities were being obeyed. This original group met with violence in Alabama and, giving up the plan to travel by bus on to New Orleans, ended this Freedom Ride by taking air transportation.

Newspaper publicity jarred the indignation of many of the same students who had conducted the "sit-ins." The Nashville branch of this student movement took up the cause of the Freedom Rides and set out to continue them. After some hesitation, CORE resumed its backing of the movement.

The response from all over the country was widespread and strongly in support of the Rides. Eventually 305 persons from every section of the nation were jailed as Freedom Riders. The largest proportion were students, but a substantial cross-section of clergymen joined the move into southern jails. At least two groups of clergymen from the Northeast went on Freedom Rides.

A group of religious leaders known as the "Mission to Mississippi" converged on Jackson in July. From South, North, and West, these men came to consult with Mississippi leaders and to give support to the Freedom Rider movement. Some of this group went to jail. Others visited Washington to plead the cause of integrated facilities with the Interstate Commerce Commission and with Attorney General Robert Kennedy. Late in the summer a group of twenty-eight Episcopal clergy on the way to their triennial convention traveled via Jackson — and ten of them via Mississippi jails.

The Freedom Rides brought out some of the strongest conflicting attitudes of recent years between churchmen who favor integration and those who oppose it. But significant differences in strategy have been exposed among those favoring integration. Many believe such massive, direct action, even though it is carefully non-violent, forces matters more rapidly than the processes of adjustment will bear. A second group believes that efforts ought to be put into voter education and registration among Negroes; Martin Luther King and the Christian Leadership Conference give priority to this approach and were at first reluctant to provide substantial support to the Freedom Rides for this reason.

Such differences and the consequent ambivalence of the churches in situations of conflict can be anticipated when the primary function of religion is understood as referring not to specific social goals and strategies, but rather revolving around our understanding of God and man. Variant contexts of social forces will lead to different applications of these larger views.

4. *The Black Muslim Movement.* A different aspect of this ambiguity with reference to social conflict of religious organizations is exemplified in the Black Muslim movement.[9] In this instance the dynamics of the movement have been almost exclusively centered on commitment, discipline, and interpretation of God and self. Little direct teaching on larger social issues has existed. As a result, the ambiguity of the Black Muslim organization, with its apparent opposition to the prevalent teachings of Christian groups, hovers ominously over the scene of American race relations.

Begun in Detroit in the early 1930's, the Black Muslim movement caught up the remnants of earlier Negro nationalist organizations and moulded them into a tightly disciplined religious structure. The movement is headed by Elijah Muhammad, the Messenger of Allah and chief minister of the Black Muslims. From Temple No. 2 in Chicago's south side, Elijah Muhammad governs a chain of temples which are now strategically located in the Negro districts of every major city in all parts of the land.

One arm of control is the Fruit of Islam, a semi-military organization headed by Elijah's son-in-law, Supreme Captain Raymond Sharrieff. Another arm is made up of the ministers of the various temples, the most noted and gifted of whom is Malcolm X of the temple in Harlem; these ministers and all members must be totally loyal to Elijah Muhammad.

The teachings of the Black Muslims combine a very high and strict personal code of behavior with a deep and potentially violent hatred of the white man.[10] Negroes are called Black Men and are understood as the "Lost Nation of Islam in North America," now found and organized in preparation for "their day of destiny."[11] Black men are superior to whites, and the teachings of Elijah Muhammad are designed to cure the infection caught during the time of the white man's enslavement of the Black.

The Muslims do not smoke, drink, or eat excessively, and delinquency or crime is a rarity among them. Members must devote considerable time and money to the movement. Sexual morality is defined in very strict terms and transgressors are disciplined by the Fruit of Islam.[12] Women are given a place of honor, but one of strict subordination to the male, and they are carefully trained for their roles in the home.

The goals of the Black Muslim movement are vague and perhaps intentionally ill-defined. The explicit goal is to reach all Black Men in America and fuse them into a "United Front." The Movement already has over 100,000 members and, according to Lincoln, is growing "at a rate which seriously embarrasses Negro leaders with more moderate programs."[13] Elijah Muhammad teaches segregation in reverse, and his doctrine and discipline have wide appeal to the Negroes, embittered by discrimination and disillusioned with American democracy and churches. Its ambiguity on social goals adds to its strength both by making it less vulnerable to prosecution as subversive and also because it does not raise issues which might prove divisive among leaders or members.

While it does not seem likely that the Black Muslim movement will win a majority of American Negroes or pose a serious threat to social order, its most significant effect may be upon non-Muslim segments of the Negro community. For one thing, it is challenging young Negroes to greater discipline of life, and this is evident in a different sort of discipline in the non-violent "sit-in" and Freedom Ride movements. The shift of method from education, persuasion, and legal action to the more aggressive, direction action of the recent protest movements represents a greater impatience in the Negro community produced in part by the Black Muslims.

The element of Negro nationalism which is explicit and blatant with the Black Muslims has also become a prominent element in the post-World War II struggle for racial justice. Increasingly, Negroes insist on leading their own battle. The bi-racial nature of the NAACP and even CORE is far less apparent in the Christian Leadership Conference and in the Student Non-Violent Co-ordinating Committee. Sometimes there is deliberate effort to prevent participation of genuinely sympathetic whites.

While the Black Muslims may well illustrate the primary function of religious organization and its resultant tendency toward ambiguity on immediate social issues, Elijah Muhammad's movement is having an impact on the American scene which is helping to alter the shape of the protest movement and appears ominous to many observers.

III THE AMBIGUOUS ROLE OF CHURCHES

Quite clearly, the protest movements for racial justice illustrate the ambiguous position toward which religious organizations tend when confronted with social conflict. The study of the Little Rock clergy by Campbell and Pettigrew [14] underscores this ambiguity with reference to the professional leadership of the churches. One need only examine the contrast between the official pronouncements of major denominations and the attitude of their southern white members to illustrate the point further. The contrast between the participation of southern Negro churches and southern white churches in the protest movement discloses the ambiguity with even greater clarity.

Agreement on doctrinal tenets, on basic affirmations about man and society, and even similar official pronouncements on race relations will not prevent churches and churchmen from taking very different positions in specific situations of social conflict. The same churchmen may even take different positions, in different contexts, as is witnessed by southern white ministers who vote for fairly bold racial pronouncements at church conventions but are far more cautious in their local parishes when surrounded by segregationists. A curious but not uncommon variation of this ambiguity is illustrated by the remark of a white Alabama Episcopal vestryman, that he expected and wanted his minister to stand for integration even though he as a southerner and a vestryman opposed it.

A brief description of the changing shape of the protest movement for racial justice may delineate further what is and what is not the role of the churches in relation to it.

1. *The method for achieving racial justice has undergone change.* Prior to 1954 the movement for integration operated in part in the social shadows, out of the public eye, because it was a minority movement often of dubious legality. During this period education and persuasion under the protection of approved social institutions was most appropriate. Public pronouncements by churches raised the issue and provided justification for those who worked toward integration. We may see inadequacies in this method today, but we ought not to underestimate its value in moving against the stream of popular sentiment. With increasing public support, legal action became possible and led to direct protests such as the bus boycotts, "sit-ins," and Freedom Rides. Here we have evidence that conflict may precipitate social change and produce a greater measure of justice.

2. *The movement for racial justice has been gathering momentum.* Little short of a quiet revolution has been taking place in racial practices all over the country. While changes have been neither so rapid nor complete as many have hoped, they have nevertheless been substantial. Great strides have been made in ending segregation in interstate transportation, in higher education, in public eating facilities, in public housing, in employment practices, in voting rights, and in the fields of entertainment and recreation. Significant steps toward integration have also been made in the churches, though our higher expectations here leave us profoundly dissatisfied. The past decade has seen the pace of change increased. One of the major factors in this increase has been the courage and vigor of the direct action protest movements. Whereas the earlier period has a place for the operation of the churches as institutions in education and persuasion, the cumbersome organization with its different points of view and resultant ambiguous social stance is less useful for the present with its greater rapidity of change and action. Now the churches are the seed-bed for the protest movement, a source of support and guidance, but not the prime movers.

3. *There are significant changes in leadership taking place within the protest movement.* On the one hand, we see leadership moving more

directly into the hands of Negroes, reflecting both a strain of Negro nationalism and a greater confidence on the part of the Negro community. On the other hand, we see the leadership moving toward the younger members of the Negro community, emerging from a greater impatience and also from confidence in the method of non-violent direct action, which can be carried out more effectively by venturesome, less settled persons.

4. *Whereas the churches were ahead of the society at large in matters of integration earlier, now the churches are lagging behind the faster pace of desegregation in public areas.* This is in part because the ideals of integration could be enunciated by a leadership minority in the churches, but actual integration requires a heavy majority to be effective in voluntary groups like the churches. There is also another reason worth noting. Although segregation has become the shame of contemporary American Christianity, the Negro churches provided the earliest and firmest bases of Negro social organization and power. The Negro community today is showing a wise reluctance to surrender these important centers of influence. Whites often think integration means letting Negroes attend white churches. It would be a sham integration unless Negroes share in positions of authority also. Perhaps this is what leads some Negroes to suggest that integration might better take place by having Caucasians join Negro churches. In any event, there is more than segregationist sentiment behind the lagging integration of our church life.

Looking back with the inadequate perspective of less than a decade on the rise and development of these protest movements, it still seems possible to say that the real turning point in the struggle came in one way with the decision on public school desegregation by the U.S. Supreme Court in 1954 and in another way with the Montgomery Bus Boycott of 1955–6. In the Supreme Court decision, the drive for racial justice received the stamp of legality and the vital factor of public moral sanction. In the bus boycott, the movement found a charismatic leader, Martin Luther King, Jr., who has further developed and theorized the method of non-violence. He has not supplanted other leaders, nor has non-violence replaced education and legal action; but King and this method have become symbols of a new era.

What had been in the making for a decade, as Negro political power emerged on the national scene and Negro leadership became increasingly well trained and assured, sprang into being after the Supreme

RALPH LORD ROY

Conflict from the Communist Left and the Radical Right

Among American Christians the word "conflict" often carries with it a decidedly negative connotation. As a result, someone justifiably might pose the questions, "What is wrong with conflict? Did not Jesus foment considerable conflict? Were not the early apostles in reality apostles of conflict? Must not all loyal followers of Christ, if they seek to be true to their faith, be promoters of conflict?" Obviously such queries as these must be answered in the affirmative. There is nothing inherently wrong in conflict, or even in dissension or division. The focus here is upon a particular kind of conflict, one which has objectives which seem to be patently undesirable. A distinction must be drawn between creative conflict which issues in social change and discord which is promoted by Right and Left-Wing extremist groups.

It is wise at the outset to define the terms Left Wing and Right Wing as used hereafter since the use of these terms often is extremely ambiguous. The Left Wing may be precisely delineated. We shall mean only the American Communist party and groups and individuals purposefully sympathetic to that party. This discussion does not focus upon Socialists nor upon such Communist offshoots as the Trotskyites nor the Lovestoneites nor the Browderites nor, of course, those interesting experiments with Christian communism in a number of early American religious communities.

Defining the Right Wing cannot be achieved as simply. The Right Wing is not intended to be synonymous with conservatism, though in one sense, of course, the Right Wing is conservative, indeed, ultra-conservative. Nor should the Right Wing be confused with anti-Communism, since there are many liberals and even leftists who share a strong disdain for the American Communist party and its final authority, the Politburo of the Communist party of the USSR. The Right Wing to be discussed here is a loose configuration of organizations and individuals, under no one leader and following no definitive "party line."

It is possible only to catalogue some of the policies most Right Wingers oppose. They are against internationalism and what they refer to as a policy of "appeasement" or the "no win" policy abroad. More specifically, they oppose co-existence with international Communism; they oppose the United Nations; they oppose foreign aid (except in the cases of Chiang and perhaps Franco and Salazar); they oppose American soldiers under a unified command, as in NATO or in SEATO; and they oppose trade with any Communist-controlled state and with any other country which carries on commerce with the Communistic bloc of nations.

At home, the radical Right Wing opposes what it sees as socialistic trends and aggressive subversive forces in our midst. Usually rightists decry any attempt of the federal government to involve itself in areas of education, agriculture, health, housing, and race relations. They are against all efforts to liberalize our immigration policies, oppose heavy taxes, and frequently object to the whole principle of the progressive income tax. They assail the Supreme Court and the State Department; they vigorously defend the House Committee on Un-American Activities. Their heroes include General Douglas MacArthur, who could have been their leader had he responded to their appeals, and more recently, General Edwin A. Walker. Except for a few rabid anti-Catholics among them, they idolize the late Senator Joseph R. McCarthy; and, except for a few fanatics and anti-Semites in their midst, they admire Senator Barry Goldwater.

I CONFLICT FROM THE COMMUNIST LEFT

The attitude of the American Communist party toward the churches of this nation has not been consistent over the past four decades. It is possible to discern eight distinctive periods from the time the party was founded until the present day.

1. The first period, and the longest period, was from 1919 to 1931. These were the *years of indiscriminate attack*. All religions and religious institutions were subjected to sharp and often crude ridicule. No distinctions were made between progressive and conservative churchmen, between modernist and fundamentalist churchmen, between Negro and white churchmen.

2. The second period was from 1931 to 1935. These were the *years of*

transition. Beginning with the Scottsboro case in 1931, the Communists discovered, much to their amazement, that it was possible to win genuine support of some churchmen on critical issues, especially in the Negro community. By 1933, the first efforts were made to entice some clergymen, both white and Negro, into supporting the American League Against War and Fascism which was formed that year. Nonetheless, the official position of the party remained one of bitter hostility toward religious dogma and toward the organized church.

3. From 1935 to 1939, the *years of the united front,* the Communists exerted their greatest efforts to involve churchmen. Hundreds of clergymen of all denominations were successfully used. The high mark was reached in October 1937, when Maurice Thorez, leader of the French Communist party, proclaimed the policy of the "outstretched hand" to the Roman Catholic church and its adherents. The American Communist party immediately followed Thorez's lead.

4. The fourth period, from 1939 to 1941, was a time of Communist *retreat and isolation.* The front apparatus of the third period collapsed almost overnight in August 1939, when Hitler and Stalin announced their pact giving the Germans a free hand in Poland and precipitating war against France and England. What remained of the united front was battered further by Russia's attack upon Finland in December 1939, and by the alliance between Russia and Japan in April 1941. The hard-core members of the party, however, still sought to influence the churches and made some little progress with their theme of "peace" and non-involvement of the United States in another "capitalist war."

5. From 1941 to 1945 World War II raged, and immediately following Germany's attack upon Russia in June 1941, the Communists became *America's super-patriots.* They assailed religious pacifists (wooed only a few months earlier) as traitors. They praised progressive capitalism (while, simultaneously, most capitalists were praising the valor of the USSR, its leader, Stalin, its Red Army, and its people). In 1943 and 1944, the Communist party for the first time — and indeed, the only time — publicized its recruiting efforts among the clergy. It was during these two years that several ministers announced that they had become members of the Communist party of the U.S.A.

6. From 1945 to 1950, the Communists again sought to establish a widespread *front apparatus,* but along more sectarian lines than in the 1930's. While not reverting to the open hostility of the 1920's, the Communists again took a strong stand against the principal leadership of both the Protestant and the Roman Catholic churches. An authoritative article in *Political Affairs* in November 1946, for example, warned that

John Foster Dulles and such leading churchmen as Henry P. Van Dusen were propelling the Federal Council of Churches and the World Council of Churches into the orbit of "Vatican-inspired fascism."

7. From 1950 to 1956, as between 1939 and 1941, the pressing issue was again *peace*. Efforts were made to exploit the pacifism still much alive in the churches. There was even a Communist effort to feed the dissatisfaction with the Korean war among adherents of the Radical Right. This was the time of the Stockholm Peace Appeal, the American Peace Crusade, peace prayer vigils, the Lobby for Peace, and scores of other peace fronts and efforts. Several hundred clergy were deceived into supporting some Communist "peace" venture. Yet it was in this period, too, that the pressures against the Communist left were heaviest. It was during this period that such Left Wing political groups as the Methodist Federation for Social Action and the Episcopal League for Social Action and such magazines as *The Protestant* and *Social Questions Bulletin* reached their low ebb.

8. Since 1956 *the Communists have had no significant contact with the churches or with more than two dozen individual churchmen*. Three events in 1956 helped cripple the party, robbing it of most of its members, its funds, and its zeal.

One was the Twentieth Congress held in Moscow in February 1956 that led to de-Stalinization. To most of the party faithful, this was as though the god you had been worshiping for a generation had been exposed suddenly as a fraud.

This was followed in quick succession by Communist admissions of widespread anti-Semitic excesses in the USSR, the one land where Communists had contended for years that there were no remaining traces of anti-Semitism.

Then came the Hungarian revolution. It stunned Communists to find the Hungarian people rising up against the government of this people's democracy, the same people who had supported the Hungarian government overwhelmingly in a "free election" only shortly before.

Since 1956, therefore, the Communist party in America has been a tiny sect, virtually immobilized everywhere and especially in its relationship to the churches.

This rapid survey of the Communist attitudes toward the American churches illustrates the vacillation of the party during the past forty years.[1] At various times, at least four different strategies were employed.

The first Communist strategy may be designated as the *strategy of denunciation*. This was rooted in the writings of Marx and Lenin and was modeled after the early anti-religious practices of the USSR. Religion, whatever form it took, was seen as an opium of the people, cleverly manipulated by the ruling class to keep the people enslaved. "To the revolutionist," a *Daily Worker* editorial said in 1928, "all creeds, all churches, all temples of ignorance and superstition and fear, no matter what god or sets of gods they profess to worship, are useful to the capitalist class." It made no difference whatever that some clergymen wanted to befriend the workers or support the labor movement or even co-operate with the Communist party. Commented one Communist writer: "If these sky-pilots know that the church is a fraud, why don't they get out of it?"

Another side of this early strategy of denunciation was Communist *emphasis upon atheism.* The Communists sought to buttress their own children and other children as well against what they described as the "bourgeois poison" of religion in the public schools and elsewhere. They met with some success. Thus, one little child wrote the *Daily Worker* in 1924: "Our first teacher died and I was at her funeral. The priest was a great fool because he said such lies. I hate all priests." In 1926 another youngster sent this letter to the *Daily Worker:* "I wish the preachers would be chased out of here or go to work, so they would make a labor school instead of a church." In a few instances "Worker Sunday Schools" were established for the propagation of anti-religious views. In 1931, the Communists proudly announced the formation of the Workers' Anti-Religious League in New York City, patterned after the League of the Godless in the USSR.

A second strategy which developed in the early 1930's may be referred to as the *strategy of discrimination or selectivity.* It was first applied to the Negro clergy. Communists should take a special interest in the "little preachers," one party spokesman wrote. They are, he said, "closer to the masses and they hate the domination of the big ministers who speak for the ruling class." Gradually this policy of selectivity was expanded to cover all Protestantism and even Roman Catholicism. There were progressive churchmen to be treated with respect and there were reactionary churchmen to be villified. The Communists still were not changing their fundamental attitude toward religion, but they were beginning to understand the diversity in American religious life and to appreciate the individuality of many clergymen.

Then, with the creation of the united front apparatus of the mid-'thirties, came the *strategy of exploitation.* This proved to be the most successful approach of the American Communists to the churches and the clergy. The party sought to exploit organized religion and its influence in the United States by securing the names of clergymen on the letterheads of front groups, by soliciting the signatures of ministers, rabbis, and priests on petitions, and occasionally by enticing churchmen to speak at Communist-sponsored protest meetings. The strategies of denunciation and of discrimination both had been essentially honest. Now the Communists adopted a deliberately deceptive approach. The idea was no longer to abuse the churches; the goal now was to use the churches. The Communists were assisted immeasurably by a tiny but active corps of ministers who were convinced of the righteousness of the Communist cause, men like Harry F. Ward of the Methodist Federation for Social Action, William B. Spofford, Sr., editor of *The Witness,* and Claude C. Williams of the People's Institute of Applied Religion. The Communists, aided by these few ministers, traded upon the idealism of the American clergy. They chose attractive causes, provided their fronts with innocent-sounding names, formulated seductive slogans, and then systematically rounded up support among churchmen.

This support was solicited in many different ways. It might be through a letter mailed to hundreds of ministers pleading for help in the case of Willie McGee, a Mississippi Negro finally executed for alleged rape of a white woman. It might be an urgent telephone call from one clergyman to another asking support for a rally against the end of rent control. It might be through a petition, circulated on the streets and even at ministerial associations, asking for an end to nuclear tests. In most cases, the cause itself was a deserving one. What the victim did not know — and what the Communists did not tell him — was that they were hoping to use his good name to help camouflage the activities of the party.

There were several cases in which this strategy of exploitation was exposed. One such case revolved around a distinguished Congregationalist minister who became a leader in the front apparatus in the 1930's. He knew that he was co-operating with Communists, but he believed that the Communists operated openly and honestly as he himself did. By 1940, he was serving as chairman of one of the principal Communist fronts. This was during the period of the Hitler-Stalin pact. Naïvely, he introduced a resolution critical of the concordat between the Nazis and the Communists at the group's annual membership meeting. To his amazement, it was shouted down. Only then was he made aware that the organization was controlled by Communists, that they had packed the meeting, and that they viewed him simply as window-dressing to hide their manipulations.

Why, one is justified in asking, were sophisticated, alert clergymen like this man ready to co-operate with Communists in the 'thirties? Why were they willing to work with a secular faith, indeed a rival faith, which had declared its intention to foment revolution, which professed atheism, and which was basically hostile to organized religion whatever the twists and turns in its current line?

Several clergymen have volunteered answers to these questions. In some instances they had become disillusioned with parish life where they witnessed so much complacency and apathy. They were aroused by the deprivation and the unemployment which they saw around them. They were angered by the racial discrimination and prejudice so prevalent in America. They were incensed by the Right Wing of the 1930's, especially the Hearst press, which led a continuing attack upon every progressive measure. Many had strong pacifist inclinations and believed that private industry, especially the munitions manufacturers, were eager for war in a drive for profits. Even more important, perhaps, was the world view of the 'thirties. While the Communists in the United States struggled and sacrificed for social progress, the Soviet Union stood out among the nations of the world as the champion of peace and progress. Russia had signed the Kellogg pact. Russia had taken the lead for disarmament at world conferences. Yet, when fascism threatened, it appeared to be only Russia who was ready to assist helpless Ethiopia; it was only Russia who intervened on behalf of the Spanish Loyalists; and it was only Russia that stood against the appeasement of the Munich pact.

There were other reasons for this co-operation with Communists that are far more subtle. There were ministers in rebellion against the middle-class morality of the church who felt a certain satisfaction when they rubbed shoulders with fiery apostles of the Left. Frankly stated, the fact that the Communist party gave clergymen top billing appealed to the ego of some. Others felt a sense of social mission and social accomplishment when they spoke out against injustice before cheering crowds. These were some of the reasons why clergymen did not find it so hard to work with Communists. There were other, often more personal reasons, as well.

There was a fourth strategy, used only rarely by the Communists, but the strategy that has created so much suspicion and led to so many false charges. This was *the strategy of infiltration*. There are only a few known instances where the Communist party actually sought to infiltrate local parishes, usually Negro parishes. One such case involved an African Methodist Episcopal church in Far Rockaway, Long Island. Here the pastor, Solomon Freeman, was recruited into the Communist party during World War II. His assignment was to enroll other ministers into the party. He failed in this, but he did succeed in forming a Communist cell of over thirty of his parishioners who met each Thursday evening in his church. After a year Freeman moved to Brooklyn, left the party because he considered the dues too high, and the cell was disbanded.

An even earlier example of attempted infiltration involved a Presbyterian church in Harlem which occurred during the mid-'thirties. A group of Communist youths sought to capture a young adult organization of the church and met with considerable success. The pastor and his wife, however, uncovered their real motives and succeeded in foiling the Communists in their plans.

Despite these efforts at infiltration, there was never any serious Communist influence in our churches, even at the height of the united front period. Today that influence is almost at the zero mark. There is only one identifiable Communist minister, the Reverend Eliot White of Arlington, Massachusetts, a man who has not served a pulpit since 1931, a man who is 92, a man who is blind. There are at the most two dozen clergymen who can be fairly described as fellow travelers. None of them is influential. Indeed, only two or three of them occupy pulpits at the present time.

II CONFLICT FROM THE RADICAL RIGHT

The high point of Right Wing hysteria in the churches was reached in 1952 and 1953 when a whole series of events, culminating in the Bishop Oxnam hearing, brought the charges of subversion in the sanctuary into the headlines.[2] With the death of Senator Joseph R. McCarthy, the hysteria waned until the publication of the Air Force Manual in 1960. In 1961 the John Birch Society was discovered by the press and the old estimate of 7000 Communist agents and dupes in the ministry was re-echoed by Robert Welch and was again spread across the press. Today we have scores of anti-Communist publications, rallies, and schools all vying with one another for power, for publicity, and, be it noted, for money.

At least two popular misconceptions should be clarified at the outset. First, contrary to the contentions of several eminent scholars, the current upsurge of the Right Wing is not to be seen as a resurgence of Protestant fundamentalism. The error in this assertion is in the failure to understand the nature of fundamentalism. Piety has been confused with theology, for many important and affluent figures on the Far Right are exceedingly liberal theologically. Biblical literalism, for example, and such doctrines as the vicarious atonement of Christ play no part in their thinking. It is important to remember, too, that many fundamentalist leaders, among them Billy Graham, refuse to join the Radical Right.

A second common misconception is that the Radical Right of the

1960's is simply a revival of the McCarthy alliance of a decade earlier. This opinion holds that after the defeat and death of the senator, many of his followers were temporarily lost in anonymity, leaderless, but no less adamant in their extreme views. Now, the argument goes, they are staging a comeback.

The movement known as McCarthyism focused upon one issue: anti-Communism. The Radical Right Wing of the 1960's, of course, shares this concern, but its protest goes far beyond hysteria over alleged subversion, State Department spies, and twenty-one years of treason.

Radical Rightists, unlike many McCarthyites of the 1950's (including McCarthy himself), embrace an ultra-conservative economic philosophy. Moreover, there are some essential distinctions between the camp followers in each instance. Many fundamentalists, and other Protestants as well, who were not attracted to McCarthy because of fear of his Roman Catholicism, have no such reservations about the Radical Right. Conversely, and of particular importance in the Northeast, many Roman Catholics who flocked to McCarthy are not as quickly wooed by such roving evangelist-patriots as Fred Schwartz or Billy James Hargis or even by a Senator Goldwater. Their views were further influenced by the election of Kennedy as President. Many avid McCarthyites in such cities as New York and Boston were Irish Roman Catholics. Many among this group feel a strong emotional identification with Kennedy and are very reluctant to believe that Communism is flourishing in Washington under the nation's first Irish Catholic President.

That the Right Wing has become more vocal and better organized since 1960 is obvious. Why has this happened? There is no one answer, and writers who trace the resurgence of the Right to any one or two factors are oversimplifying a complex picture.

One factor is clearly the international situation. America is only one generation removed from isolationism and the refusal to join the League of Nations. Combined with this isolation is aggressive nationalism that contradicts isolationism in a sense, but in another sense buttresses it. Together they produce a "go-it-alone" attitude. Somehow, if the United States were not subverted by its enemies and strangled by its alleged friends, America would not have all the difficulties it faces today. World problems are easy to solve, is the argument. One simply does what is right.

We would have followed such a righteous course, the argument continues, if we were not sold out at Yalta by Roosevelt, if our State Department had not been subverted by Communist agents like Alger Hiss, if our atomic secrets had not been stolen by the Rosenbergs, and if we were allowed to win the war in Korea by Truman and Eisenhower. Spies, fellow-travelers, liberals, college professors, and bleeding-heart preachers have somehow conspired against us and we cannot regain our national sanity until we clean them out. Meanwhile, the Radical Rightists indignantly point their fingers of accusation in many different directions.

A second factor has been the national controversy over integration. Not long ago, internationalism and liberal domestic policies received strong support from the South. That support has been waning, and one factor is the success of extremists in enlisting southerners under the banner of states' rights. The fear is that Communists, "pinks," and liberals will not be content until we have a nation of mulattoes.

A third factor in the rise of the Radical Right has been the emergence of capable spokesmen on its behalf. Writers for the *National Review* head the list—men like William Buckley, William Henry Chamberlain, William Rusher, Orval Watts, and many others. They have been able to give the Right an intellectual respectability which it lacked for many years. The appearance of Senator Goldwater on the national scene has been important also. He is as honest and as genuine as the late Senator Robert A. Taft, but he is more attractive and his views are even more palatable to the Far Right.

A fourth factor is the sense of insecurity and frustration experienced by many Americans. John Glenn was not the first man to encircle the earth in space. Our rocket was not the first to hit the moon. There is widespread fear that our weapons may not be as powerful as those of the Soviet Union. In addition to these frightening developments in the race for world supremacy, the Right sees socialism creeping forward at home. They blame Eisenhower for not stopping it; indeed, he encouraged it. With Kennedy as President, aggressive liberalism is again in control and conservatives are panicky. To all this is added an insecurity arising out of prosperity—a fear that what we have may be taken away, a fear that through taxes and red tape Big Brother Government is enslaving all of us.

Fifth, there are many psychological and sociological roots which have contributed to the rise of Right Wing extremism in American life.[3] One scholar has suggested that the Radical Right feeds on a fear among white Protestants that they have lost their privileged position in American society. Others see its resurgence as a protest against the defeat of rural, moralistic America by an urban America where ethical relativism is powerful.

It might be suggested that with the days of pioneering over, with the safety valve of the westward movement no longer available, with revivalism and dogmatic religion no longer in vogue as it was a century ago, the zeal and the dogmatism and the vigor of many Americans has to find a new channel for expression. People are looking for a cause, a goal, a purpose, a certainty amid so much uncertainty.

More money and more leisure time and modern means of communication play an important role, too. The money enables the Radical Right to propagandize widely and effectively; the free leisure time means that more people can spend more time attending anti-Communist schools and reading rightist literature; modern means of communication enables the radicals to reach new millions through television and radio and inexpensive paperback books.

Various psychologists see the upsurge of the Right Wing as evidence of self-hate or of feelings of guilt. It may even be described in terms of the breakdown of the American family.

A final factor contributing to the resurgence of the Right Wing merits a more detailed examination. For many years, extremists have been focusing upon certain issues year after year. By 1960 they seemed to be breaking through to the American people. Once this happened, a "bandwagon psychology" developed and dozens of new patriots began to peddle their wares across the nation.

Money became more plentiful as big business and little business both, alarmed by what they heard and read, generously began to contribute to hucksters of hysteria. The more money contributed, the more literature is published. With more literature reaching more people, more people become alarmed and more people give and more literature is published and still more people become alarmed — and on it spirals.

There are many different ways of categorizing the hundreds of groups that collectively feed the Radical Right. Motivation is one index. As in most movements, motives doubtless are mixed. Certainly some leaders and certainly thousands of followers are fully sincere. They dedicate their time and their talent and their money to defend something dear to them which they believe is threatened. But other motives are apparent also. Some rightist leaders enjoy the publicity and the notoriety. Some make a handsome living. A few probably are affected by some mental illness.

Just as motives differ, so do methods. Some groups engage in wholesale, wanton, malicious slander. They move from town to town, sowing confusion and dissension wherever they go. Others speak in more general terms; indeed, most of what they say about Communism is correct. The problem is that they approach the subject with an emotion and with an urgency that generates hysteria when reason and common sense are so urgently needed.

These extremist groups may be categorized in many different ways.

There are, first, the "far out" groups. These include the anti-Semites who have been claiming that Communism is Jewish for many years. The Jews, they claim, control an "Invisible Government" which manipulates all the nations of the world. The Jews are responsible for all evil. Bernard Baruch has been the "dictator" of the United States. Justice Frankfurter controlled the Supreme Court until Justice Goldberg succeeded him. The Jews caused World War I to give power to the Bolsheviks — this was the first Zionist War. They then led America into World War II to destroy Stalin's only serious obstacle, Adolph Hitler in Europe and the empire of Japan in Asia. In 1950, they caused the "third Zionist War," the Korean War, which they then deliberately sabotaged.

Others who may be classed as "far out" are virulent and even violent segregationists who view integration as a Communist plot. There is an amazing assortment of medical quacks who believe that fluoridation of the water is sponsored by Communists to "poison" the American people. Others warn against the Salk polio vaccine as a Communist maneuver; they endorse fake cancer treatments; they sell all kinds of bizarre health foods.

Finally, of course, there are groups such as the Minute Men, who are prepared to conduct guerrilla warfare against the Communists; or the Conservative Society of America, which proposes the lynching of Chief Justice Warren (because impeachment is too good for him); and others such as the John Birch Society, whose leader describes former President Eisenhower as a consciously Communist agent.

A group of fundamentalists comprise the second category. They see the issue in theological terms. The world is a battlefield and there are two contestants. One is God, who leads the legions of good. The other is Satan, who will face ultimate defeat but who will meanwhile gain major victories. Satan, who is the father of Communism, works in very deceptive ways. To prepare the way for Communism in other parts of the world, Satan has devised a remarkable scheme. He is spreading modernism and disbelief across our land. He is using Christian clergymen to deny the fundamentals of the Christian faith — the virgin birth of Christ, his physical resurrection, the inerrancy of the Word of God. When faith is thus polluted, it can be destroyed. Just as the serpent Satan stole into the Garden of Eden, so has the serpent Satan stolen into the very center of our religious life.

Many fundamentalists, as pointed out before, are not identified with the Radical Right. The most persistent rightist among them has been Carl McIntire, who was ousted from the ministry of the Presbyterian Church in the U.S.A. in 1936 for creating dissension within that denomination. Since that time he has not ceased in his attacks upon all of the major churches. McIntire's influence on the Radical Right is limited by his insistence upon assailing the Roman Catholic Church. Tactically, the leaders of the Radical Right find it unwise to be anti-Catholic in the 1960's.

Third, there are dozens of extremely conservative groups in America, some of them, like the Committee for Constitutional Government, with a long history. Many of these groups are quasi-anarchistic in their ideology, though they would hotly dispute this characterization. They frequently oppose public schools and libraries as socialistic. Some even oppose public highways as socialistic. They insist upon the repeal of the Sixteenth Amendment as quickly as possible, for the income tax, a plan "originally proposed by Karl Marx," is seen at the root of all our major evils.

In the churches the most vocal extreme economic conservatives are found allied with Spiritual Mobilization and with the Christian Freedom Foundation, publishers of *Christian Economics*.[4] These groups are well-financed. Their publications are quite literate, even sophisticated in spots, always pious.

Finally, conflict and discord among people in general, including church people, have been fostered by persons who lay claim to special firsthand experience. They may be divided into groups: certain ex-Communists and certain ex-FBI agents.

Some articulate ex-Communists are ready to place their confessions on sale and appear as speakers in cities and towns across the nation to tell their listeners of unnamed ministers whom they knew to be members of the party. Their estimates of Communist infiltration usually are staggering. Their main spokesmen have included Louis F. Budenz, a former editor of the *Daily Worker* who returned to the Roman Catholic church; Joseph Kornfeder, known in the party as Joseph Zack, who was ousted from the party for alleged Trotskyite sympathies in 1934; and former general secretary of the party, Benjamin Gitlow, also ousted from the party when he refused to follow a Moscow directive that control of the party should be handed over to William Z. Foster in 1929.

The ex-FBI agent is even more difficult to cope with than the ex-Communist. Herbert Philbrick, for example, can speak in generalities about the menace of Communist influence in the churches and millions of Americans will believe him.

We have not attempted to touch upon many issues related to the topic. What should be the response of our churches and of Americans generally to the Left and particularly to the current avalanche from the Radical

Right? What is the appropriate course of action for the parish clergyman? The seminary teacher? The church editor? The concerned layman?

Can the resurgence of the Right, together with the virtual disappearance of the Communist Left in the United States, have some positive results? What kind of judgment on the churches is implicit in the inroads of the Right among churchmen?

It should be re-emphasized, in summation, that conflict is a welcome part of American life. Indeed, the churches and their clergy and laity must, in one sense, always be at odds with the established order of things. There are times when the demands of justice must outweigh the desire for unity, when churchmen must choose light at the expense of sweetness. Yet, the Judeo-Christian tradition demands that conflict be rooted in reason and in truth and in charity, not in hysteria and in falsehood and in hate. Herein rests the basic difficulty with both the Communist Left and the Radical Right.

NOTES

1. For a fuller discussion, see my *Communism and the Churches* (New York: Harcourt, Brace, 1960).
2. For a discussion of the earlier situation, see my *Apostles of Discord* (Boston: Beacon, 1953). Also, see John Higham, *Strangers in the Land* (New Brunswick: Rutgers University Press, 1955).
3. Daniel Bell, ed., *The Radical Right* (Garden City: Doubleday, 1963), and Robert Lee, "Social Sources of the Radical Right," *The Christian Century* (May 9, 1962), 595–7.
4. George Younger, "Protestant Piety and the Right Wing," *Social Action* (May 15, 1951).

SEYMOUR MARTIN LIPSET

Religion and Politics in the American Past and Present *

I INTRODUCTION: INTERACTION OF RELIGION AND POLITICS

The interrelationship between religion and politics in the United States has been of interest to most analysts of American culture. To a considerable extent there has been general agreement that the fact of a pluralistic religious culture — the existence of many competing denominations — has contributed to the development and stability of American democracy. All American religions have been numerical minorities for much of our history, and hence have an "interest" in democratic liberties. Tocqueville's comment on the source of American Catholic commitment to democratic rights applies to most groups: "They constitute a minority, and all rights must be respected in order to ensure them the free exercise of their own privileges." [1] The prevalence of voluntary associations, many of which have played major roles in shaping political issues, seems causally related to the pattern of voluntary benevolent and

* I am grateful to Barclay Johnson for research assistance and to Earl Raab for editing a much longer manuscript. IBM cards from various surveys which have been used for secondary analysis came from the Roper Public Opinion Library at Williams College, and research funds were obtained from a "basic research" grant from the Behavioral Science Division at the Ford Foundation. I am also indebted to the Survey Research Center of the University of California for their assistance. The relationship of American church structure, historic patterns of participation, and theology to the basic traits in American society is dealt with in S. M. Lipset, *The First New Nation: The United States in Historical and Comparative Perspective* (New York: Basic Books, 1963), pp. 140–69, 79–83.

moral associations which developed around the various denominations.

But if there is abundant discussion of the impact of religion as an institution on the general character of the polity, there is an understandable reluctance to deal with the way in which religious interest or belief enters directly into the main stream of political controversy, determining and structuring the nature of party conflict. No political party now wants to be in the position of explicitly alienating any religious group, and no religious denomination wants to acknowledge an identification with one political party.

Yet it should be obvious that simply as an important value-generating institution and source of status and power, religion cannot exist without seriously affecting the nature of political discourse. Tocqueville, Bryce, and many other sophisticated foreign commentators on nineteenth century America discussed the interaction between party choice and religious affiliation. A host of moral issues which separated the parties were clearly associated with religious belief. The modern assumption that a relationship between religion and politics violates "separation of church and state," has only in recent decades served to suppress serious intellectual inquiry into the interaction of these two key institutions.

Nothing is so revealing of the strength of the taboo on this subject than the story of the way in which the pollsters and others who have been gathering statistics on voting behavior had to be forced by the analysis of their data to accept the fact that religious affiliation had an independent effect on vote choice.

For many years, George Gallup, the head of the first permanent polling agency in the United States, did not inquire regularly concerning the religious affiliation of respondents in his election and other opinion surveys. The first major academic study of voting preference based on interviews, that of Lazarsfeld and his associates in 1940, found a large difference in the party choice of Protestants as compared to Catholics, no matter what other factors, such as education and economic status, were held constant. This came as a considerable surprise to them, since there was no issue related to religion, as such, in this election.[2] As recently as 1959, Elmo Roper, who directs a second national survey group, wrote that there was no relationship between religious affiliation and voting.[3] And, of course, in writing about determinants of partisan choice in past elections, historians, other than those writing directly on religion, tended to concentrate on variations among socio-economic groups, regions, and to some extent ethnic groups. Systematic investigation of the interrelationships of these factors with religion has only occurred in the last two decades.

But if the relationship of religion to politics was a relatively neglected subject, social scientists have pointed up for some time the fact that there is variation in other aspects of behavior associated with religious background. That is, when one is seeking to analyze what makes people behave differently, whether it be their work habits, parent-child relationships, size of family, achievement aspirations, and the like, religion must be included among the list of explanatory variables. At the least, such research has demonstrated that religious denominations must be regarded as sub-cultural units which serve as important reference groups for their members. That is, these are the social groups whose approbation a member seeks, or from whom he takes his standards of judgment in many aspects of behavior. Political behavior clearly falls into the area of those heavily linked to religious background. However, to say this is not to explain anything. The tendency of different political identities is not, of course, a product of historical whimsy. There are at least three kinds of variation among religious groups which bear on their political differentiation:

1. *Different Social Characteristics.* Different church groupings have definable differences in the socio-economic and ethnic composition as well as in the geography of their memberships.

2. *Different Historical Experiences.* The Episcopalian and Congregationalist churches were state-established churches in early America; the Baptist and Methodist churches were not. In the 1930's, world Jewry was under attack by Adolf Hitler. These secular experiences have had a relationship to political identification.

3. *Different Religious Values.* Different religious groups vary in religious ideology in such spheres as public morality and social welfare. Methodists and Baptists have been concerned with the evils inherent in liquor and gambling; Catholics reject birth control and divorce as sinful.

The close interdependence of these three factors for any given religious group is obvious. It is the continuing task of religious history and sociology to probe the shifting relationships among these factors, but it is sufficiently clear that they have operated to make religious variation a matter of political significance in America.

Tracing the religious-political pattern in the United States is the chief concern of this chapter. The political history of the country is so short that this pattern is almost a matter of variations on one basic design. The first part of the paper deals with the establishment of that design: the formative years and the one major realignment which took place around the middle of the nineteenth century. This is a sweeping attempt to describe the development of the basic religious-political pattern, without detailing the variations or passing contradictions which must attend any such broad historical generalization.[4]

This examination finds that such variable factors as these served to affect the basic political differentiation among American religious bodies: (1) social status, (2) economic class, (3) anti-Catholicism in both its religious and ethnic form, (4) level of concern with "public morality." The interplay of these and other factors in the religious-political pattern of twentieth century America is then substantively examined. It becomes abundantly clear that political variation among religious groups is not just a matter of statistical curiosity, but it is closely related to the broad shaping of American political life.

II THE BASIC DESIGN

A. The Formative Years. America's first experience with political differentiation among religious groups began with the founding of the nation. The Episcopalian and Congregationalist churches became identified with the conservative Federalists and Whigs, while the Baptist, Methodist, and Presbyterian churches were linked with the Jeffersonians and Jacksonians. Initially, this divergence was in some part the result of the different social characteristics of these religious groups, and in some part related to the fact that the former had been state-established churches. Both before and after the formation of the United States as a nation, it was not only a country whose population was largely Protestant, but specific Protestant denominations were the official state church. Almost all of the colonies had an established church, the Church of England in the South and the Congregationalists in the North. Though we now think of the Constitution as having outlawed religious establishments when it laid down the principle of separation of church and state, in fact, it did not. The Bill of Rights states that *Congress* shall make no laws with respect to the the establishment of religion. Until the passage of the Fourteenth Amendment in 1866, this provision did not affect the individual states.

In some states these established churches were not disestablished until the second decade of the nineteenth century — in the final case of Massachusetts not until 1833, forty-four years after the adoption of the Constitution.[5] The struggle for the disestablishment of the churches on the state level was related to party politics of its day. The original party fight was between the liberal Democratic-Republicans, led by Jefferson and Madison, and the conservative Federalists, led by John Adams, Alexander Hamilton, and others. One of the differences between the Democratic-

Republican leaders, who in a sense were the left wingers of their day, and present liberal political leaders, is that many of the former were Deists in their religious belief. They tended to look upon much of organized religion and most of the theologies of their day as outmoded medieval beliefs which would dwindle away. They were children of the Enlightenment intellectually. As in the case of the scholars of the European Enlightenment, they saw the modern world of the late eighteenth or early nineteenth century as growing beyond the superstitions which were regarded as hangovers from feudalism, medievalism, and a monarchical society.

On the other hand, the more traditionalistic Federalists were concerned with maintaining various values and behavior patterns that persisted from colonial times. Many of them favored the preservation of established religions. The Congregationalist church was the established church for many years in three Federalist strongholds—New Hampshire until 1817, Connecticut until 1818, and Massachusetts until 1833.[6]

The defeat of the Federalists, first in the South where the Jeffersonians were dominant, then later in New England, was related to the disestablishment of the churches. It should be noted that while there was, in this period, a decline of religious institutions generally, the elimination of established religion was not in itself a defeat of religion; the Protestant denominations which were *not* established predictably supported the disestablishment of the state church.

The resolution of the Establishment issue in the early nineteenth century did not, of course, end the relationship between various denomination and party politics. Evidence drawn from an analysis of voting records would suggest that the link between the traditional high status churches, Anglican and Congregationalist, and the more conservative party continued after the demise of the Federalists. Conversely those denominations which were associated with lower status groups, either in terms of ethnic origins, more recent immigrant status, or class composition, tended to be identified with the Democrats. Catholics, largely Irish, though not yet the major force they were to become, still were a noticeable group in some of the larger cities such as Boston and New York, and then as later were largely Democratic.

These relationships between religion and party were, like all such statistical associations, a product of a number of factors. In part, they reflected an "interest" struggle among denominations; the established churches, past or present, were linked to the party of the Establishment, the Federalists. To some degree they were determined by traditions or values associated with certain denominations; the Calvinist groups, in particular, viewed Catholicism as representing great evil, the "anti-Christ" in Rome. Further, they flowed from class or status elements; the more well-to-do, who were also disproportionately members of the established churches, tended to support the more conservative party, while the poorer strata, who adhered to the new sects or the Catholic church, were Jeffersonians. The linkage between Catholics, plus others of more recent immigrant stock, and the Democrats was cemented at this early period in American history by the fact that the Federalists openly and avowedly tried to make life difficult for them, while the Jeffersonians defended their interests and rights.[7]

All the studies of voting behavior during this period agree that religious affiliation played a major role in differentiating the supporters of the two parties. The most detailed of them, that by Manning Dauer covering elections around 1800, reports that the Federalist party benefited considerably from Congregationalist support.[8] The Episcopalians, who had been the established church in the southern states, also gave heavy backing to the conservative party. "The other religions whose members originally supported the Federalists were the German Reformed, Dutch Reformed, and Lutheran denominations . . . the Quakers, strongest in Pennsylvania, were generally Federalist, except when war threatened."[9] In areas which backed the Jeffersonians "the chief denominations were the Baptists . . . the Methodists and Presbyterians . . . concentrated in the back country geographically; and these same denominations plus the Irish Catholics in the towns."[10] It is difficult to estimate the extent to which such apparent differences in denominational political allegiance were directly related to the interest or theological positions of the churches, or reflected variations in socio-economic position. The denominations which backed the Democrats all had an "interest" in disestablishment; they were largely composed of the less well-to-do; the Baptists and the Methodists were new sects whose ministers and adherents ranked low in the social hierarchy; the Presbyterians were largely a low-status Scotch-Irish immigrant group who had been rejected by the Puritans of New England and "were natural recruits for a leveling party."[11]

One would expect, however, that these groups would be among the most moralistic, and dislike the secularistic attitudes and policies of many Democratic leaders. The binding link between the "out-group" sects and the Deist party leaders would seem to have been a common dislike of the power and influence of the once established or traditional denominations. Insofar as the state enforced Christian norms, it reflected the past strength of the Establishment, and a decisive break between church and state meant the triumph of religious equalitarianism.

The highly visible character of the link between politics and religion may be seen in the comments of two ministers, one Congregationalist and the other Methodist, concerning the politics of the early nineteenth century. The Congregationalist recorded that the Jeffersonians included "nearly all the minor sects, besides the Sabbath-breakers, rum-selling, tippling folk, infidels, and ruff-scruff generally." The Methodist minister wrote: "The great mass . . . of the Methodist church and her adherents were Republicans. Every convert to Methodism in those times became a Republican if he was not one before . . . On the other hand Calvinism and Federalism were yoked together." [12]

There is an abundant literature of sermons and articles which testifies to the close tie between Congregationalism and Federalism. The Jeffersonians were denounced from many pulpits as advocates of atheism and immorality. Inequality was defended as part of the divine scheme of things. Alexander Hamilton saw in the formation of a Christian Constitutional Society the salvation of the Federalist party. Even irreligious conservatives "considered religion indispensable to restrain the brute appetites of lower orders." [13]

Differences over the relationship of the church and state played a major role in structuring the revived two-party system which formed around supporters and opponents of Andrew Jackson. One of the first major revivals of the Jacksonians, the anti-Masonic party, which was to become one of the major constituent elements in the Whig party, sought to bring together those who favored an alliance between church and state. And the Whig party basically took over this task.

> Battlegrounds shifted over time, but the lines drawn in the 1830's between "the Church and State party" and the "Jackson Party" held fast. Struggles over Sunday laws, the sustained effort to open public assemblies with prayer, Jackson's refusal to act against Georgia for imprisoning missionaries to the Cherokees — on these and like issues, party differences were distinct, passionate and enduring.[14]

The northern Whig spokesmen, like the Federalists before them, gave voice to the values of the dethroned Puritan Establishment. They argued that the state was a proper instrument to eradicate moral evils such as gambling and "grogselling," while the Democrats sought to limit the role of the state to the prevention of evils which resulted from individuals or groups being interfered with by others. The religious feeling and action that underlay the Federalist and Whig moralistic concerns may be seen in the activities of Lyman Beecher, who, as a key figure in the Congregationalist church, also was involved successively in Federalist, Whig, and later Republican politics. He, like many others of the New England theocrats, "sought to reestablish a clerically dominated social order by means of voluntary social and moral reform societies that would give the clergy an influential role in forming public opinion and molding public legislation. The many 'benevolent societies' of the [Jacksonian] Period, which sought to evangelize the unchurched, to save the heathen, to sober the drunkard, to rescue the wayward female, to purify the Sabbath, to end dueling, to inaugurate Sunday Schools, and to send freed slaves back to Africa . . . [were composed largely of] the ministers and leading laymen and women of the Congregational churches." [15]

The party struggle was clearly not between religion and irreligion, although apparently most free-thinkers and their organizations supported the Democrats, while the very devout, particularly among the older once-established groups, backed the Whigs.[16]

It is important to recognize that there was considerable congruence between the Jacksonian concern for secular equalitarianism and the struggle against the domination of the theocracy in religion. As McLoughlin puts it, "Here was the essence of the quarrel between the Whigs and the Jacksonians: the fight against aristocracy and privilege in politics had a clear parallel in religion." [17]

B. The Great Re-Alignment. The early religious-political pattern in America, therefore, found the more evangelical Protestants, particularly the Baptists, the Methodists, and the Presbyterians, backing the Jeffersonians-become-Democrats, along with the emerging Catholic population. The more deeply established and less evangelical Protestants, notably the Congregationalists and the Episcopalians, supported the Federalists and Whigs-become-Republican. But by the time the two-party system had been recast in its durable Republican-Democratic mold after the Civil War, the northern Methodists, Presbyterians, and Baptists were predominantly Republican. Since most American Protestants had by then become Baptists and Methodists, this realignment meant that native-born Protestants in general had become predominantly Republican.

There were, of course, a number of reasons for the shift of these several Protestant bodies. To begin with, both their socio-economic level in society and their symbolic status rose rapidly. The high-status churches, Episcopal, Congregational, Quaker, and Unitarian, had not participated in the evangelical revivalism and expansion which the other Protestant groups underwent during the first half of the nineteenth century. The once-established churches remained disproportionately concentrated in the cities of the East, and declined in relative numerical importance. At the same time the influx of Roman Catholic immigrants, especially the Irish, swelled the working class. Thus, in terms of relative standing in the social scale, Methodists and Baptists, particularly the former, were both pulled and pushed upward. Simultaneously, these groups underwent in varying degrees the familiar shift from sect to denomination, a shift which was consonant with the forces changing their social position from without. In fact, these groups attained something of the status of "established churches" themselves. By 1850, two-thirds of the Protestants were Baptists and Methodists. Both groups had a sizable middle-class membership, and the Methodists possessed considerable urban strength.

With the increase in numbers and influence of these ascendant Protestant groups went a corresponding increase in willingness to use state power to enforce "their morality." There was still a kind of parallel between the fight against the political establishment and the fight against the (now unofficial) religious establishment, but the Baptists and Methodists began to move to the "other side" of the fight as they became more "established" themselves. They joined older-established Protestant churches and the prevailing conservative political party in raising moral concerns as public issues. A purely religious dimension entered as a differentiating factor here. The Episcopalian church (like the Lutheran and the Catholic churches) had come out of a tradition of having been state and total society churches, and never did see their religious mission as prescribing behavior, in the same way that the sects or denominations with sectarian origins typically do. Thus, in the early part of the nineteenth century, the surge of organizational movements to raise public morality — e.g., for temperance, peace, abolition of slavery, and maintenance of the Sabbath — were predominantly fostered by members of the old Federalist upper class and Congregational ministers, aided by the Presbyterians.

For example, the early nineteenth-century concern with the drinking habits and general state of morality among the population had strong class and political links. "The Federalists reasoned that if they could wean men from profanity, vice, and inebriation, the former sinners would be amenable to changing their political allegiance."[18] Reports of the day indicate that temperance and Federalism were closely identified by friends and foes alike.[19]

This early temperance movement had been dominated by members of the old Calvinist denominations, but its social base began to change in the 1840's. The rising evangelical sects also turned against the sin of drink. It was "becoming a potent sign of middle class status, distinguishing the abstainer from the lower levels of the ne'er-do-wells, the unambitious and the irreligious." [20]

As a matter of fact, the Baptists and the Methodists called for more drastic measures than did the earlier temperance leaders. The former favored total abstinence and eventually the passage of prohibition legislation, whereas the latter had advocated education to secure moderate drinking.[21]

Similarly, the leadership of the abolitionist organizations, begun in the 1830's, was drawn from substantial upper-middle class and distinguished Federalist families, predominantly Congregational, Presbyterian, and Quaker, even though they included many Methodists, and were supported of course by Transcendentalist-Unitarian intellectuals.[22] However, a number of studies have associated the subsequent mass growth of the anti-slavery movement in the North with the emergent evangelical denominations.[23] Abolition had particular strength in areas which had been subject to successful revivalist campaigns.[24]

While the more evangelical denominations fostered abolitionist sentiment in the North, it is significant to note that membership in the very same churches was related to support for slavery in the South. Thus the three churches which split into the northern and southern wings were the Presbyterians, Baptists, and Methodists. The Presbyterians suffered their first division in 1837–38. "Although the split of New School and Old School was ostensibly along theological lines, in fact the South remained with the Old School and the alliance of abolitionism and revivalism shaped the New School General Assembly." [25]

The Baptists and Methodists also separated long before the Civil War as a result of "contrasting attitudes on the part of the two sections of the church (North and South) on a moral question, slavery." [26] The positions of each of these evangelical denominations on opposite sides of the abolition question partly reflect the "settling in" of these groups, North and South, and their consequent support of their respective political establishments. It is notable, however, that abolition was an issue that lent itself to deep "moral" feeling on both sides, and was one therefore in which these denominations were able to commit themselves more thoroughly and with more religious vehemence than the Episcopalian, the Catholic, or the Lutheran bodies.

The clue to understanding these reactions lies in the attitudes toward sin which had emerged among the deeply religious evangelical American Protestants:

> The most significant characteristic of the Protestant attitude was a consciousness of the evil nature of sin. Protestant expounders made a simple and

clear-cut distinction between right and wrong. Man was either saved or damned. Righteousness would be rewarded, sin punished. Sin must be fought. . . .

Urged on by conscience, the dissatisfied soon found that the [basic community] sin was the sin of slavery. This cancer of society should be cut out, and stern duty called upon foes of sin to remove it. . . . These intense foes of the South were going to do everything possible to destroy slavery. They found their duty all the more compelling as the sin was largely in the body politic of the South, and attack upon it must weaken those who held power.[27]

Just as evangelical Protestantism helped to make the conflict "irrepressible" by bolstering the moral fiber of abolitionism, it served the same role south of the Mason-Dixon line by defining the sectional conflict as one of God versus Satan as well:

The South, men said and did not doubt, was peculiarly Christian; probably, indeed, it was the last great bulwark of Christianity. . . . From pulpit and hustings ran the dark suggestion that the God of the Yankee was not God at all but Antichrist loosed at last from the pit. The coming war would be no mere secular contest but Armageddon, with the South standing in the role of the defender of the ark, its people as the Chosen People. . . .

Every man was in his place because He had set him there. Everything was as it was because He had ordained it so. Hence, slavery, and indeed, everything that was, was His responsibility, not the South's. So far from being evil, it was the very essence of Right. Wrong would consist only in rebellion against it.[28]

Roy Nichols has pointed up the specific denominational sources of the support of slavery:

The bitter resentment welling up in the South was intensified by the fact that its people shared the prevailing Protestantism. . . . The Methodists, Baptists, and Presbyterians particularly set much store by preaching, and they stressed the Protestant tenets earlier described, emphasizing morals, conscience, and the hatred of sin. Stung to anger by attacks upon their institutions and by slurs upon their moral integrity, their pulpits became rostrums of defense. Thus southern clergymen fought northern ministers in the same Protestant vocabulary, but their themes differed. Southern divines became increasingly satisfied that slavery was ordained of God and justified in the Bible. God would condemn those who bore false witness against the South — the northern hypocrites who attacked the South as morally delinquent.[29]

Whatever other effects issued from this deep commitment of the major Protestant groups to the abolitionist issue, it certainly served to both facilitate and dramatize their great realignment in the North and West with the Republican party.

The shift away from the Democrats was made easier by the emergence of a number of "third parties," of which the Liberty party in the early 1840's and the Free-Soil party in 1848 were the most prominent. The latter ran Martin Van Buren, Jackson's Secretary of State and successor as President, as its presidential candidate, and drew into its ranks many Democrats. In addition, the tremendous increase in immigrant population, particularly Irish Catholics, made the evangelical Protestants more receptive to nativist propaganda, and presumably less happy within a party in which the immigrant groups played a major role. All during this period, "third" nativist parties such as the American or Know-Nothing party also probably served as a halfway house for a movement by Protestant Democrats away from their traditional party home to the Republican successors of the Whigs. The northern Know-Nothings included many foes of slavery, and the party disintegrated in the North because it refused to take a strong stand against the extension of slavery. While the Democrats were losing support among the once less privileged sects, the Whigs and Republicans retained the support of the members of the higher-status denominations.

These conclusions concerning changes in the voting allegiances of the various Protestant groups should be regarded as an informed guess. As yet, no hard analysis exists of this period other than Lee Benson's study of the election in New York State in the early 1840's. Examining the areas which give disproportionate support to the Liberty party, a small abolitionist organization, in the 1844 election, he reports that "its strongest support came from areas most likely to respond to the doctrines preached by New York rural evangelical sects. During the early 1840's, Baptists apparently led the anti-slavery hosts; Presbyterians and Methodists followed closely." [30]

The temperance and prohibition issues also played a major and interrelated role in recruiting evangelical Protestants to the anti-Democratic ranks. To a considerable extent, those active in abolition groups also strongly backed prohibitionist organizations, and vice versa. Anti-slavery candidates were often also advocates of prohibition. "In the 1850's, various combinations of antislaveryism, antiforeignism, and prohibitionism were electing hundreds of . . . men to office." [31]

But if these interrelated moral issues associated with the parties of the well-to-do and better educated resulted in defections from the Democrats of native-born adherents of the evangelical sects, the Democrats were able to recoup their losses from the heavy waves of immigration.

The overwhelming support which the Democrats secured from non-Anglo-Saxon immigrants, largely Germans and Irish Catholics, may be related to three factors which differentiated parties in the decades before the Civil War. The Democrats, as opposed to the Whigs and the Republicans, were much more oriented to serving the needs of the poor and new immigrants, they tended to oppose restrictions on liquor, whereas as we have seen their opponents supported them, and perhaps most important of all as far as the immigrants and Catholics were concerned, the Whigs and Republicans were often explicitly allied with various nativist and anti-Catholic organizations, such as the Native Americans and the Know-Nothings.

When the anti-foreign, anti-Catholic Know-Nothings broke up over the slavery question, the vast majority of them seem to have joined the Republicans in the North. Election data indicate that they had "served as a bridge between the old Whig party and the Republican party." [32] In New York state, where the Know-Nothings had received 34 per cent of the vote in the state elections of 1855, there was a heavy drop-off in their support the following year, since "the Know-Nothing voters were deserting nativism to join the new favorite," the Republican party.[33] In the northwestern states in which there was a heavily foreign, particularly German, settlement, "the Know-Nothings cast their lot with the Republicans rather than nominate candidates of their own. Under their influence the Republican party in many northwestern states took on a decided nativist tinge. . . ." [34] In Indiana, the early Republican party was "tinged with the anti-foreign Know-Nothingism." [35] In Pennsylvania, the Republican and American parties co-operated closely in the election of 1856 on the state level. The Republicans officially endorsed a plan for a joint ticket of presidential electors for the two parties.[36] In Massachusetts, where the Know-Nothings had been stronger than anywhere else in the North, they formed "a *de facto* coalition with the rising Republican party." [37]

Before the 1860 presidential elections, Republican midwestern leaders, including Lincoln, made valiant efforts to destroy the impression that the party was anti-Catholic or anti-foreign, since in addition to the principle of equality itself, many of them realized that the foreign-born vote, particularly the German, could lose them the election if it went decisively against them. A detailed analysis of voting returns in Wisconsin indicates that this Republican effort, which was led by Carl Schurz, was unsuccessful. The Wisconsin Domesday Book project, "a superior Gallup Poll," indicates that five-sixths of the Germans backed Douglas against Lincoln, "because of the Know-Nothing nativism which the Republicans had absorbed." [38]

Even four years of war did not affect the basic correlates of party support. An analysis of voting returns in a number of states in the 1864 presidential election indicates relationships between various social factors and party presidential choice similar to those which differentiated Democrats and Whigs in the 1840's and were to distinguish Republicans and Democrats following the war. Lincoln's support came disproportionately from Protestants of New England and Anglo-Saxon background living in rural areas and small towns and "the better residential districts of the greater cities." Catholics, those of non-Anglo-Saxon recent immigrant background, particularly the Germans, and those living in the poorer districts of the large cities, were disposed to vote for McClellan, the Democratic candidate.[39]

In the late nineteenth and early twentieth centuries, outside of the one-party South, anti-Catholic and anti-immigrant politics which continued to exist tended to find a home inside of the Republican party. And on the issue of Catholic efforts to secure state funds for parochial schools, "often the local and State Democratic parties became allied with the Catholic point of view or at least were not hostile," while the Republicans took "the opposite stand."[40] "Running for governor of Ohio in 1875, Rutherford B. Hayes worked fiercely to smear the Democrats as subservient to Catholic designs. President Grant struck a similar campaign note at a veterans' reunion that fall by hinting darkly that unless the public schools were kept free from sectarian influence the nation might face a new civil war between the forces of patriotism and intelligence on the one side and superstition and ignorance on the other. . . . During the election of 1876 occasional Republican(s) charge(d) that the 'Romanish Church' was using the Democratic party to overthrow the American school system. . . ."[41]

In that year, James G. Blaine, the Republican leader in the House of Representatives, introduced a constitutional amendment which specified that no governmental authority could allow any public property, revenues, or loans, to be used for the support of any school or other institution under the control of any religious sect. Though seeking to outlaw support for private religious schools, the amendment explicitly permitted the "reading of the Bible in any school or institution," a clause which "revealed the Protestant inspiration of the resolution," since Catholics had opposed Bible reading which almost invariably meant use of a Protestant version.[42] The Blaine proposal "failed to secure the necessary two-thirds majority in a strictly party vote, Republicans voting for and Democrats against it."[43] Republicans were not loath to continue the religious issues in the campaign since their election platforms in 1876 and 1880 called for the passage of the constitutional amendment proposed by Blaine, and more significantly, perhaps, Rutherford

Hayes, their Presidential candidate in these elections, had openly identified himself with anti-Catholicism in 1875. And Blaine, the author of the anti-Catholic amendment, was the Republican candidate in 1884.

The largest single anti-Catholic organization of the late nineteenth century, The American Protective Association (A.P.A.), was organized in 1887. Politically, the A.P.A. operated as a faction of the Republican party. "During the presidential campaign of 1892, the A.P.A. showed itself very friendly to the candidacy of Benjamin Harrison, a friendship that was stimulated, so it seems, by liberal assistance from the Republican campaign."[44] As it grew the effort to capture "Republican primaries and conventions was . . . the predominant activity of the A.P.A. during the years 1893–95. . . . The Democratic party helped, by its strong anti-Know-Nothing attitude, to drive the A.P.A. wholly into Republican ranks."[45]

While the A.P.A.'s effort to dominate the party ultimately failed in its objective of converting the national level of the Republican party to its cause, it succeeded, in local elections both in western and eastern states, in fostering the Catholic issue, particularly as it related to the question of parochial schools as a basis of division between the parties.

As to the constant relationship between the Republican party and various nativist efforts to restrict immigration, John Higham in his detailed study of post-Civil war nativism concluded:

> From the outset the Republican party provided the main vehicle for restrictionist sentiment. It never monopolized or committed itself wholly to the movement, but it supplied the principal leaders, most of the energy, and most of the votes. Throughout the North and West the party tended to attract those who thought of themselves as "the better sort." It seemed the guardian of respectability, morality, and standing. . . .[46]

It should not be surprising that a recent study of immigrant groups concludes that the two major Catholic ethnic groups, the Irish and the German, remained loyal to the Democratic party for the half-century after the Civil War. The former, of course, played an increasingly important role within the party organization in the large cities, where like "their Irish co-religionists, German Catholics tended to regard the Republican party as a vehicle for intolerant Puritans bent on prohibition, Sunday closing, and immigration restriction."[47]

III THE DESIGN AT WORK: THE TWENTIETH CENTURY

The basic religious-political pattern crystallized in the latter part of the nineteenth century was one of increasing Catholic identification with the Democratic party as the party least antipathetic to newcomers and increasing Protestant identification with the Republican party as the party most closely allied with the American middle-class status quo of the time.

Following the Civil War, the link between Protestant orthodoxy and Americanism as a political ideology became closer than ever. The victory of the North was taken by many in the northern churches as clear evidence that they had been fighting God's crusade and "it was but another short step to the enshrinement of the political instrument which, in the hands of Providence, had guided the Union to victory over slavery and disunion." [48]

Sidney Mead concludes that there is general agreement among historians "that at the time Protestantism in America achieved its greatest dominance of the culture [the second half of the nineteenth century], it had also achieved an almost complete ideological and emotional identification with the burgeoning bourgeois society and its free enterprise system, so that in 1876 Protestantism presented a massive, almost unbroken front in its defense of the social status quo. . . .[49]

James Bryce probably represented the informed consensus on the subject in the post-Civil War period, when he reported of the 1880's: "Roman Catholics are normally Democrats, because, except in Maryland, which is Democratic anyhow, they are mainly Irish. Congregationalists and Unitarians, being presumably sprung from New England, are apt to be Republicans. Presbyterians, Methodists, Baptists, Episcopalians . . . are mostly Republicans in the Northern States, Democrats in the South." [50] It is, however, difficult to be precise concerning the relation between party support and religious and ethnic group memberships from the Civil War to the Smith campaign in 1928. Historians, political scientists, and sociologists, have in the main failed to analyze the basic data. The existing research does indicate, however, that lines of division held fairly firm during these decades. A summary of electoral researches in post-Civil War and early twentieth-century Wisconsin points this up clearly:

> During these late nineteenth-century decades, and persisting many decades later, much of Wisconsin's two-party division of the vote derived from circumstances usually described as "traditional." As elsewhere among northern voters, the Civil War had equated Republicanism with patriotism and respectability. This was especially true in the Wisconsin counties settled by Yankees from New England and upstate New York. Here identification with the cause of the Union often confirmed a preference for Republicans as the heirs of the Whigs, or perhaps of the Know-Nothings or even the abolitionists.

The liquor issue also served to solidify the support which the temperance-minded, native American Protestant accorded the Republican party.

Conversely, the traditional Democratic support was heavily derived from those outside the scheme of values represented by the Yankee conscience. Both German and Irish immigrants found the Democratic party relatively congenial. Numerically the German element was more important, and even into the early part of the twentieth century, particularly until World War I, the rural counties settled mainly by Germans (Protestant or Catholic) turned out Democratic votes more or less in the pattern established by 1860. The city of Milwaukee also provided a substantial Democratic following of a similar traditional sort. . . .[51]

In Indiana, between 1868 and 1900 "an astonishing parallelism appears in the county-by-county division of party strength," and Key and Munger account for these continuities in party voting strength by the phenomenon of geographic concentrations of groups with similar cultural and religious origins who adhered to historic voting ties."[52]

Though continuities such as these are prevalent in American political history, it is clear that occasionally religious and ethnic groups do shift party or ideological ties. The linkages between the German-Americans and the Democratic party were broken when the United States entered a war against Germany under a Democratic President in 1917. Much earlier, one may point to a decisive permanent change in the allegiance of a religious group, the Mormons, who gave up their identification with the Democratic party. The historic commitment of the Mormons to the Democrats was based on the fact that Joseph Smith, the founder of the church, had been a Democrat, that much of the persecution of the church had occurred under Republican administrations, and that Utah was admitted to the Union under a Democratic President, Grover Cleveland. This tie was decisively broken in 1900. In that year, McKinley carried the state against Bryan, though four years earlier Bryan had secured 80 per cent of the vote from the largely Mormon electorate.[53] The state remained Republican until 1932, with the exception of the election of 1916. Similarly, Negroes, who had retained their historic allegiance to the Republican party from the end of the Civil War until the election of 1932, shifted to support the Democrats in successive contests.

But though such major changes occur, the available evidence suggests that there were no major adjustments in the pattern established in the nineteenth century outside of the Solid South of disproportionate Catholic backing for the Democrats and Protestant preference for the Republicans. The strength of the correlation between the Catholic-Protestant division and party support undoubtedly rose and fell, but the difference remained basic. It has been argued that the election of 1896 was one of the "critical elections" in American political history in the sense that significant groupings growing out of the first Bryan-McKinley contest made long-term changes in loyalties.[54] In general, the candidacy of Bryan, who came out of the Midwest Bible Belt Populist tradition, resulted in a sizable increase in the Democratic vote in the Plains and Mountain states, and in a heavy loss in the East, where his inflationary program is presumed to have had a negative rather than a positive appeal to the less debt-ridden farmers and urban strata. The contest, however, probably did not affect the long-term relationship between religious-ethnic factors and party support; in fact, it may have even increased the correlation in the eastern states. An analysis of changes in the vote between 1892 and 1896 in Massachusetts, which differentiated according to size of community, indicates that the Democrats lost most heavily in smaller communities, and retained considerable support in the larger communities in which they had previously been strong.[55]

TABLE I

Shifts in Democratic Strength, 1892–1896, in Relation to Population Size of Towns

Population Size Groups	Mean Democratic Percentages 1892	1896	Mean Change 1892–1896	Per Cent 1896 Loss of 1892 Vote
1–999	34.0	14.7	19.3	56.8
2000–2999	38.8	18.3	20.5	52.6
10,000–14,999	46.7	26.9	19.8	42.4
50,000 plus	47.7	30.1	17.6	34.8

Source: V. O. Key, Jr. "A Theory of Critical Elections," *Journal of Politics*, 17 (1955), p. 14. Key did not compute the last column.

Since, according to V. O. Key, size of community was a rough index of religious and national origin variation—the small communities were largely Anglo-Saxon and Protestant, the larger cities had sizable segments of foreign-born Catholics—the evidence (see Table I) would suggest that the campaign of 1896 may have actually reinforced the ethnic-religious correlations with party voting, at least as far as Massachusetts is concerned. On the national level, a study of this election which compared the vote in communities with more or less than 45,000 population within each state found that "in states in which the foreign-born constituted larger proportions of the population in comparison with other states, the urban population (more than 45,000) gave Bryan a larger proportion of the vote than he received in rural areas (less than 45,-000)."[56] And the assumption that findings such as these reflect consistency in the ethnic-religious correlation is reinforced by an analysis of the vote within one large city, Boston. In Boston, the correlation between percentage of Democratic vote and percentage of foreign-born (principally Catholic) in each ward was about as high in 1892 as one ever secures when relating such factors, 0.88; in 1896 the relationship was slightly lower, although from a statistical point of view the difference was so small as to suggest practical identity, 0.82.[57]

The Democrats clearly lost heavily among the poorer, immigrant, and Catholic population, as they did among those with the opposite characteristics, but the fact of this decline, particularly in the eastern states, did not change the previously existing relationships. Unfortunately, the one detailed historical study of the statistical association between proportion of foreign-born (largely Catholic) and party voting, that by Robert Dahl of New Haven, begins with the election of 1904. His data indicate a high correlation (about 0.80) for 1904, which then dropped some in 1908, remaining "moderately close and steady until 1928," when the Smith campaign raised it to new heights.[58] Dahl suggests too that the seemingly radical candidacy of Bryan resulted in permanent losses to the Democratic party from more conservative Yankee Democrats. In general, the increasing identification of the Democratic party with the tremendous mass of Catholic immigrants and Irish leadership in eastern cities served to convert most Yankees to the Republican standard. Protestant British, Scandinavian, and German immigrants, becoming accepted as members of the old stock, also joined the Republicans.[59] And the rural midwestern Protestant votes which Bryan brought to the Democrats from the Populists in 1896 and 1900 returned to the Republican fold with the candidacy of Theodore Roosevelt in 1904.[60]

It is important to note in evaluating elections such as those of 1860, 1896, 1932, or 1952, in which one party made decisive gains, that the sheer fact of a large switch in votes from one party to another need not mean that there has been any change in the *relative* relationship of any given social group to a party. The increase may come more or less proportionately from all segments, so that the correlations between factors such as class or religion and party choice will remain relatively constant. This seems to have occurred in Boston between 1892 and 1896, when the Republicans gained greatly in all wards of the city but the correlation between proportion of foreign-born and Presidential vote remained almost identical. In addition, it is possible that a major increase in the support of a given party may result more from the party's intensifying its support among strata previously identified with it, than from gains from traditionally negative strata. Thus, the elections of 1928 and 1960 clearly increased the existing relationship between religious affiliation and voting.

World War I and its aftereffects appear, however, to have affected the relationship of ethnic, and therefore religious, groupings to the two parties. Wilson had been elected in 1912 on a minority vote, the normal Republican majority being divided between Taft and Roosevelt. However, in 1916, Wilson ran on an anti-war platform, while Charles Evans Hughes and the Republican party were much more sympathetic to the cause of the Allies led by Great Britain. The available evidence would suggest that various groups of non-Anglo-Saxon origin—the Irish who disliked Britain, the Jews who viewed Czarist Russia as the major anti-Semitic power of its day, and German and Scandinavian Americans who favored Germany—shifted to or remained with Wilson, while conversely there may have been an intensification of Anglo-Saxon "Yankee" backing for the Republicans.[61] Since the move to the Democrats included many traditionally Republican Scandinavian Lutherans, it is hard to estimate whether the Democrats gained or lost among Protestant voters.

Entry into war under Wilson, however, resulted in a major alienation of traditional Democratic Irish and Catholic support. In 1920, the Republicans won their greatest victory in history, securing 61.2 per cent of the national vote. In Massachusetts, with its large Irish Catholic population, the party was unable to even nominate candidates for many local and congressional posts.[62] In Iowa, the "mainstay of the Democratic party has always been the German-Americans, particularly Catholic Germans. So violent was their reaction against Wilson in 1920 that in some parts of Iowa the Democratic party all but disappeared. Candidates were not available to run for Congress on the Democratic ticket."[63]

James M. Cox, the Democratic candidate in that year, has himself well described what happened to him and his party:

> Leaders of three racial groups, Germans, Irish and Italian, had gone over to the Republican side. The Germans were angry with Wilson because of the war. The Irish were inflamed because Wilson did not make the independence of Ireland part of the Versailles treaty. The Italians were enraged because Fiume had been taken away from Italy. The Italians were practically solid.[64]

In 1924, the Democrats remained weak among the groups which had defected in 1920. Many of them voted for Senator Robert La Follette, on a third party ticket.[65] He had been a major leader in resisting entry into the war, had campaigned vigorously for the independence of Ireland, and perhaps most important of all, was the presidential candidate most avowedly opposed to the Ku Klux Klan, and most denounced by the Klan.[66] In Massachusetts, as in Illinois, most of his votes seem to have come from traditional centers of Democratic strength.

The rise of the Ku Klux Klan to prominence during the 1920's undoubtedly played an important role in preventing the Republicans from making permanent inroads among disaffected Democrats of Catholic and recent immigrant background. In much of the Northeast and Midwest, the Klan, like the A.P.A. before them, largely worked through the Republican party and had considerable influence in some of the state organizations. "In the East, where the Democratic Party was controlled largely by Irish Catholics, the Klan inevitably associated itself more closely with the Republicans." [67] In addition, the Republicans had fostered both Prohibition and quota restrictions on immigration which were biased in favor of entrants from the Nordic Protestant nations, while the northern Democratic members of Congress had shown opposition to these measures which were clearly unpalatable to most Catholics and others of recent immigrant stock.

The decline of the Democrats in presidential voting, particularly among Catholics and recent immigrant groups, did not mean that the party had lost its following among them. Some political analysts who have focused only on the presidential races have erred in suggesting that strong Catholic Democratic loyalties stem from 1928, the year Al Smith ran for President. They overlook the fact that the Democratic vote for state offices in many areas with large Catholic populations remained extremely high in the years during which the party declined heavily on the presidential level. In Massachusetts in 1922, the Democratic percentage of the two-party vote for Governor was 17.6 higher than in the 1920 presidential race. And the party gained much more in cities which had a large majority of foreign-born population than it did in communities which were predominantly native-born.[68] Similarly in 1924, when the Democratic presidential candidate secured only a quarter of the state's vote, the party's senatorial candidate, an Irish-American, captured almost half the vote, losing by only 18,000 in a poll of over a million. In New York State, Al Smith was defeated for re-election as Governor in 1920 by less than 100,000 votes, while Harding's majority over Cox was over one million; two years later Smith was returned as Governor with the largest majority in the history of New York's gubernatorial races.[69]

The results of these state contests suggest that despite the scrambled results of the 1920 and 1924 presidential contests, the traditional links between religion, ethnic group membership, class, and party support actually continued. The Democratic party remained as the party through which Catholics, those of recent immigrant stock, and the poorer strata secured recognition, social mobility, and local interest representation. Key and Munger in their analysis of Indiana voting behavior indicate that this pattern of persistent loyalty to the state party, even when there are strong religious or ethnic pulls away from the party on the presidential level, occurred in 1928 and 1940 as well. In the former election the differentials between the presidential and state office vote "strongly suggest that Protestant Democrats and perhaps Catholic Republicans responded to the situation by splitting their tickets. After the religious issue subsided, national and local party appeals were more nearly congruent and ticket splitting declined." [70] In the 1940 election, a largely Germanic area showed a large drop in support for Roosevelt, while the vote for the Democratic candidate for Governor was much higher. In an analysis of public opinion survey data in the 1950's Angus Campbell reported similar findings based on interviews with individuals. That is, the vote for state office and congressional contests remained linked to the usual correlates of party choice, while the presidential vote varied considerably.[71]

The story of the 1928 election in which Al Smith ran as the first Catholic to hold a presidential nomination of a major party has been told and analyzed by many.[72] This election aroused strong emotions and prejudices around the related issues of attitudes to Catholicism and Prohibition. The Smith campaign activated the poor, Catholic, Jewish, urban, immigrant groups, and alienated the small town and rural native Protestants.[73] Lubell has argued that a profound "social upheaval stirred beneath the Smith vote. What Smith really embodied was the revolt of the underdog urban immigrant against the top dog of 'old American' stock. His Catholicism was an essential element in that revolt." [74]

The election of 1928 played a major role in structuring the subsequent alignment of American voters. It clearly brought back to the national Democratic party all of the immigrant, Catholic, and Jewish vote which it had lost after World War I — and then some.[75] Although many contemporaries blamed Smith's defeat on the success of a bitterly anti-Catholic campaign waged by the Ku Klux Klan and by many Protestant churchmen, the evidence does not sustain this thesis.[76] In fact, Smith secured 41 per cent of the national vote, more than any previous Democratic candidate in the twentieth century, except for Wilson running for re-election in 1916. It is likely that, as in the case of John F. Kennedy, thirty-two years later, Smith's religion won him more votes among co-religionists and other opponents of the Protestant Yankee Establishment than it lost him. Given the fact that the country was still in the midst of its greatest prosperity in history, Smith's ability to increase Democratic strength in the cities and much of the North may be perceived as an indicator of the decline both of Prohibitionist and anti-Catholic sentiment.

In 1932, Roosevelt retained the Catholic-Jewish and recent immigrant vote which had supported Smith, and, of course, secured a considerable body of votes from other groups as a result of the reaction to the Great Depression. V. O. Key reports data from the various New England states which indicate that, in comparing the 1932 with the 1928 vote by varying types of communities, "the proportion of new Democrats did not differ significantly among the groups of towns examined." [77] That is, the Smith campaign had restored more intensively than before the correlations which had previously existed between presidential party voting and religious affiliation before the reactions to World War I had upset them. The correlations continued under Roosevelt, as Samuel Lubell has pointed out, for regions such as New England where a sizable Catholic population faced a previously dominant Yankee Protestant one: "Between 1932 and 1944, New England's Democratic vote did not shift by more than 2 per cent in any election, in the main, the bedrock cleavage in the East remains a Catholic-Protestant one." [78]

Analysis of the various elections discussed thus far has had to rest on ecological considerations. The only method used to infer the relationship between social characteristics such as ethnic origin or religious affiliation and voting habits was to compare the social characteristics of different voting areas. This approach has many methodological weaknesses; the inference that one may deduce the behavior of individuals from the correlates of areas or communities may not be valid in any given case.[79] From 1936 on, however, a more reliable measure of the correlates of vote decision exist, the data from public opinion surveys. Using such materials, it is possible to analyze the relative contribution of class as distinct from religious factors, the variations among different denominations, and so forth. Time and space do not permit the detailed types of analyses which available data make feasible.

For purposes of this essay, however, I have re-analyzed public opinion materials for each presidential election from 1936 to 1960, plus the congressional races of 1954 and 1958. Unfortunately, most of the available surveys do not contain detailed denominational information for Protestants, or if they do, the size of the sample interviewed is too small to permit any reliable interpretation of the differences among denominations. A denominational analysis must involve holding some measure of class position constant, since the Protestant denominations vary greatly with respect to the average socio-economic level of their adherents.

To compare the effects of class and religion, I have followed a method, first used by Robert Alford, in which urban voters are divided between those in manual and non-manual occupations, and these groups plus rural voters are divided between Protestants and Catholics.[80] These measures of religious and class voting presented in Table II are only rough and relative measures of underlying social forces. Of all the forces affecting voting, only two are here analyzed (albeit two of the most important ones). Obviously different kinds of social circumstances might affect the operation of these forces. For example, if a depression (which would ordinarily increase class voting) and a Catholic candidate for President (which would increase religious voting) occurred simultaneously, the two indices would not increase as much as they would if either event were to take place without the other. Thus, there is no absolute standard; the effects of religion and class should be compared over time and in light of auxiliary knowledge, and a certain margin of error is to be expected.

Southerners and Negroes have been excluded from tables because some of the relations we are concerned with are different among them. Negroes, though predominantly Protestant, have voted overwhelmingly Democratic since 1936. Southerners, ironically, continue their post-Civil War pattern of voting Democratic though this traditional loyalty has greatly declined in presidential contests.

TABLE II

Per Cent Voting Democratic Among Protestants and Catholics Within Farm, Manual, and Non-manual Occupations (Nonsouthern Whites Only)

Occupations	Total	Catholics	Protestants	Religious Voting (Difference between Catholics and Protestants)
		—1936—		
Farm	53 (330)	56 (32)	46 (190)	plus 10
Manual	71 (556)	86 (138)	63 (243)	plus 23
Non-manual	47 (732)	71 (122)	34 (401)	plus 37
Class Voting (Difference between manual & nonmanual)	plus 24	plus 15	plus 29	
Total		76 (292)	45 (834)	plus 31

Occupations	Total	Catholics	Protestants	Religious Voting (Difference between Catholics and Protestants)
		—1940—		
Farm	47 (363)	56 (34)	47 (213)	plus 9
Manual	67 (692)	85 (178)	53 (295)	plus 32
Non-manual	44 (990)	62 (174)	32 (523)	plus 30
Class Voting	plus 23	plus 23	plus 21	
Total		72 (386)	41 (1031)	plus 31
		—1944—		
Farm	39 (158)	61 (18)	36 (95)	plus 25
Manual	63 (458)	74 (111)	55 (178)	plus 19
Non-manual	43 (398)	60 (70)	31 (217)	plus 29
Class Voting	plus 20	plus 14	plus 24	
Total		68 (199)	41 (490)	plus 27
		—1948—		
Farm	48 (138)	62 (13)	47 (123)	plus 15
Manual	64 (306)	75 (77)	57 (205)	plus 18
Non-manual	46 (448)	59 (107)	35 (291)	plus 24
Class Voting	plus 18	plus 16	plus 22	
Total		65 (197)	45 (619)	plus 20
		—1952—		
Farm	32 (90)	36 (14)	31 (75)	plus 5
Manual	52 (370)	63 (150)	43 (202)	plus 20
Non-manual	28 (336)	35 (85)	18 (211)	plus 17
Class Voting	plus 24	plus 28	plus 25	
Total		52 (249)	30 (488)	plus 22
		—1954—		
Farm	38 (69)	33 (12)	38 (56)	less 5
Manual	62 (265)	74 (89)	54 (167)	plus 20
Non-manual	45 (236)	57 (65)	36 (148)	plus 21
Class Voting	plus 17	plus 17	plus 18	
Total		64 (166)	44 (371)	plus 20
		—1956—		
Farm	45 (62)	78 (9)	39 (52)	plus 39
Manual	50 (294)	60 (101)	44 (185)	plus 16

TABLE II (*continued*)

Occupations	Total	Catholics	Protestants	Religious Voting (Difference between Catholics and Protestants)
Non-manual	33 (210)	49 (61)	21 (124)	plus 28
Class Voting	plus 17	plus 11	plus 23	
Total		57 (171)	35 (361)	plus 22
		—1958—		
Farm	55 (53)	67 (6)	53 (45)	plus 14
Manual	66 (282)	59 (95)	57 (178)	plus 24
Non-manual	48 (271)	59 (81)	35 (156)	plus 24
Class Voting	plus 18	plus 22	plus 22	
Total		71 (182)	47 (379)	plus 24
		—1960—		
Farm	36 (120)	69 (13)	32 (106)	plus 37
Manual	58 (719)	84 (240)	43 (438)	plus 41
Non-manual	40 (565)	78 (159)	19 (336)	plus 59
Class Voting	plus 18	plus 6	plus 24	
Total		81 (412)	33 (880)	plus 48

Sources for Table II: 1936—A.I.P.O. (Gallup Poll) #141; 1940—A.I.P.O. #248; 1944—A.I.P.O. #323K; 1948—A.I.P.O. #454K; 1952—Michigan (Survey Research Center) Election Study, 1952; 1954—A.I.P.O. #539K; 1956—A.I.P.O. #573K; 1958—A.I.P.O. #608K; 1960—A.I.P.O. #638K.

In using the 1936 sample, it was necessary to define farmers as persons living on farms but not possessing manual or non-manual jobs.

In using the 1952 sample, it was necessary to define farmers as farm owners. Four states on the North-South border had to be excluded from this sample, but were included in the others.

Comparing the internal variations within the Protestant and Catholic groups, it seems evident that the pattern described for much of the nineteenth century has continued during the past twenty-four years. Class factors consistently differentiate among Protestants. That is, the middle-class Protestants have always been much more likely to back the Republicans than manual workers with similar religious loyalties. Among Catholics, however, class differences in party support, while present, are somewhat less powerful. Alford, who reports similar findings in his analysis of survey data from 1944 to 1960 (including Negroes and

Southerners), comments that the lesser strength of the class-party relationship among Catholics is "consistent with the presumed ethnic and minority sentiments among Catholics which override class sentiments as a basis for political loyalties." [81] As "out-group" minorities, Catholics, Jews, and Negroes are much more likely to respond politically in terms of their ethnic-religious group identification than are the majority white Protestant population. Other bases of diversity, of which class is historically the most significant, should affect Protestant reactions more than they do the others.

Examining trends within both major religious groupings confirms the thesis elaborated by Lubell, from his examination of the votes of different geographical area, that the Smith-Roosevelt effect on voting patterns reached a climax in 1936. Working people and Catholics completed the swing to the Democrats which had been triggered off in 1928. Both class and religious voting were extremely high in 1936. There was a difference of 52 percentage points between the Democratic vote of Catholic manual workers (86) and middle-class Protestants (34). Four years later, the differences were practically as great, although the Democrats lost part of their national majority. Various writers have suggested that this drop was a result of "isolationist" ethnic groups turning away from the interventionist anti-German and anti-Italian foreign policy of Roosevelt as they had once moved away from Wilson. This change did not affect the relation between religion and party support since presumably it included the Catholic Italians and the predominantly Lutheran Germans. The index of religious voting dropped considerably from 1940 to 1944, from a difference of 31 per cent in 1936 and 1940 to 23 per cent in 1944, a figure which then remained fairly steady for both presidential and congressional elections until the election of 1960. The change from 1940 to 1944 suggests that the issue of America's policy toward Communism may have affected Catholics even before the war ended. Class differences, as measured by the gross indicator of manual vs. non-manual divisions, also declined during this period, although the drop was smaller and less consistent than that of religion.

The gross character of the indicators of class and religious voting makes it impossible to reach any definitive conclusion concerning the relative weight of "class" as contrasted with "religion" as a determinant of party choice. An examination of the data presented in Table II does suggest that the Catholic-Protestant difference has been somewhat more important than the manual vs. non-manual cleavage from 1936 to 1960. However, this result is in some part a consequence of the fact that the two factors have been dichotomized. When the impact of class is estimated by dividing the population into more classes, e.g., upper, upper-middle, middle, upper-lower, and lower, or in terms of a number of occupational classes, e.g., large business, free professionals, down to unskilled workers, the variations linked to class become much greater. Well-to-do businessmen often vote from 80 to 90 per cent Republican, while semi-skilled and unskilled workers who are union members will vote 75 per cent Democratic.[82] Such differences are clearly larger than the variations between Catholic and Protestants. Similarly, the impact of religious affiliations on voting varies with degree of involvement in religious activities. Although the relationship differs with degree of commitment — the more religious members of a group are more likely to follow the dominant tendency of the group than the less religious or the irreligious — a correlation between voting and religion is not intensified as consistently or to the degree that occurs with the increased specification of class.

Some estimate of the effect of these factors may be seen in the statistics reported in Table III, which were drawn from an analysis of a large opinion survey. Completed in 1954, it is based on a sample of 9,852 interviews in eleven states outside of the South. With a sample of this magnitude, it is possible to examine the variation among a large number of classes within each major religious grouping.

An examination of Table III suggests that there is somewhat more variation within each religious group between the highest and lowest class than between Protestant and Catholics in the same class. Thus Catholics vary between 36 per cent Democratic in sympathies among "upper class" non-manuals to 69 per cent within the lower manual stratum, or a difference of 33 per cent. The corresponding difference among Protestants between the highest and the lowest group is 36 per cent. Within any one stratum, the largest variation in per cent Democratic between Catholics and Protestants is 25 per cent, but most intra-class differences are less. A comparable analysis (not reported here) for actual vote in the 1952 election resulted in differences of comparable magnitude.

The usual concentration on the Protestant-Catholic-Jewish trichotomy serves to conceal variations among the Protestant denominations. When these are separated, the available survey evidence would suggest that the average socio-economic status of the members of a given denomination is an important determinant of the relative position of the denomination with respect to support of the two major parties. However, there is some evidence that Protestant denominational differences do exist which are independent of class position. A large national sample of the electorate

TABLE III

Relationship Between Socio-Economic Status and Traditional Party Preference for the Three Major Religious Groupings
Per Cent Democratic and Republican — 1954 (White Respondents Only)

Stratum	Protestant Dem.	Protestant Rep.		Catholic Dem.	Catholic Rep.		Jews Dem.	Jews Rep.	
Non-manual									
Upper	14	61	(169)	36	39	(39)	31	0	(13)
Upper-Middle	24	49	(714)	36	27	(232)	55	10	(58)
Lower-Middle	25	44	(910)	50	18	(406)	63	5	(79)
Lower	45	40	(62)	64	7	(28)	X	X	
Manual									
Upper-Middle	36	37	(300)	49	10	(144)	X	X	
Lower-Middle	40	30	(1696)	63	11	(945)	66	2	(44)
Lower	50	24	(361)	69	10	(267)	X	X	
Farm									
Upper	24	41	(34)	X	X		X	X	
Upper-Middle	29	44	(168)	38	44	(16)	X	X	
Lower-Middle	32	43	(402)	58	20	(96)	X	X	
Lower	34	41	(129)	44	12	(25)	X	X	

Source: Computed from the data of a survey conducted in eleven states by International Research Associates in 1954. The states are California, Michigan, Minnesota, Massachusetts, Iowa, New Mexico, Illinois, Ohio, Oregon, Pennsylvania, and New Jersey. Independents are included in the base. They are the difference between the two party totals and 100 per cent.

interviewed in the spring of 1952 was asked which party the respondents have most often favored between 1936 and 1952. When this sample was differentiated among those in manual and non-manual occupations, the data indicated that the two "lowest status" and most fundamentalist groups of Protestants, Baptists and those classified under the heading of "other Protestants," contained the smaller proportion of Republicans within the manual and the non-manual strata. Conversely, the denominations of the more well-to-do, the Episcopalians, the Presbyterians, and the Congregationalists, contributed heavily to Republican support. A substantial majority of the manual workers who adhered to the latter groups indicated they had voted Republican most of the time. Lutherans seemed more Republican than one might have predicted from knowledge of their socio-economic position, while Methodists fell in a middle position with respect to Republican propensities.

To a considerable extent the data reported in Table IV below would seem to confirm the generally accepted assumptions concerning intra-

TABLE IV

Predominant Past Voting Behavior, Religion and Occupation — 1952 (Nonsouthern Whites) Per Cent Two-Party Vote

Denomination	Blue Collar Dem.	Blue Collar Rep.		White Collar Dem.	White Collar Rep.	
Baptist	61	39	(31)	35	65	(23)
Lutheran	51	49	(29)	18	82	(45)
Methodist	48	52	(52)	32	68	(62)
Episcopal	40	60	(15)	24	76	(41)
Presbyterian	33	67	(28)	28	72	(39)
Congregational	27	73	(11)	21	79	(28)
Other Protestant	65	35	(39)	27	73	(56)
Total Protestant	50	50	(215)	26	73	(294)
Catholic	81	19	(170)	53	47	(106)
Jewish	83	17	(6)	74	26	(43)

Source: Data for analysis are from a 1952 survey by Elmo Roper Associates.

Protestant political variation, that the general political set of a Protestant denomination is determined largely by the average socio-economic status of its adherents. When segregated by denomination and occupational status, it is clear that every Protestant group is more disposed to back the Republicans than Catholics or Jews are. The differences between all of the Protestant denominations and the Catholic and Jewish group are greatest among the white-collar strata. However, intra-Protestant variation is greater within the manual groups than in the middle classes. A substantial majority of workers adhering to the three highest-status churches, as determined by data concerning the average socio-economic level of their adherents (the Episcopalians, the Presbyterians, and the Congregationalists), had cast most of their votes for Republican candidates.

These findings would suggest that worker members of predominantly high-status churches are greatly affected by the modal opinion of the group, or perhaps, that the workers who adhere to such denominations do so in part because they are "upward mobile," that they seek to identify with the more privileged classes. Conversely, working-class members of the three lowest-status (in terms of average socio-economic position) churches (the Baptists, the Methodists, and the Lutherans) are much more likely to be Democrats. The poorest denomination, the Baptists, is the most Democratic of all the major sects. Two groups, the Lutherans and "other Protestants" behave in a puzzling way. Workers so classified tend toward the Democrats, white-collar adherents are overwhelmingly Republicans. The behavior of the "others" may be a result of the conglomerate nature of the classification. "Other Protestant" workers are most probably members of low-status, small fundamentalist sects whose membership is almost entirely composed of relatively poor people. Such groups rank below the Baptists in social status. On the other hand, middle-class adherents of small Protestant groups are disproportionately members of high-status denominations such as the Unitarians, the Christian Scientists, the Quakers, and the like. If these assumptions are valid, then there is in fact no discrepancy between the Democratic predisposition of manual workers and the Republican orientation of white-collar ones. The former belong with the Baptists, the latter with the Episcopalians. The variation between the voting behavior of Lutheran workers and middle-class persons is more difficult to explain. It may be that part of the answer lies in the different synods of the Lutheran church. As far as interaction is concerned, these are, in effect, separate groups. The members of the more fundamentalist ones, principally the Missouri Synod, are less well-to-do on the average than are those who adhere to the more liberal Synods. It is possible, therefore, that the sources of the class variation among Lutherans are similar to those which explain the differences among the "others."

There clearly are significant differences among Protestants in comparable class positions which are associated with denominational affiliations. It would appear, however, that such differences are not a function of variation in theological beliefs, of the difference between ascetic and non-ascetic, or religious liberal and conservative doctrines. Groups like the Baptists or fundamentalists who have stressed ascetic morality and anti-Catholicism — doctrines which should dispose them to favor Republicans — are, in fact, seemingly more inclined to support the Democrats.

Benton Johnson offers an explanation of the apparent paradox that the more fundamentalist and ascetic Protestant groups are disproportionately Democratic. He first points to another paradox, that the churches of the more well-to-do have also been more liberal not only in their theology but in their social and economic pronouncements. The liberal National Council of Churches, though representing the wealthier Protestant denominations, has given considerable support to the Social Gospel movement.[83] An analysis of the highest-status church in the United States, the Episcopal church, based on questionnaire data from clergy and laymen, demonstrates convincingly that the clergy of this predominantly well-to-do denomination are very liberal in their political views.[84] On the other hand, the churches of the poorer Protestants, predominantly the Baptists and the smaller but numerous fundamentalist groups, have on the whole opposed the social gospel, and have taken conservative positions on economic and political issues.

Johnson argues that the political position of these groups are congruent with historic theological elements in ascetic Protestantism. The liberalism of the churches of the more well-to-do derive from the fact that their ministers are often men "who have received their training from the more influential and prestigeful seminaries . . . , many of which are close to large universities, [and] have participated in the trend toward liberal humanitarianism that has been going on in intellectual circles for many years." [85] The churches of the poor, on the other hand, prefer a simple unintellectual theology which defines Christianity in traditional terms, and preaches good versus evil, God against Satan. Both parishioners and clergy tend to be low in educational attainments, and the seminaries of these groups are often deliberately removed from contact with secular university life.

The fact that there is a general correlation between the average socio-economic status of the members of different denominations and the religious and political liberalism of their clergy and official church bodies suggests the hypothesis that the more integrated an individual is in the religious life of the liberal high-status churches, the more liberal he should be in his outlook, holding other factors constant; conversely the opposite pattern should occur among the adherents of the low-status and more fundamentalist sects.

An analysis of interviews drawn from one city, Eugene, Oregon, sustains these assumptions. As in the national data presented above, members of low-status Eugene churches are more likely to be Democrats than those adhering to the high-status ones. These tendencies hold up within classes as well. Manual workers and those in non-manual occupations belonging to fundamentalist groups are more Democratic than those in the same class adhering to the liberal denominations. However, when the supporters of the liberal churches are divided on the basis of church attendance, frequent churchgoers show a lower Republican propensity than do those who go rarely. Among the fundamentalist groups, the exact opposite occurs: frequent attenders are more likely to vote Republican, while those who are rarely seen in church retain a strong Democratic allegiance. This relationship holds up even when class position is held constant.

The data presented in Table V clearly suggest that religious practice and class position operate independently to affect partisan choice. As

TABLE V

Percentage of Two-Party Vote of Liberal and Fundamentalist by Frequency of Church Attendance and Class Position

Occupational Class and Frequency of Attendance	Party Identification (per cent Republican)		Voting Behavior (per cent Republican)	
Liberal:				
White-Collar				
Attend Frequently	54	(29)	62	(26)
Attend Seldom	63	(16)	93	(14)
Blue-Collar				
Attend Frequently	44	(9)	38	(8)
Attend Seldom	56	(9)	63	(8)
Total Liberal:				
Attend Frequently	51	(37)	56	(34)
Attend Seldom	60	(25)	82	(22)
Fundamentalist:				
White-Collar				
Attend Frequently	65	(17)	71	(17)
Attend Seldom	44	(16)	55	(11)
Blue-Collar				
Attend Frequently	48	(27)	53	(17)
Attend Seldom	27	(11)	33	(6)
Total Fundamentalist:				
Attend Frequently	55	(44)	62	(34)
Attend Seldom	37	(27)	47	(17)

Source: Benton Johnson, "Ascetic Protestantism and Political Preference," *Public Opinion Quarterly*, 26 (1962), pp. 43–4. Voting behavior is based on a scale derived from reported votes in four elections between 1952 and 1958.

Johnson points out, the varying Protestant religious beliefs serve to reduce the relation between class and party among church attenders. Low-status fundamentalist churchgoers vote less Democratic than their class position calls for, while high-status Protestants who attend religiously liberal churches are less Republican than one might anticipate, given their social position.

The finding presented earlier that adherents of different denominations are disposed to follow the predominant political choice of the denomination may be shaped mainly by those who identify with, but are not involved in, the religious life of a given church. To be a non-practicing Episcopalian or Congregationalist means to have a public high-status attribute; nominal church affiliation affects one's self-conception and public image, but apparently it does not much affect one's values. Hence non-practicing supporters of such churches are among the most Republican of individuals with comparable socio-economic traits. Conversely, to remain identified with a low-status church means to retain a status-ascribing characteristic that lowers one's general social status. An individual who so defines himself is presumably less oriented toward upward mobility, toward the values of the higher-status groups. Consequently such people are among the most prone to vote Democratic within their stratum.

Religion, therefore, would seem to affect political choice in two independent ways, as a source of beliefs and as a determinant of status. And the two variables operate at cross-purposes among Protestants. Active membership in a liberal high-status church pulls one toward political liberalism; nominal adherence primarily serves as a source of status and hence strengthens the political conservatism associated with high position. And the opposite pattern operates among the inactive and active adherents of the more fundamentalist low-status groupings.

Since differences in ethnic background have been stressed by some commentators as being of greater significance than variations in religious affiliation in determining party choice, it is relevant to examine their contribution to party vote here. In fact, some have argued that correlations between religious affiliation and party choice are actually a consequence of ethnic background. Those belonging to low-status, more recently immigrant ethnic groups, presumably more Catholic than Protestant, are more likely to be Democratic. An analysis of the variations by ethnic background within the two major Christian groupings, however, does not confirm this suggestion.

TABLE VI

Relationship Between Party Affiliation and Ethnicity Among Religious and Class Groupings — 1954 — Per Cent (Whites Only)

Classification	Democrat	Republican	N
Non-manual Catholics			
Ireland	47	19	(189)
Italy	44	17	(87)
Great Britain	49	17	(75)
Germany and Austria	33	36	(127)
Poland	44	13	(32)
Other East Europe	48	21	(42)
No Answer on Origins	43	21	(85)
Totals	45%	21%	(707)
Non-manual Protestants			
Ireland	29	38	(138)

Classification	Democrat	Republican	N
Great Britain	22	52	(637)
Germany and Austria	21	46	(390)
Scandinavia and Holland	26	50	(254)
East Europe	26	39	(38)
Other West Europe	19	53	(77)
No Answer on Origins	30	39	(314)
Totals	24%	47%	(1860)
Manual Catholics			
Ireland	61	10	(244)
Italy	62	11	(251)
Great Britain	65	10	(152)
Germany and Austria	58	11	(192)
Poland	69	8	(167)
Other East Europe	68	10	(101)
Other West Europe	61	11	(113)
No Answer on Origins	60	13	(118)
Totals	63%	10%	(1373)
Manual Protestants			
Ireland	44	23	(219)
Great Britain	37	32	(699)
Germany and Austria	35	36	(491)
Scandinavia and Holland	40	34	(362)
East Europe	49	26	(61)
Other West Europe	49	24	(113)
No Answer on Origins	48	24	(438)
Totals	40%	30%	(2386)
Farm Catholics			
Ireland	67	8	(24)
Germany and Austria	46	16	(50)
East Europe	55	30	(20)
Other West Europe	45	34	(38)
Totals	52%	21%	(147)
Farm Protestants			
Ireland	28	42	(57)
Great Britain	26	49	(201)
Germany and Austria	39	40	(200)
Scandinavia and Holland	29	37	(123)
Other Europe	25	53	(28)
No Answer on Origins	33	45	(132)
Totals	32%	43%	(744)

Source: Calculated from INRA 1954 Eleven State Study. Independents not reported but included in calculations.

The data summarized in Table VI do indicate some variation within strata and religious groupings which is linked to ethnic background (as measured by responses to the question: "From what country did your ancestors come?"). However, it seems clear that there is no consistent pattern, and that in any case the variations are not large. Although studies of some cities have indicated relatively strong Republican support among Italian Catholics as compared to Irish, this finding does not hold up for the eleven states dealt with here.[86] The one group of Catholics who show any special Republican tendency is from Germany and Austria, a fact which may reflect the persistence of antagonism to the Democrats for having led two wars against Germany. Manual worker Catholics from eastern Europe show a greater Democratic propensity than do other Catholics in their stratum, but the difference is not very great. Among Protestants, curiously enough, those of Irish background, historically most opposed to the Irish Catholics of any group, give the Democrats somewhat more backing than Protestants of British, German, and Scandinavian origin, a phenomenon for which I cannot even suggest a slightly plausible *ex post facto* reason. And German urban Protestants, like Catholics of the same national background, are somewhat lower in support of Democrats than others of their religious group; farmers with the same ethnic religious background, however, do not seem to share this antagonism.

The findings from the eleven state survey are reiterated by the results of the analysis of data from the 1952 Roper survey which secured information concerning ethnic origin by asking for birthplace of father and grandfather. This study, however, does not permit an intensive analysis of many national backgrounds since the sample size was much smaller, and the largest single group was composed of fourth-generation background. However, a comparison of those of fourth-generation American (and British) ancestry with those of Irish and continental European background suggested little difference between those of old American or Anglo-Saxon background and those with other forebears within class and religious groupings.

The slightly greater propensity of Catholic workers of recent immigrant background to vote Democratic is contributed largely by twenty respondents of Irish background who are almost all Democratic. The Republican discrepancy among non-manual recent immigrant Protestants is largely a product of the behavior of fourteen Scandinavians who are equally heavily Republican. Whatever the sources of the remaining relatively small variations among different ethnic groups, it seems obvious that the differences in party support which are linked to ethnicity are

TABLE VII

Relationship of Ancestry, Religion, Class, and Past Voting Record (Whites — Non-southern) Percentage — 1952

	Democratic	Republican	
Catholics			
Non-manual			
4th Generation American or British	51	49	(41)
All others	49	51	(47)
Manual			
4th Generation American or British	76	24	(54)
All others	82	18	(85)
Protestants			
Non-manual			
4th Generation American or British	29	71	(205)
All others	22	78	(69)
Manual			
4th Generation American or British	49	51	(147)
All others	51	49	(47)

Source: 1952 Study by Elmo Roper Associates.

much less significant than those tied to class and religion. Though national ancestry may continue to affect political reactions, particularly with regard to foreign policy issues, this is one source of party diversity which time seems to be eliminating. It is significant to note that the largest remaining differences are among the farm population, a pattern which may reflect the maintenance of ethnic cultural communities in rural areas. The assumptions of those who contend that Americans no longer divide among themselves in national origin terms, that the country has blended in three melting pots — Protestant, Catholic, and Jewish — would seem to be borne out by these data.

Class and religious differences then remain as the two most significant correlates of party support. An examination of the survey data from 1936 to 1958 reported in Table II suggests that there was little change in the relationship of these two variables and party support during this period, although the parties varied in strength from election to election. Thus in the 1950's, Eisenhower gained among all groups — Catholics and Protestants *and* those in manual and white-collar occupations. With the exception of the small number of Protestant farmers, each class and religious category increased its Republican vote when Eisenhower was running (1952 and 1956) and decreased when he was not (1954 and 1958). As Philip Converse concludes from a national survey of a panel of voters conducted by the University of Michigan's Survey Research Center in 1956, 1958, and 1960:

> Of those citizens considering themselves to be Democrats and thereby voting Democratic unless they perceived compelling reasons to do otherwise, over one-quarter had defected to vote for Eisenhower in 1952 and 1956. Two facts stand out about this massive defection. First, it was a defection and in no sense a conversion. Democrats voting for Eisenhower continued to think of themselves as Democrats, and continued to vote Democratic at other levels of office, particularly when Eisenhower was not on the ticket. Our subsequent data since 1956 have made it clear that Eisenhower's appeal was rather completely dissociated from the Republican Party: even among Democrats most attracted to him, it is hard to find evidence of any change induced in personal loyalties.
>
> Second, and most important for our purposes here, the Democratic defections of the Eisenhower interlude seem to have occurred quite independent of religious background. That is, rates of defection were essentially the same for Protestant and Catholic Democrats alike. By sample estimates, Catholic defections were slightly less frequent than Protestant defections in 1952, and slightly more frequent in 1956. However, neither difference exceeds sampling error. More generally, it may be shown that the Democratic rates of defection to Eisenhower were remarkably similar across all the commonly studied social groupings: he enjoyed an "across-the-board" appeal which paid no visible respect to the major social boundaries.[87]

However, the data presented in Table II do suggest that among Catholics there was a somewhat greater return to the Democrats in 1958 than there had been in 1954. Since this return was concentrated among Catholic manual workers it is tempting to suggest that the eclipse of McCarthyism, which had considerable support from the poorer Catholics, may have accounted for the return of this group to its normal pattern.

The 1960 election produced a major convulsion in the previously stable level of religious voting. The measures of religious differences in voting in Table II among both manual and non-manual workers are far higher than in any other of the elections recorded. If the 1956 results are contrasted with those of 1960, one might be tempted to conclude that the shift in religious voting was entirely due to changes among Catholics. If, however, the 1954 and 1958 elections, in which Eisenhower was not running, are regarded as the "normal" pattern, we can see that both Catholic groups moved toward the Democrats (although the shift among manual workers was a small one), and that both Protestant groups moved toward the Republicans. Using results of a panel study interviewed in 1956, 1958, and 1960, Converse reaches a similar verdict:

> Instead of concluding that political choices of Catholics were profoundly affected by the candidacy of a Catholic while Protestants were left unaffected, we must conclude that the impact on the two religious groupings was rather more equal, although opposite in direction.[88]

At the end of the Eisenhower years, Catholics returned to and went far beyond their normal Democratic vote, while Protestants moved in the opposite direction.

Let us attempt to account for the Catholic shift toward the Democrats. Kennedy was a member not only of a minority religion, but also a minority ethnic group, albeit a highly acculturated one. He was our first Catholic President and our first President with Irish ancestry. Perhaps his national origin gained him support independent of his religion. Converse reports, however, that there is only a "mild sign that Irish Catholics were more affected by the Kennedy candidacy than were non-Irish Catholics." Italians and other non-Irish Catholics voted overwhelmingly for him, as thirty-two years earlier they did for Al Smith. Converse concludes therefore:

> While it is plausible to suppose from these data, then, that the ethnic factor contributed some extra "push" to Catholics in 1960, there is of course no question but that its role was entirely eclipsed, like an eddy in a torrent, by movement along broader religious lines.[89]

Given the unique pattern of Catholic voting in 1960, which is apparently not explicable in terms of class differences (which, of course, are controlled in the table) or ethnic loyalties, the reaction presumably can be accounted for only in terms of some more narrowly religious linked factors. In 1958, Converse found no consistent relationship between political party preference and church attendance, or between party preference and "identification with the Catholic community." The latter variable was tapped by two questions intended to measure "the sense of proximity and common interest which individual members feel vis-à-vis the group." However, in examining the *deviation* of the 1960 vote from the 1958 party preferences, Converse reports that both church attendance and community involvement were related to Kennedy voting.[90] He accounts for this result by suggesting that when the direct relevance of an election to the interests or values of a group is high, then conformity to its political norms will be related to involvement in the group, but if direct political relevance is low, this relationship is reduced. Thus in 1960, the nomination of a Catholic gave the group tie increased relevance, and the relationship between conformity to political norms and involvement in the group was intensified.

Since Protestants are much more diverse in their values than are Catholics, the intensity of their reaction against Kennedy was striking. In spite of the long-term decline in anti-Catholic feeling in America, the rapid rise of Catholics into a position of social prominence and power seems to have set off a new wave of uneasiness. Writing before Kennedy was nominated (the index of his book does not list his name) Will Herberg perceived this trend:

Protestantism in America today presents the anomaly of a strong majority group with a growing minority consciousness. "The psychological basis of much of American Protestantism," *Social Action* (Congregational) somewhat ruefully pointed out in 1952, "lies in a negative rejection of Roman Catholicism . . . The one emotional loyalty that of a certainty binds us Protestants together . . . is the battle against Rome." The fear of "Rome" is indeed the most powerful cement of Protestant community consciousness, and it seems to loom larger today than it has for some time. Discussion of Protestant communal affairs moves increasingly under the shadow of the "Catholic problem," and Protestant attitudes tend more and more to be defined in terms of confrontation with a self-assured and aggressive Catholicism. The tension has become really acute.[91]

In a survey administered during the 1960 campaign direct references to Kennedy's religion were avoided, yet almost half of the white Protestant respondents spontaneously mentioned the matter. Over three-quarters of those who did mention it were coded as "unequivocally negative."[92]

The data which have been presented on voting trends suggest that deviations of Protestant manual and non-manual workers caused by the candidacy of a Catholic were of about equal size. But the crude division into only two occupational groups seems to conceal a more complex relationship between status and voting deviation. Negative references to Kennedy's religion were given most frequently by unskilled workers, but least often from persons in the middle of the occupational scale, clerical and sales workers. The anti-Catholic reaction of the upper-middle-class occupations is at first glance surprising. In rural areas, and especially in the South, the expected relationship of low status and religious involvement to anti-Catholicism could be seen, but

where Catholics reside in large numbers and have come to compete for some of the forms of secular power, the anti-Catholics reaction fell much less clearly along lines of religious involvement in the narrow sense. This was particularly true of the upper middle class in the non-Southern metropolis, where the Catholic encroachment has been most notable. Here, despite the highest education level, the Protestant business and professional community responded in a manner which suggests a threat along a broad front, not simply a challenge to religious orthodoxy.[93]

The evidence strongly suggests that there were two types of anti-Catholicism in 1960. The lower-class non-urban kind is the religious anti-Catholicism of American history, tied to a lack of education, strong commitment to one's own Protestant church, and little direct contact with the targets of one's feelings. Presumably, this attitude has been declining in importance in recent years and, with the spread of education and urbanization, will continue to decline.

Anti-Catholic sentiment among higher-status persons may be a different matter. Probably this is the response of Protestants to their "growing minority consciousness" discussed by Herberg later in this volume. The same forces which cause the old nativist anti-Catholicism to decline help the new form to flourish: the outdated stereotype of the Catholic immigrant as a drunk and a bum fades away, but a new picture emerges of a community which is fully American, yet not Protestant, in which the Catholic and the Jew continue to increase their visible importance.

IV THE INFLUENCE OF RELIGION ON POLITICS

A. Social and Group Factors. It is obviously impossible to discuss the nature of political life in America without paying special attention to the influence of religious groups and values. This relationship has in fact hardly been investigated. There is much to be done before we can iron out the interrelated effects of religion, class, ethnicity, sectionalism, and the variety of other elements which shape American political behavior. But just as it is possible to construct a class or economic interpretation of political conflict and consensus in America, it would also be practical to do the same for religion; this, however, remains to be done.

At the moment we can say that broadly speaking there have been two main sets of facts relating religious influences to politics. The first may be described as *social or group factors,* and the second are *theological or value elements.* A number of processes affect the way in which the first set of factors operate.

1. The social situation of the dominant group within a given religion may lead to an identification between the denomination and given political tendencies. Thus, the needs of immigrants and workers have been identified with the politics of the Democratic party. Churches primarily composed of such groups have tended to back the Democrats in this country, and the more left party in other nations.

2. One party or ideological tendency may give more support than others to explicit needs of religious groups. Northern Democrats have been prone to give more support to government aid to religious schools than have Whigs or Republicans.

3. Direct linkages to a given political party may become a conventional method of mobility for aspiring members of different religious or ethnic groups.

A link betweeen parties and religious groups may reflect a conscious identification by the members of a religious group with issues directly involving the group as such. It may, however, also result unwittingly from the common life experiences of members of the same group. That is, individuals belonging to a given religious group tend to have similar experiences and to react in the same way, without feeling that they are reacting as members of a religious community. In large measure, the indirect impact of a religious group on its members rests in the fact that membership in a church helps determine the social interaction of members of the group. Church members are more likely to interact with members of their own church than with others. Thus, the fact that a man is a Catholic generally means that he belongs to a Catholic family, most of whose members are Democrats, and that he is more likely to associate with other Catholics, the majority of whom are Democrats. In large measure the traditional identification of a religious group with a political tendency is mediated through primary groups without individuals being aware of the fact that religious factors motivate their political behavior.

This process will be accentuated if the linkage between the religious group and its model pattern of political behavior becomes manifest. For much of American history, as we have seen, various ethnic groups associated with the Catholic church have dealt primarily with the Democratic party, and the party, in turn, has sought ways of retaining their loyalty. Catholics, historically, have been much more likely to gain office through the Democratic party. As Peter Odegard pointed out in 1960, before Kennedy was nominated:

> It is no accident that over 80 per cent of the Catholic members of Congress are Democrats. Nor is it surprising that under Democratic Presidents Franklin Roosevelt and Harry Truman one out of every four judicial appointments went to a Catholic as against one out of every 25 under Harding, Coolidge and Hoover.[94]

The relationship between religion and composition of party representation in Congress makes manifest the sharp difference between the parties in this respect.

TABLE VIII

Relationship Between Religion and Party Among Members of Both Houses of Congress from Different Sections as of January 1960

Section	Per Cent Catholics of Democratic Members	Per Cent Catholics of Republican Members
East	56	12
West	13	3
South	5	0
Midwest	38	7
Total	26	7

Source: John H. Fenton, *The Catholic Vote* (New Orleans: The Hauser Press, 1960), p. 89.

Clearly, involvement in the support from Democratic urban machines has played a considerable role in facilitating social mobility among Irish and other Catholic groups. This process has been described and documented in detail for what has been, perhaps, the most extreme example of a state in which politics and social mobility have been intimately tied to ethnicity and religion, Massachusetts.[95]

The creation of a visible identification between one party and various ethnic-religious groups, however, may create a negative reference image for others, which presses them to support the other party. Thus, a study of British immigrants in nineteenth century America reports that many of them joined the Republican party because they saw the Democrats in the hands of the Irish Catholics.[96] More recently, Adam Clayton Powell, Congressman from Harlem and Minister of Harlem's largest church, the Abyssinian Baptist, appealed to the white Protestants of New York to unite to gain political influence since almost no major judgeships or other major New York appointive offices were in the hands of Protestants.

B. Variant Religious Values. In addition to the various social and historical factors that have shaped the political identity of religious groups, there are very direct relationships between different religious beliefs and value systems and different political tendencies. Such relationships may take two forms: (1) explicit religious formulations which carry with them political directives; and (2) the indirect effect of religious systems in creating the dispositional base for the acceptance of certain secular political ideologies.

The most obvious example of the first type are the encyclicals of the

Roman Catholic pontiffs. A number of them, especially in the late nineteenth and twentieth centuries, have dealt with political matters. For example, the Papacy has condemned socialism and communism as materialistic and anti-religious movements which no Catholic may support. The condemnation of socialism has, of course, been redefined so as to include only materialistic or atheistic socialism, and the bishops of the British Commonwealth have explicitly stated that their social-democratic or Labour parties do not fall under this ban since they are not Marxist or materialistic. Nevertheless, there can be little doubt that the encyclical denunciations of socialism have affected the political behavior of Catholics in many countries. They have made it difficult for socialists to make inroads among Catholics on the European continent, and within the British Commonwealth Labour parties Catholics have generally played a conservative role, resisting efforts to define these parties as socialist in a Marxist sense.

Conversely, the economic ideology expressed in many encyclicals, while anti-socialist, has tended to favor what has come to be known as the welfare state. Since Pope Leo XIII, the Catholic church has condemned the exploitation of labor by business, and has urged state protection against the insecurities of old age, unemployment, and the like. The Popes have also favored trade unions. In large measure, the theology of the Catholic church, stemming from pre-capitalist feudal and aristocratic origins, has been against what it calls "materialistic socialism *and* capitalism." It is difficult to describe the best state envisaged by the pontiffs, but in general it would appear to be a Christian state with church control of education and of the young, and with economic legislation which protected the lower classes against economic exploitation. A linkage between papal social encyclicals and American Catholics was provided in the statements of the American Bishops which called for the adoption of "welfare state" measures long before they had a serious chance of enactment. Thus the yearly statement of the American Catholic Bishops in 1917 advocated liberal economic measures which were not put into effect until the party of the Protestant majority was finally defeated in the 1930's. The bishops suggested a heavier graduated income tax, social security, unemployment insurance, and minimum wage legislation.[97]

It should be recognized, however, that there has been considerable diversity of opinion among the Catholic clergy, even on church related matters. For decades they have recognized a divergence between "conservative" and "liberal" persuasions on such questions as the wisdom of continuing the Index of Prohibited Books, the moral propriety of state-run schools, and participation in interfaith activities.[98]

Among the laity, too, striking evidence of diversity can be found. Efforts by the church have kept laws on the books forbidding private physicians from dispensing contraceptive information in two states, Massachusetts and Connecticut. Yet, when Gallup interviewers asked a national sample in 1943, "Would you like to see government health clinics furnish birth control information to married people who wish it?" fully 45 per cent of the Catholics questioned responded in the affirmative.[99]

It is impossible to know how much effect official church positions have had on the political behavior of Catholics in different countries. Practicing Catholics have covered the range of the political spectrum from left-wing socialism to fascism. Local bishops have interpreted official church dogma to justify support of almost every political ideology except communism. There can, however, be little doubt that these church pronouncements have had some effect, given the authoritative aura of the church. For example, the sympathy which Catholic doctrine has had for trade union objectives, as contrasted with the greater emphasis on individualism inherent in Protestantism may in some part explain why even non-union middle-class Catholics are more supportive of union rights in this country.

A detailed study of the relationship between religious affiliation and vote in an Ohio referendum on anti-union "right-to-work" legislation held in 1958, found that regardless of what other factors also influenced the vote, the "religious factor" invariably emerges as an important determinant of voting behavior on the right-to-work issue . . . Ohio's counties were segregated (for analytic purposes) into twenty different levels of urbanism, income, and rural farm, and in all twenty of these groups the more Catholic counties exceeded the least Catholic in their opposition to right-to-work.[100]

Perhaps more important in their effect on politics and other areas of life than the directly political manifestoes of religious leaders are the ways in which religious doctrines operate to predispose adherents to favor one secular pattern rather than another. Many observers, for example, have called attention to the processes through which Protestantism has contributed to individualism, self-reliance, feelings of personal responsibility for success and failure, and interpretation of social evils in terms of moral turpitude. Catholicism, on the other hand, has tended to stress community responsibility, and does not emphasize individual morality. Emile Durkheim has pointed out the link between the differing stresses inherent in Protestantism and Catholicism in relation to variation in suicide rates. Durkheim's thesis is that Protestants are more prone than Catholics to commit suicide, for, among other reasons, Protestantism places greater responsibility on individuals for the consequences of their actions.

Similarly, it may be suggested that the differences among American Protestants and Catholics in their reaction to the welfare state may flow from a more or less conscious rejection of reliance on organized social action and the welfare state among Protestants. Studies of the 1948 and 1952 presidential elections indicated that Protestant Republicans were more opposed to social welfare measures than Catholic Republicans.[101] Even when moral matters rather than welfare measures are at issue, white Protestants are less likely to support state action than are Catholics. In a study of the influence of religion on behavior Gerhard Lenski found that Protestants who thought that certain kinds of behavior, i.e., gambling, moderate drinking, Sunday business, were "always or usually wrong" were less likely than Catholics to favor legal suppression of the immoral practice.[102] Similarly, white Protestants in this survey were more liberal than Catholics with respect to matters of civil liberties, including issues such as attacks on religion, criticism of the President, and rights of free speech for fascists and communists.

Further evidence for the thesis that religious background may indirectly affect secular behavior may be found in a study of productivity among workers. Melville Dalton notes that Protestant workers have higher rates of productivity than Catholic workers, and suggests that this is a consequence of greater individualism among the Protestants. The same survey also reports that Republican workers (most of whom were probably Protestants) were higher in productivity than Democratic ones.[103] Similar differences in economic orientation are suggested in Lenski's study. He finds, when comparing Protestants to Catholics, holding class background and length of family immigrant history constant, that Protestants are more likely to have positive attitudes toward work, to be less active in unions, to expect to agree with businessmen rather than with unions on various issues, and to be critical of installment buying. After considering the various environmental factors which might create such differences between the two major religious groups, Lenski concludes that the traditional differences in religious ethos continue to play an important role in affecting attitudes such as these.[104]

Historically, as we have seen, the moralistic values of ascetic Protestantism have been fostered by the conservative parties — Federalists, Whigs, and Republicans. All of the major Protestant crusades, against drink, against slavery, and against the increase in Catholic and non-evangelical segments of the population through immigration, have found much greater support from these parties, and have most often been opposed by the Democrats. Even today, public opinion survey data indicate that Protestants, particularly those living on farms or in small communities, or adhering to the more fundamentalist denominations, tend to be opposed to drink or gambling. According to a Gallup survey, as recently as 1959, 34 per cent of all Protestants favored national Prohibition as contrasted with 9 per cent of all Catholics. Three-fifths of all Protestant farmers supported such a law, as did 42 per cent of those living in towns of less than 10,000 population.[105] The varying attitudes toward work, success, individual responsibility, and public morality between Catholics and Protestants, especially Protestants adhering to the ascetic sects, may dispose the Catholic more than the Protestant to accept or support the welfare state. Consequently, the allegiance to the Democratic party may be facilitated by Catholic values, while ascetic Protestant values may contribute to the continuing disproportionate support which Republicans draw in the North from white Protestants, even among manual workers who belong to unions.

An indirect relationship between politics and religion may be found in the role of new sects which split off from the Anglican church. The name given them in Britain is an insightful one, "Nonconformists," or "Dissenters." Most new or dissenting religions tend to appeal to those groups in society who are in an underprivileged position. While religious protest may be couched in purely theological terms, it may give expression to feelings of resentment against various aspects of the social or economic structure. By breaking sectors of the population from the traditional religious system, it removes in part their tie to other aspects of the social order.

A number of studies of radical and left-wing movements in Britain and on the European continent including Czarist Russia have presented data which suggest the validity of this thesis.[106] Protestants are true protestors, not only against traditional religion, but against aspects of the social structure as well. It is important to note, however, that the relationship between theological and secular protest is rarely manifest. The Methodists, who contributed much to the growth of British labor, for example, were both conservative and apathetic toward politics, and in large measure most sectarian movements are hostile to worldly matters. The connection to politics seems to lie in these religions providing the first break with a portion of the established order, and in their giving lower-class individuals the opportunity for self-expression in organizations of their own.[107]

On the other hand, it has been suggested by some observers, that discontent which expresses itself in religious terms is often contained by religion. That is, a religion which promulgates transcendental doctrines, such as only the poor but honest will be rewarded, may reduce the pressures for social reform by enabling the discontented to project a future equitable situation in Heaven. Given the combination of transcendental elements and the hostility to worldly matters often found in fundamentalist or revivalist sects, such religious groups may reduce the level of lower-class political protest. In effect, they constitute a functional equivalent for such protest for many of their members.

An examination of history suggests that American Protestant sects have more often served to draw off antagonism from the social arena to the religious order, rather than forming the beginning of a breakthrough against the secular order. New sects have developed more readily here than anywhere else in the world. For the most part, these are drawn from economically and socially depressed strata, and their theology reflects transvaluational beliefs, such as the belief that wealth or ornate living is sinful or part of a corrupting process. During the last Great Depression, when efforts to form significant protest parties failed totally, the sectarians grew while other religions declined or showed no change.[108] Such movements have played a role as a "transmission belt" not for the left, but for the radical or extremist right wing. The differences between the American and European reactions reflect many factors, but two which seem important are the relationship of the dominant religion to the state, and the class composition of the sects. In much of Europe, the dominant religion, Anglican, Lutheran, Catholic, or Orthodox, had been a state church closely identified with the traditional ruling strata. Hence, the new sects were necessarily rejecting an institution which was part of the old social order, and their fight against established religion was also a fight against the conservative parties allied with established religion. In America, this issue did not arise after the early nineteenth century. Second, much of the support of fundementalist Protestantism as well as of new sects have come from the lower non-metropolitan middle and lower classes. The urban working class has been disproportionately Catholic. And the more dissatisfied, possible downwardly mobile or aging members of the lower-middle class have politically identified with traditional old values rather than with new ones. Hence, perhaps, the propensity discussed earlier for sectarianism and right-wing politics to join forces.

The one important exception to these generalizations has been the Negro churches. Negroes have been even more inclined than whites to find the need to back transvaluational new churches. But such forms of religious innovation have often played a role in facilitating secular political or race protest movements. In a sense, these have played a role comparable to lower-class based new Protestant groups in Europe. The Southern Bible Belt has, in fact, thrown up two forms of religiously linked protest, a rightist white one, and a leftist Negro one. And since one group seeks to return to the old status quo, while the other seeks a new world, the reasons for the difference are not hard to comprehend.

C. Some Implications. In concluding the discussion of the influence of religion on politics, it may be important to point out that its important effect may not rest with its influence in determining the basis of party division. Many further avenues of exploration are suggested, e.g., the extent to which the unique character of pluralistic American Protestantism has contributed to exacerbating the nature of controversy.

The emphasis on making politics an arena in which men seek to enforce the moral has been distinctly American, and over time has come to influence many groups which have no historic ties to Puritanism. Most recently, a distinguished French Dominican student of American religion has criticized American Catholics for having absorbed this American Protestant view of religion and morality. He worries that they are becoming more like American Baptists and Presbyterians than like European or Latin-American Catholics, that they have accepted Puritanism:

> What is Puritanism? A French Jacobin, Saint-Just gave the most perfect definition of it that I know: "Either virtue or a reign of terror." . . . Sin must be repressed by all possible means of force and of civil and social legislation. One must force people to be virtuous. Virtue and sin are identified with human law.
>
> . . . [The] Puritan influence is very deep in America. Many non-Catholics suffer from it and would like to free themselves from it. Now, you would think that they should be able to count on the Catholics in this endeavor. But such is not the case and one often has the impression that American Catholics are more Puritan than anybody else and that they are close to setting themselves up as the champions of Puritanism. . . .
>
> . . . (An) instance of the same thing was the enthusiasm whipped up by McCarthy among certain American Catholics: "Either virtue or a reign of terror." [109]

This tendency to enforce virtue by law runs like a red letter throughout American history. Insofar as an issue has been linked to the moral sense of religious people it has given rise to movements designed to eradicate evil, whether the cause be abolition, white supremacy, temperance, or anti-Popery. Such behavior suggests an identity between religious commitment and intolerance of ambiguity. The more committed an individual is to a religious belief the less likely will he be to appreciate the rights of "error," whether in the religious or secular arena. Lenski in his analysis of the impact of religion suggests that "*tolerance* and *secularism*" are closely interrelated, that both are fostered by modern urban society.[110]

There is considerable evidence which attests to the validity of this thesis with respect to the behavior of individuals today. In a comprehensive examination of the attitudes of the American people and their civic leaders toward civil liberties for unpopular views made in 1954, Samuel Stouffer found "that more churchgoers are intolerant of . . . nonconformity . . . than are nonchurchgoers" and that this relationship holds "when education, age, region, and type of community are taken into account." [111] The same relationship between church attendance and intolerance occurred among community leaders as well. There was no consistent variation between Catholics and Protestants in this survey.

It has often been pointed out that moralist fervor linked to religion has typically marked the emergence of new American social movements, from Temperance to Birchism. These social movements have also been marked by leadership from "displaced" groups in America, groups which have for one reason or another lost an earlier status.[112] At certain times religious groups, as such, have felt a sharp loss of status. Perhaps Protestantism as a whole is feeling such a loss today. In addition, as has been noted, the conservative in America has historically allied himself with religious and moralistic causes even more than with class issues—out of a necessity flowing from the nature of American society. These implications for American political life have to be further explored against the specific background of America's persistent religious-political design.

The discussion in this essay of the various political behaviors which are related to religion may be subjected to the criticism that we are not properly speaking of "religious factors" at all. In large measure, the "religious" attitudes which affect political choice have been determined by special historical circumstances which affect many members of particular denominations because they were predominantly immigrants, workers, or businessmen, or lived in a certain part of the country. As Gibson Winter has noted: "If Protestant attitudes were really grounded in a religious factor, the positions of White and Negro Protestants would not be diametrically opposed on all issues." [113]

Clearly from the point of view of the theologian, of the "true believer," much of what has been discussed here, or in other writings of social scientists on religion, is not really dealing with religion as the area of men's experiences in which he deals with God. However, if we recognize that the sociologist cannot deal with this subject as such, that in fact he must deal with religious groupings as one of the sources of men's sub-group identifications, an identification which involves the special way in which different groups see their relationship to the transcendental, then much of sociological analysis of religion becomes a specification of the way in which different religious communities have absorbed their various experiences, and the consequent effect of such absorption on their behavior in other "non-religious" arenas.

Religion is of obvious particular interest to the sociologist since it is the one institution which is explicitly concerned with values, with stating and teaching proper modes of thinking and acting. And whether the religion of the privileged or deprived, it translates experiences into value terms, into concepts of right and wrong. Since religious groups must define the right as divinely inspired, their structure serves to institutionalize reactions to historical experiences as norms which are passed on to subsequent generations.

The United States as a nation was in some part formed out of the historic experiences of the English dissenting Protestant sects. The very emphasis on morality in politics which so distinguishes much of our domestic and foreign politics is a consequence of our being a Protestant nation without an established church. And elements in the Protestant tradition together with the focus on the voluntary principle have meant that Americans have come to define reactions to new experiences in religious terms, often through creating or joining a new religion. Thus even when the reasons men support a given political party may be explained almost totally with respect to their economic or status position, the fact that their position in the stratification hierarchy is in part mediated through a religious affiliation affects the quality of the secular political response. In this way the "religious factor" has affected the character of American politics. To attempt to explain American political history without a discussion of the relationship of politics and religion is wrong; the fact that men have done so only serves to demonstrate that to study a subject does not necessarily mean that one understands it.

There is obviously no simple solution to the study of the "religious factor" in American politics. Much of its influence must be perceived as part of the total value system affecting everyone. As we have seen, membership in the same denominations stimulated feeling for and against slavery before the Civil War. Today, southern Negroes and whites adhere to the same denominations, and both are largely Baptist and Methodist. Foreign Catholic observers have noted to their dissatisfaction that many American Catholics have taken over Protestant Puritanical attitudes, that the American Catholic's tastes, reactions, and ideas on moral issues are colored by people around him, and thus he is more like an American Baptist than, let us say, a Latin American or European Catholic. The problem which co-variation of diverse elements with religion poses for analysis was explicitly recognized by Alexis de Tocqueville when he attempted to make sense out of American political life in the 1830's:

> There is in each religion a political doctrine which, by affinity, is joined to it. This point is controvertible in the sense that where nothing interferes with this tendency, it surely shows itself. But it doesn't follow that it is impossible to separate religious doctrines from their political effects. On the contrary, in all the countries of the world, material interests have been seen to operate this separation. The Catholics in . . . the United States are the invariable supporters of the "democratic" party. Does it follow that Catholicism leads to the "democratic" spirit? No, but that the Catholics are poor, and come almost all from a country where the aristocracy is Protestant.[114]

The combination of the "political doctrine," which, as Tocqueville suggests, is inherent in every religion, with the fact that denominations in pluralistic America are variously located in the social and economic structure, and the continuing strong sense of commitment to an identification with religion, means that religion remains, today, as in Tocqueville's time, one of the main sources of party cleavage and of political tone. And I would venture the prediction that analysts of American political life will continue to find evidence of its impact for generations to come.

NOTES

1. Alexis de Tocqueville, *Democracy in America* (New York: Vintage Books, 1954), I, p. 312.
2. Paul F. Lazarsfeld, Bernard Berelson, and Hazel Gaudet, *The People's Choice* (New York: Columbia University Press, 1948), p. 21. See the discussion of this development in Peter Rossi, "Four Landmarks in Voting Research," in E. Burdick and A. J. Brodbeck, eds., *American Voting Behavior* (Glencoe: The Free Press, 1959), p. 18. Rossi reports that "Dr. Lazarsfeld related that George Gallup expressed disbelief when he told him of his finding that this religious factor was independently related to voting behavior." P. 438.
3. Elmo Roper, "The Myth of the Catholic Vote," *Saturday Review of Literature* (October 31, 1959), p. 22.
4. In this essay, I ignore most factors other than religion which have affected the varying social bases of support of American parties. This may give the unwarranted impression that I am trying to suggest that religion is the predominant factor. Obviously, this is not so, although it and class position are the two

most important continuing ones. For an analysis of the significance of class factors see S. M. Lipset, *Political Man* (Garden City: Doubleday-Anchor Books, 1963), esp. pp. 303–31.

5. See Euarts B. Greene, *Religion and the State* (Ithaca: Great Seal Books, 1959), pp. 78–93.
6. See W. W. Sweet, *The Story of Religion in America* (New York: Harper, 1950).
7. John C. Miller, *Crisis in Freedom* (Boston: Little, Brown, 1951), pp. 43–4, 46–8.
8. Manning Dauer, *The Adams Federalists* (Baltimore: Johns Hopkins Press, 1953), p. 25. See also Anson Stokes, *Church and State in the United States* (New York: Harper, 1950), I, pp. 408–10.
9. Ibid. pp. 28–9.
10. Loc. cit. on the Irish, see Carl Wittke, *The Irish in America* (Baton Rouge: Louisiana State University Press, 1956), p. 106.
11. See Lawrence H. Fuchs, "Some Political Aspects of Immigration," in Joseph Fiszman, ed., *The American Political Arena* (Boston: Little, Brown, 1962), p. 523, for a discussion of the role of the Scotch-Irish as "the core ethnic group of the Democratic Party."
12. Stokes, op. cit. I, p. 676.
13. Arthur Schlesinger, Jr., *The Age of Jackson* (Boston: Little, Brown, 1946), p. 16. See also Henry Adams, *The United States in 1800* (Ithaca: Great Seal Books, 1955), pp. 56–9.
14. Lee Benson, *The Concept of Jacksonian Democracy: New York as a Test Case* (Princeton: Princeton University Press, 1961), p. 196.
15. William G. McLoughlin, "Introduction," Charles G. Finney, *Lectures on Revivals of Religion* (Cambridge: Belknap Press of Harvard University Press, 1960), p. xviii.
16. Benson, op. cit. pp. 198–207.
17. Op. cit. p. xix.
18. Clifford S. Griffin, *Their Brothers' Keepers* (New Brunswick: Rutgers University Press, 1960), p. 37; John A. Krout, *The Origins of Prohibition* (New York: Alfred A. Knopf, 1925), pp. 83–100.
19. Alice Tyler, *Freedom's Ferment* (Minneapolis: The University of Minnesota Press, 1944), p. 317; Joseph Gusfield, "Status Conflicts and the Changing Ideologies of the American Temperance Movement," in David Pittman and Charles R. Snyder, eds., *Society, Culture and Drinking Practices* (New York: John Wiley, 1962), pp. 105–6.
20. Gusfield, op. cit. p. 107.
21. Griffin, op. cit. pp. 131–4.
22. David Donald, *Lincoln Reconsidered* (New York: Vintage Books, 1961), pp. 27–9.
23. Franklin Hamlin Littell, *From State Church to Pluralism* (New York: Doubleday-Anchor Books, 1962), p. 57; Tyler, op. cit. p. 505; Benson, op. cit. p. 212.
24. Gilbert Barnes, *The Anti-Slavery Impulse, 1830–1844* (Gloucester: Peter Smith, 1957), p. 107; Littell, op. cit. p. 64.
25. Littell, op. cit. p. 64.
26. H. Richard Niebuhr, *The Social Sources of Denominationalism* (New York: Meridian Books, 1957), p. 194.
27. Roy Franklin Nichols, *The Disruption of American Democracy* (New York: Collier Books, 1962), pp. 35, 43.

28. W. J. Cash, *The Mind of the South* (New York: Doubleday-Anchor Books, 1954), pp. 91–3. See also Kenneth Stampp, *The Peculiar Institution* (New York: Alfred A. Knopf, 1956), pp. 158–62.
29. Nichols, op. cit. p. 48; see also Stanley Elkins, *Slavery* (Chicago: University of Chicago Press, 1959), p. 36.
30. Benson, op. cit. p. 212.
31. Griffin, op. cit. p. 220
32. Lawrence F. Schmeckebier, "History of the Know-nothing Party in Maryland," *Studies in Historical and Political Science,* Johns Hopkins University, 17 (1899), p. 40; Wilfred Binkley, *American Political Parties, Their Natural History* (New York: Alfred A. Knopf, 1947), p. 163.
33. Louis D. Scisco, *Political Nativism in New York State* (New York: Columbia University Press, 1901), pp. 29–31.
34. Ray Allen Billington, *The Protestant Crusade 1800–1860* (New York: Rinehart, 1952), p. 395.
35. Kenneth M. Stampp, *Indiana Politics During the Civil War* (Indianapolis: Indiana Historical Bureau, 1949), p. 5.
36. Henry R. Mueller, *The Whig Party in Pennsylvania* (New York: Columbia University Press, 1922), pp. 233–4.
37. Oscar Handlin, *Boston's Immigrants* (Cambridge: The Belknap Press of Harvard University Press, 1959), p. 204.
38. See Joseph Schafer, "Who Elected Lincoln?" *American Historical Review,* 47 (Oct. 1941), p. 51. Lincoln's advocacy of abstinence and Prohibition Legislation in Illinois could not have endeared him to the German voters.
39. William F. Zornow, *Lincoln and the Party Divided* (Norman: University of Oklahoma Press, 1954), pp. 208–15. "Lincoln lost most of the counties where at least one-third of the population was foreign-born, or he polled a percentage less than he received for each state as a whole." P. 212.
40. R. Freeman Butts, *The American Tradition in Religion and Education* (Boston: The Beacon Press, 1950), p. 142.
41. John Higham, *Strangers in the Land* (New Brunswick: Rutgers University Press, 1955), pp. 28–9; Stokes, op. cit. II, p. 68.
42. Butts, op. cit. p. 143.
43. Stokes, op. cit. II, p. 68.
44. Humphrey J. Desmond, *The A.P.A. Movement* (Washington: The New Century Press, 1912), pp. 67–8.
45. Ibid. p. 33.
46. Higham, op. cit. pp. 98–9.
47. Maldwyn Jones, *American Immigrants* (Chicago: University of Chicago Press, 1960), p. 166.
48. Sidney E. Mead, "American Protestantism since the Civil War: From Denominationalism to Americanism," in Abraham Eisenstadt, ed., *American History. Book II: Since 1865* (New York: Thomas Y. Crowell, 1962), p. 174.
49. Ibid. pp. 186, 187.
50. James Bryce, *The American Commonwealth,* Vol. II (Toronto: The Copp, Clark Company, 1891), p. 36. Bryce also mentions that the support of the Democrats by "the Roman Catholic Germans [is due] to the tacit alliance which has subsisted in many districts between the Catholic Church and the Democrats." p. 32.
51. Leon D. Epstein, *Politics in Wisconsin* (Madison: University of Wisconsin

Press, 1958), pp. 35–6. Epstein is here summarizing "the careful and detailed studies of Joseph Schafer," published in a number of articles cited by Epstein on page 164. These loyalties were not simply maintanied by tradition. In the early 1870's the Republicans passed a law "regulating saloons in a manner hostile to the German-Americans," and in the 1890's religious tensions were exacerbated by "a Republican law assumed to be hostile to the maintenance of parochial schools." Footnote 5, p. 163. Samuel Lubell describes the traditional mainstay of the Iowa Democratic party before World War I as "the German-Americans, particularly the Catholic Germans." *The Future of American Politics* (New York: Doubleday-Anchor Books, 1956), p. 180.

52. V. O. Key, Jr., and Frank Munger, "Social Determinism and Electoral Decisions: the Case of Indiana," in Eugene Burdick and Arthur Brodbeck, eds., *American Voting Behavior* (Glencoe: The Free Press, 1959), p. 283.
53. This shift has been explained as resulting from the fact that Utah and the Mormon Church (as the largest economic as well as religious group in the state) were particularly concerned with protective tariffs for one of the state's major crops, sugar beets. The McKinley administration passed tariff legislation protecting domestic suppliers, while the Democrats opposed such tariffs.
54. V. O. Key, Jr., "A Theory of Critical Elections," *Journal of Politics,* 17 (1955), pp. 1–18.
55. In Illinois, on the other hand, Bryan appears to have done much better in rural areas than in urban ones, a pattern which was probably true for much of the West. For Illinois see Duncan MacRae, Jr., and James A. Meldrum, "Critical Elections in Illinois: 1888–1958," *The American Political Science Review,* 54 (1960), pp. 679–81.
56. William Diamond, "Urban and Rural Voting in 1896," *American Historical Review,* 46 (1941), p. 303.
57. Key, op. cit. p. 15.
58. Robert Dahl, *Who Governs?* (New Haven: Yale University Press, 1961), p. 45.
59. J. Joseph Huthmacher, *Massachussets People and Politics* (Cambridge: The Belknap Press of Harvard University Press, 1959), pp. 14–15.
60. Though this was apparently true for the country as a whole to judge by National voting statistics, it was apparently not true of Illinois. See MacRae and Meldrum, op. cit. p. 680.
61. Samuel Lubell, op. cit. pp. 143–4.
62. Huthmacher, op. cit. p. 33.
63. Lubell, op. cit. pp. 180–81.
64. James M. Cox, *Journal Through My Years* (New York: Simon and Schuster, 1946), pp. 272–3.
65. In Illinois La Follette's vote came "from elements of the population which might have voted for Al Smith had he been nominated. . . . La Follette . . . obtained heavier support . . . from urban counties with heavy foreign-born population." The vote correlated 0.68 per cent with pro-wet sentiment on a 1922 referendum, and 0.54 per cent Catholic. MacRae and Meldrum, op. cit. p. 677.
66. Lubell, op. cit. pp. 138, 149, 180; Huthmacher, op. cit. p. 101.
67. Ibid. p. 89; see also Emerson Hunsberger Loucks, *The Ku Klux Klan in Pennsylvania* (Harrisburg: The Telegraph Press, 1936), p. 99; John B. Martin, *Indiana* (New York: Alfred A. Knopf), pp. 193–4.

68. Huthmacher, op. cit. p. 74; for Illinois data see MacRae and Meldrum, op. cit. pp. 676–7.
69. Ibid. p. 94.
70. Key and Munger, op. cit. pp. 294–5.
71. Angus Campbell, "Surge and Decline: A Study of Electoral Change," *Public Opinion Quarterly,* 24 (1960), pp. 397–418.
72. For a description of the campaign see Edmund Moore, *A Catholic Runs for President: the 1928 Campaign* (New York: Ronald, 1956).
73. Key, op. cit. pp. 4–6, 11–12, 13; Lubell, op. cit. pp. 36, 37, 41, 42.
74. Ibid. pp. 37, 41.
75. A number of studies indicate that the most consistent correlate of Democratic vote over the long term, and of the Smith gain over the past two elections in particular, was the proportion of foreign-born in the population. This has been found for Illinois, MacRae and Meldrum, op. cit. p. 675; for New Haven, Dahl, op. cit. pp. 49–50; and most recently in a detailed national ecological study for the country as a whole. See Ruth C. Silva, *Rum, Religion, and Votes* (University Park: Pennsylvania State University Press, 1962).
76. S. M. Lipset, "Some Statistics on Bigotry in Voting," *Commentary,* 30 (1960), pp. 286–90; William F. Ogburn and Neil S. Talbot, "A Measurement of the Factors in the Presidential Election of 1928," *Social Forces,* 8 (1929), p. 176; Peter Odegard, *Religion and Politics* (New Brunswick: Oceana Publications, 1960), pp. 165–7; Edward J. Richter and Berton Dulce, *Religion and the Presidency* (New York: The Macmillan Co., 1962), pp. 96–7; MacRae and Meldrum, op. cit., p. 675; Silva, op. cit., *passim.*
77. Op. cit. p. 9; for Illinois see MacRae and Meldrum, op. cit. p. 678.
78. Op. cit. p. 43. "After 1932, the presidential vote [in Illinois] continues to reflect the same cleavage of the electorate through 1956, even while the proportions obtained by Democrats and Republicans fluctuate." MacRae and Meldrum, op. cit. p. 678.
79. William S. Robinson, "Ecological Correlations and Behavior of Individuals," *American Sociological Review,* 15 (1950), pp. 351–7.
80. See Robert Alford, *Class Voting in Four Anglo-American Countries* (Ph.D. dissertation in Sociology, University of California, Berkeley, 1961).
81. Op. cit. p. 255.
82. S. M. Lipset, *Political Man,* pp. 303–6; and Harold Sheppard, Arthur Kornhauser, and Arthur Mayer, *When Labor Votes* (New York: University Books, 1956), pp. 42–3.
83. Benton Johnson, "Ascetic Protestantism and Political Preference," *Public Opinion Quarterly,* 26 (1962), pp. 38–40.
84. Benjamin Ringer and Charles Glock, "The Political Role of the Church as Defined by Its Parishioners," *Public Opinion Quarterly,* 18 (1954–55), pp. 337–47.
85. Johnson, op. cit. p. 39; for an analysis of the sources of the liberalism of American academics and other intellectuals, see Lipset, *Political Man,* pp. 332–71.
86. Dahl, op. cit. p. 60.
87. Philip Converse, "Religion and Politics: The 1960 Elections," (Unpublished dittoed paper: Survey Research Center, University of Michigan, 1962), pp. 4–5. An analysis of the effects of moving to the suburbs by Catholics based on a survey in metropolitan St. Louis in 1956 reports that even in this Eisenhower year: "In voting, both central city and suburban Catholics remain heavily

Democratic. When we control country of origin, generation since migration, and education, only in the suburbs and in the most extreme classes, do we find small Republican pluralities among Catholics — those with northern and western European backgrounds, those who are third generation, those with college educations. And these are far less Republican than their counterparts among the non-Catholics." Scott Grear, "Catholic Voters and the Democratic Party," *Public Opinion Quarterly*, 25 (1961), p. 623.

88. Converse, op. cit. p. 9.
89. Ibid. p. 29.
90. Ibid. pp. 32–3.
91. Will Herberg, *Protestant, Catholic, Jew* (New York: Doubleday-Anchor Books, 1960), p. 234. Herberg's foreword is dated October, 1959. The passage he quotes is from "Christian Faith and the Protestant Churches," *Social Action*, 18 (May 1952), p. 1.
92. Converse, op. cit. p. 39.
93. Ibid. pp. 50–51.
94. Peter Odegard, op. cit. p. 121. The same tendency has been documented in detail for the New England states. See Duane Lockard, *New England State Politics* (Princeton: Princeton University Press, 1959), pp. 32, 66–7, 98, 134, 198–9, 241. See also Samuel Lubell, op. cit. pp. 83–4.
95. See Oscar Handlin, op. cit.; Earl Lathem and George Goodwin, *Massachusetts Politics* (Medford: Tufts Civic Education Center, 1960); Joseph Huthmacher, *Massachusetts People and Politics 1919–1933* (Cambridge: The Belknap Press of Harvard University Press, 1959); and Murray B. Levin, *The Complete Politician. Political Strategy in Massachusetts* (Indianapolis: Bobbs-Merrill, 1962).
96. Rowland T. Berthoff, *British Immigrants in Industrial America, 1790–1950* (Cambridge: Harvard University Press, 1953), pp. 196–8.
97. Robert D. Cross, *The Emergence of Liberal Catholicism in America* (Cambridge: Harvard University Press, 1958).
98. Ibid. pp. 75, 105–8, 212.
99. Source: A.I.P.O. Study No., 308KT, 1943.
100. John H. Fenton, *The Catholic Vote* (New Orleans: The Hauser Press, 1960), pp. 37–8.
101. A. Campbell, et al., "Political Issues and the Vote, November 1952," *American Political Science Review*, 47 (1953), pp. 374–5.
102. Gerhard Lenski, *The Religious Factor* (New York: Doubleday, 1961), pp. 177–8. However, as I note later, Protestants as a group were much more likely than Catholics to think that gambling and moderate drinking were wrong.
103. See Melville Dalton, "Worker Response and Social Background," *Journal of Political Economy*, 55 (1947), pp. 323–32.
104. Lanski, op. cit. pp. 75–119.
105. Calculated from the data of A.I.P.O. Survey No. 622K, 1959.
106. For further discussion and references, see S. M. Lipset, *Political Man*, op. cit. pp. 106–8.
107. See A. D. Belden, *George Whitefield the Awakener* (London: S. Low Marston and Co., Ltd., 1930), pp. 247ff. See also William Kornhauser, *The Politics of Mass Society* (Glencoe: The Free Press, 1959), pp. 137ff.
108. W. W. Sweet, *The American Churches* (New York: Abingdon-Cokesbury, 1947), p. 73; A. T. Boisen, *Religion in Crisis and Custom* (New York: Harper 1955); also Argyle, op. cit. pp. 138–40.

109. R. L. Bruckberger, "The American Catholics as a Minority," in Thomas T. McAvoy, ed., *Roman Catholicism and the American Way of Life* (Notre Dame: University of Notre Dame Press, 1960), pp. 45–7.

110. Lenski, op. cit. p. 9.

111. Samuel Stouffer, *Communism, Conformity, and Civil Liberties* (New York: Doubleday, 1955), p. 147.

112. Together with Earl Raab, I am currently involved in a research project which seeks to analyze the sources of "extremist" and moralistic movements and politics in America. Our preliminary conclusions are that aspects inherent in American Protestantism have played a major role in predisposing Americans to take part in such movement. Because of problems of length and overlap I have left out of this essay almost all the materials bearing on this dimension of the relationship of religion to politics. For my earlier published writings bearing on some of these issues, see S. M. Lipset, "The Sources of the 'Radical Right,'" and "Radical Rightists of Three Decades — Coughlinites, McCarthyites, and Birchers," in Daniel Bell, ed., *The Radical Right* (New York: Doubleday, 1963).

113. Gibson Winter, "Methodological Reflection on 'The Religious Factor,'" *Journal for the Scientific Study of Religion,* 2 (1962), p. 56.

114. Citation from Tocqueville's American diary as quoted in George W. Pierson, *Tocqueville in America* (New York: Doubleday-Anchor Books, 1959), p. 289. He makes the same point with less stress on the problem of methodolgy in the *Democracy* itself. "Most of the Catholics are poor, and they have no chance of taking part in the government unless it is open to all the citizens. They constitute a minority, and all rights must be respected in order to ensure to them the free exercise of their own privileges. These two causes induce them, even unconsciously, to adopt political doctrines which they would perhaps support with less zeal if they were rich and preponderant." Alexis de Tocqueville, op. cit. p. 312.

BENJAMIN A. REIST

Church and State in America: A Theological Inquiry

The vantage point from which this chapter is written should be clarified at the outset. The author stands within the Reformed tradition, and he writes particularly in the light of his involvement in the work of the Special Committee on the Relations Between Church and State of the General Assembly of the United Presbyterian Church, U.S.A. His assumptions were long held before this, but they have been clarified and enhanced by virtue of the responsibilities attending membership in the committee. Most simply stated, this contention is that the problem at hand is primarily and decisively *theological* in character.

I INTRODUCTION

By way of introduction, there are two points on which we must be clear. The first of these has to do with Calvin's doctrine of the state, or more properly, his doctrine of civil government. Though it would take us too far afield to elaborate this in detail, it cannot be emphasized strongly enough that Calvin's position on this matter was of the utmost significance, both historically and theologically. Unlike Luther, who saw the political order as the result of the sin of man, Calvin understood it strictly in terms of the providence of God. This he stated categorically and unequivocally:

> . . . it has not come about by human perversity that the authority over all things on earth is in the hands of kings and other rulers, but by divine providence and holy ordinance. For God was pleased so to rule the affairs of men, inasmuch as he is present with them and also presides over the making of laws and the exercising of equity in courts of justice.[1]

Calvin's point was of the utmost *theological* significance, since in understanding the political order in the framework of the doctrine of providence he championed the view that the state is *not* to be regarded simply in terms of the nature of man, but decisively in terms of the activity of God. This meant that Calvin regarded the state to be intensely positive in character. (In the *Institutes of the Christian Religion* his doctrine of civil government is precisely analogous to his doctrine of the church.) Such a view carries with it both the possibility and the necessity of a never-ending, theologically ordered critique of the state, whatever its level of development. It is this dimension of Calvin's thought which generated the political and social involvement of the Reformed tradition at large, from its earliest phases through the present.[2]

A second introductory point has to do with a problem which, while Biblical in origin and character, and thus prior to what we have just noted, is nonetheless particularly modern in its effect and significance. I refer to the problem of the tension in Christian ethics between *gospel* and *law*. The church commits no greater error than when it treats the teachings of Jesus as if they had a significance unto themselves, apart from the fact of the identity and nature of the one who uttered them. The teachings are not independent of the Teacher! The gospel — the good news that Jesus of Nazareth is indeed the Christ — does not dispose of the law, but it does so radically re-orient it that it can be neither understood nor utilized as before. Jesus Christ was not a new Moses, and His teachings did not embody a new law, at least not in the Old Testament sense. Indeed, the significance of the teachings of Jesus in the New Testament has to do with the clarification of just who He was. The Christian life is a life which bears witness to its Lord, nothing less, and an isolated ethical maxim or set of maxims can never be substituted for the person and event, Jesus Christ.

The recognition in our time of what has always been the fact of the matter as far as the New Testament is concerned has led to the vigorous assertion of the *contextual character* of the Christian ethic, most notably in the case of Professor Paul Lehmann.[3] Such a view "regards the concrete complex of the actual situation out of which the ethical problem arises as itself ethically significant."[4] As Lehmann sees it, the problem of just how the specific acts of Christians are to be ordered is the problem of explaining "how to live constructively in the gap between the will of God, theologically understood, and the concrete human situation, pragmatically understood."[5] His position as a whole is epitomized by the following:

Love is God's concrete action in Christ, establishing a bridgehead of forgiveness in the world. And life in the *koinonia* (i.e., the existing, concrete fellowship of Christians, viz. the church) is first of all, simply being oneself on this bridgehead; and then doing whatever one does with all the pragmatic resourcefulness required by God's unyielding maneuvering, on the one hand, and the actualities of enemy resistance on the other. The aim is to extend the bridgehead until the enemy and all the territory under enemy occupation are brought into the orbit of God's reconciling action in Jesus Christ.[6]

In this formulation the dynamic element of the Christian ethic is uppermost. Christians must call the world's attention to what God has done and is doing in Jesus Christ. It is the genius of the claim that the Christian ethic is a contextual ethic to insist that Christians are summoned to the activity of *witnesses,* and not to the attempt to apply universally applicable principles to the given complexities of human existence.

The contention of this paper is that these two points — the one as old as the Reformed tradition itself, and the other the result of a profoundly contemporary struggle with the ethical legacy of the New Testament — have a direct bearing on the problem with which we are concerned, that is, the problem of relating Christian faith to the relationship now in existence between church and state in the United States.

II THE PROBLEM

It will come as a surprise for many, and a shock for some, to recognize along with John Bennett that "There is no Protestant doctrine concerning Church-State relations." [7] The fact, nevertheless, is true: Protestantism is still groping for an authentically evangelical doctrine of the state which is intelligible in the modern world. The beginning of wisdom on the question before us lies in the recognition of this fact.

This is not to say that there has never been an authentically evangelical doctrine of the state. We have already cited Calvin's view, for example. It is to say, though, that the doctrine of the state, even Calvin's, becomes theologically problematical at the point of its being intelligible *in the modern world.* As regards Calvin's position we simply must understand that the context within which he labored and our own are two entirely different situations. This fact necessitates at the very least a thoroughgoing reformulation of his view before its intelligibility for modern Christians can be assured. And what is true of Calvin's position is true of Christian thought at large. The fact is that the great prototypes for the solution of the church-state problem are all pre-modern, and accordingly remote from the standpoint of our present involvement.[8]

The American scene itself is a good demonstration of what is here at stake. The specifically American heritage of the separation of church and state has primarily secular origins. Theological motivation is clearly discernible, to be sure, in the receptivity of the American churches of the colonial period for this development, and equally clearly, it accounts to a large extent for the active and noble involvement of men such as Witherspoon in the whole process. But one could hardly maintain that theological reflection alone either would or could have generated what came to pass in the formative phases of the development of the American republic.

The severely problematical character of the mandate which the General Assembly of the United Presbyterian Church, U.S.A., handed to its Special Committee on Relations Between Church and State is traceable at least in part to the colossal void beneath the comfortable but false assumption on the part of many Presbyterians that the separation of church and state is a fundamentally Protestant and decisively Presbyterian idea. Any significant assault on such issues as the observance of religious holidays in public schools, or the question of tax exemption for church property is bound to generate controversy. This in itself suggests the lack of a basic theological consensus on a contemporary Reformed doctrine of the state.[9]

In the face of the emergence of the modern world out of the collapse of medieval Christendom the concept to be most ruthlessly challenged — now no longer tenable — is the very concept which has had such impressive use in the history of Christian thought, and which is irrevocably central in all contemporary Roman Catholic reflection on the problem of church and state. This, of course, is the concept of *natural law* (the *lex naturae*). John Bennett's sketch of the issue in his *Christians and the State* helpfully illuminates the impasse which has been reached, though one cannot be quite sure that he sees it as an impasse. "Catholic teaching," he writes, "emphasizes the natural law as the criterion of all positive law and as being itself the law of God, known to the reason and confirmed by revelation." [10] There are two points to be emphasized in this statement. The first is the equation which operates in Roman thought between the natural law and the law of God; the second is the assumption which controls Roman theological reflection at large, namely, the positive relationship between man's natural knowledge and the knowledge which man has as a result of revelation. Both of these are traceable to the finest flowering of medieval Catholicism's theology, the thought of Thomas Aquinas, and the latter explicitly controls the entirety of his massive doctrinal expression, the *Summa Theologica*. Furthermore, it is of crucial significance to know that Thomism was for all intents and purposes absolutized for modern Roman theological reflection by Pope Leo XIII in one of his earliest encyclicals, *Aeterni Patris,* dated August 4, 1879.[11]

On the Protestant side perplexity reigned in the past and vigorous challenge dominates the present. Bennett's summarizing paragraph here is worth quoting in full:

> Protestant thinking about the law and about its relation to the law of God, to the natural law or to standards of justice above the positive law is confused or non-existent. Protestants, unlike Catholics, have no common tradition about the natural law which might be relevant to the discussion. They are no more moral relativists in their ultimate outlook than Catholics, and they take for granted that there is a difference between just and unjust laws, that in some sense the law of the state is under the divine judgment. But it is difficult for Protestants to find a structure of thought into which all of these convictions can be fitted.[12]

Bennett's words are well chosen. The real query is this: Why have Protestants had difficulty finding "a structure of thought into which all these convictions can be fitted?" It is, to be sure, a highly debatable point as to just what role, if any, the concept of natural law, or something approximating it, played in the thought of the Reformers. But one thing is clear: in reasserting the normative significance of scripture the Reformers divorced themselves once and for all from any such easy blending of Biblical and philosophical elements as that forming the necessary precondition for the Roman utilization of the concept. This is reflected in Bennett's delineation of what he regards as the two basic reasons for the general Protestant suspicion of natural law theory.

> Protestants have been troubled by the conception of the natural law for two reasons which strengthen each other. The first is that they do not have the rationalistic confidence that the natural law is universally known without such knowledge being seriously distorted by human sin and finiteness . . . The second reason . . . is the tendency to rigidity in the way it is applied. It does not make room for the endless variation in human situations, for the dynamic nature of history.[13]

Bennett has correctly pinpointed the two major foci of the Protestant critique of natural law theory, but each of the points needs more forceful statement than he provides, either in the passage noted or in his book as a whole. As regards the first, this must be said: both Luther and Calvin were informed by a thoroughgoing Pauline conception of the grace of God. Neither one of them is intelligible apart from the controlling idea that man is justified by the grace of God alone. Man's knowledge of himself and of his world is, accordingly, radically reoriented by the revelatory act of God in Christ. There is more at stake, then, than Bennett suggests in his first explanation of Protestant disquiet with the concept of natural law. The issue is not that human sin and finiteness simply distort what can be and is universally known. The issue is rather that in God's disclosure of himself in Christ man learns something he neither did nor could know on the far side of that revelation. If this is true, any appeal to the wisdom of man in general for clarity regarding the specifically *Christian* understanding of the political order — even if it be to the noblest expressions of this wisdom — must be ruthlessly challenged.

The second point which Bennett notes is also far more compelling than his formulation implies. No one who is informed by the fact of the dynamic character of God's act in Christ can rest easily with the attempt to superimpose yesterday's insights on today's problems. And yet this is precisely what happens when one attempts to operate on the church-state problem with a natural law theory. Bennett's illustrations of the tendency toward inflexibility which accompanies natural law theory are worthy of citation, demonstrating as they do the fact that the problem is not confined to Roman Catholicism:

> In the context of Roman Catholic thought this rigidity is seen in its most extreme form in Catholic teaching about birth control and about medical ethics. But there is also a tendency to absolutize the type of medieval society in which the Church was most at home. In quite another context ideas of natural law became frozen in the western legal tradition in terms of a one-sided individualism. This was a very great handicap to the American courts as they dealt with the problems of industrial society.[14]

The real issue involved in this inflexibility is the fact that it does violence to history. The context in which it was valid has disappeared. And it is just exactly the disappearance of that "type of medieval society in which the Church was most at home" with which we must come to terms.

The most powerful expression of the profound shift in temperament involved in the movement from medieval to modern society is to be found in the writings of Ernst Troeltsch (1865–1923), whose monumental work, *The Social Teaching of the Christian Churches,* published in 1912, was the first, and is so far the only, massive attempt to chart the history of Christian social thought. A partial picture of his insight, and this will suffice for our purposes, is contained in his relatively brief essay on "the significance of Protestantism for the rise of the modern world." [15] The point which concerns us may be paraphrased as follows. As over against classical Protestantism, modern Protestantism, from the end of the seventeenth century on, had to come to terms with existence in the midst of a new context. This was the context of the non-sectarian, religiously indifferent state. In this context Protestantism transferred in principle the whole activity of religious organization and the formation of religious communities to the realm of voluntarism and personal conviction. It did so under the influence of the basic acknowledgment of both the possibility and the fact of different religious convictions and communities existing side by side. It acknowledged at the same time the fact of a completely emancipated secular life existing alongside of itself — a manner of existence which it did not attempt to dominate, either directly or indirectly, through the intervention of the state.

Now certainly it must be obvious that Troeltsch's argument has the limitations of all sweeping generalizations. Even so, when one is pondering the broad sweep of the transition from the medieval to the modern world his case is a compelling and virtually invulnerable one. And in its light, Bennett's second point receives added clarity and force. One of the basic reasons why Protestants must resist the rigidity and inflexibility of natural law theory is that, by its very yearning for that "medieval society in which the Church was most at home," it denies the providential significance of the powerful historical forces which swept Protestantism at large toward the emergence of an utterly new situation. For better or for worse, the Protestant stance as over against both the arrival of the nonsectarian and religiously indifferent state and the rise of a completely emancipated secular life came to be one of co-existence.

For the two reasons which Bennett suggests, then, Protestants stand opposed to the utilization of the concept of natural law in the development of a modern theological understanding of the state. Both the purely theological questioning of the validity of man's natural knowledge apart from the knowledge of God in Christ, and the theologically informed positive evaluation of the movement from the medieval to the modern world form the basis of this rejection.

But the fact of the twofold co-existence, which, drawing on Troeltsch, we have just noted, itself suggests the form which our problem now must take. There is an observable double response to this co-existence. On the one hand, the political facts of life are here to stay. The modern state has a particularly robust origin in the very cross-currents of thought which challenged and ultimately conquered the last remnants of medieval Christendom in the time of the Enlightenment. There are few modern Christians who would willingly return to medieval civilization even if such a return were a live option, which it is not. This is particularly true of American Protestants, whose churches have flourished in the heritage of political liberty.

On the other hand, however, modern Christians have never been overly comfortable in the presence of the secularism which is an integral part of the modern world. What does it mean to live as a Christian in a world where Christianity and a completely emancipated secular life exist side by side? Protestant theology shifted into a new key when, beginning with Schleiermacher as the nineteenth century got under way, it began to struggle in the direction of articulating itself in terms of this question. This conversation is still going on, and will probably last as long as the modern period itself.

III BONHOEFFER: THEOLOGY AND THE MODERN WORLD

Is it possible to develop a theologically ordered understanding of the state which both challenges the dominant secularism of our time and yet takes fully into account the point to which God in his providence has brought us? Or, to put it another way, is it possible to stand with Calvin in asserting that the state must be understood within the framework of the activity of God without espousing a peculiarly Protestant return to the medieval scene? When the question is faced in this fashion there is one voice which clamors for attention out of the welter of discussion on the broad theological issues at hand.[16] This is the voice of the unforgettable German martyr, Dietrich Bonhoeffer.

In one of his early works, *Creation and Fall,*[17] embodying a theological interpretation of the first three chapters of Genesis, Bonhoeffer argued for a radically Christological interpretation of the doctrine of creation. That is, he insisted on the view that creation must be understood strictly on the basis of what God has done in Christ. In so doing, Bonhoeffer was following the lead of the celebrated Swiss theologian Karl Barth, but the implications he drew from this contention were peculiarly his own. For Bonhoeffer the most impressive thing about the creation is the fact that the Creator has not destroyed it! He was struck, that is to say, by the fact that the result of man's fall was not the Creator's destruction of his creation, but his preservation of it. As Bonhoeffer saw it, this meant that the value of the creation itself can never be understood apart from the knowledge of the purpose of its preservation. In short, the creation and everything in it can be correctly appraised only in the light of Christ. This led Bonhoeffer to insist that the structures or forms of human existence in the created world must be understood as *orders of preservation,* rather than as *orders of creation.*

God preserves the world by affirming the sinful world and directing it into its limits by means of ordinances. But none of these ordinances any longer have any eternal character because they are only there to preserve life. . . . For us (the preservation of life) is directed only towards — Christ. All the orders of the fallen world are God's orders of preservation on the way to Christ. They are not orders of creation but of preservation. They have no value in themselves. They are accomplished and have purpose only through Christ.[18]

By the time of the writing of his *Ethics,*[19] Bonhoeffer had arrived at the point where he was willing to specify what he understood the orders of preservation to be, though he preferred now to designate them "mandates." The world is relative to Christ. The mandates give concreteness to the relationship between Christ and the world.

The world, like all created things, is created through Christ and with Christ as its end, and consists in Christ alone (John 1:10; Col. 1:16). To speak of the world without speaking of Christ is empty and abstract. The world is relative to Christ, no matter whether it knows it or not. This relativeness of the world to Christ assumes concrete form in certain mandates of God in the world. The Scriptures name four such mandates: labour, marriage, government and the Church.[20]

What is most instructive is to note why Bonhoeffer had dropped the term "order" in favor of the term "mandate." The latter is preferable, he argued, because here the accent is placed on the purpose which alone gives meaning and significance to the concrete forms of the relation between Christ and the world.

We speak of divine mandates rather than of divine orders because the word mandate refers more clearly to a divinely imposed task rather than to a determination of being. . . . It is not because labour, marriage, government and the church *are* that they are commanded by God, but it is because they are commanded by God that they are. And they are divine mandates only in so far as their being is consciously or unconsciously subordinated to the divinely imposed task.[21]

Now this is a step of signal importance. The trouble with understanding the state as an "order of creation" is that almost invariably the major emphasis will fall on the doctrine of man. In the case of Emil Brunner this operates in such a way that the relationship between Christian faith and the political world is one which leaves the *status quo* intact.[22] Bonhoeffer's point is reminiscent of Calvin's; the problem of the doctrine of the state is to be solved not in the framework of the doctrine of man, but in that of the doctrine of God. It is a function of His activity.

The decisive implication of all this is that the state must be understood *eschatologically*. Eschatology is, simply, that part of theology at large in which the future dimension of God's revelation in Christ is emphasized, involving the fact that *Christian hope* is a necessary part of any authentically theological reflection, and the conviction that while God alone can ultimately fulfill His own purpose, He will do so in the light of what He has already done in Jesus Christ. To say that the state must be understood eschatologically is to insist along with Bonhoeffer that the forms and structures of human existence in the world "have purpose only through Christ."

The utmost care must be taken, however, in clarifying what such a view entails. The trouble with eschatological thinking is that all too often its use tends to divorce Christians from their world. Most emphatically this was not the case with Bonhoeffer, either in his life or in his theology, which is the outstanding reason for citing him here.

Bonhoeffer's eschatology is an eschatology-in-the-present-tense. To put the matter this way is to anticipate reversing the phrase for the sake of emphasizing his point. The only "present" which he can and will discuss is a present which is itself eschatologically conditioned. Bonhoeffer's way of asserting this occurs in his discussion of the relationship between the *penultimate* and the *ultimate*.[23]

Bonhoeffer observed that the relating of the penultimate to the ultimate in the Christian life is capable of "two extreme solutions." On the one hand there is "the radical solution," which proves invariably to be utopian and therefore irrelevant; on the other hand there is "the compromise solution," which so easily comes to terms with the world as it is that things are left exactly as they were. In neither case are the penultimate and the ultimate effectively joined, and accordingly each of the extreme solutions must be categorically rejected. They must be rejected because they separate what in Christ is united. The fact of Jesus Christ precludes the possibility of treating the penultimate and the ultimate as if they were mutually exclusive. Life in the light of Jesus Christ is life beyond either of the two extreme solutions. This is why it must be contended that the present is eschatologically conditioned.

> In Christ the reality of God meets the reality of the world and allows us to share in this real encounter. It is an encounter beyond all radicalism and beyond all compromise. Christian life is participation in the encounter of Christ with the world.[24]

There is one other factor in Bonhoeffer's thought which has particular relevance for us. His eschatological position, as we have just noted, demands the recognition of the full involvement in the given world as an absolutely necessary part of the life of a Christian. Only so can a Christian participate "in the encounter of Christ with the world." That it is specifically *the modern world* which must be the arena of the activity of modern Christians has been stated most trenchantly by Bonhoeffer. The unforgettable passage occurs in a letter which he wrote from a German concentration camp on June 8, 1944:

> The movement beginning about the thirteenth century . . . towards the autonomy of man . . . has in our time reached a certain completion. Man has learned to cope with all questions of importance without recourse to God as a working hypothesis.

Bonhoeffer regarded the all-pervasive character of this fact to be self-evident, noting wryly that within the last century it has penetrated even into religious questions. He then summed up the situation as a whole:

> . . . it is become evident that everything gets along without "God," and just as well as before. As in the scientific field, so in human affairs generally, what we call "God" is being more and more edged out of life, losing more and more ground.

What was particularly irritating to Bonhoeffer, that phase of the problem to which he was most sensitive, was the manner in which Christians have characteristically reacted to this situation. For Christians have almost uniformly treated this development as a "great defection," with the inevitable result that "the trend itself considers itself to be anti-Christian."

> Christian apologetic has taken the most varying forms of opposition to this self-assurance. Efforts are made to prove to a world thus come of age that it cannot live without the tutelage of "God." Even though there has been surrender on all secular problems, there still remains the so-called ultimate questions — death, guilt — on which only "God" can furnish an answer, and which are the reason why God and Church and the pastor are needed.

Bonhoeffer's reference to the present time as being one in which the world has come of age is one of the most often pondered flashes of insight to be found in the remarkable theology of this figure. Its implication as he saw it is equally incisive. Christian apologetics in the form which it has usually taken in the modern world is utterly reprehensible because it involves an assault which denies both the world and Jesus Christ:

> The attack by Christian apologetic upon the adulthood of the world I consider to be in the first place pointless, in the second ignoble, and in the third un-Christian. Pointless, because it looks to me like an attempt to put a grown-up man back into adolescence, i.e. to make him dependent on things

on which he is not in fact dependent any more, thrusting him back into the midst of problems which are in fact not problems for him any more. Ignoble, because this amounts to an effort to exploit the weakness of man for purposes alien to him and not freely subscribed to by him. Un-Christian, because for Christ himself is being substituted one particular stage in the religiousness of man, i.e. a human law.[25]

The aggressive overtone of Bonhoeffer's thought is unmistakable. Christians, simply because they know that in Jesus Christ their Lord God has reconciled the world to Himself, must assert that they know better than the world knows what it means for the world to be the world! The over-against-ness between the church and the world remains, but it must be vigorously positive, and can never imply the suggestion of a retrogression to the past. Thus,

. . . when Christianity is employed as a polemical weapon against the secular, this must be done in the name of a better secularity and above all it must not lead back to a static predominance of the spiritual sphere as an end in itself.[26]

How much more aggressive can one be! But note well that new problem which this generates: Just what is this "better secularity"? Or, to put it another way, "how can we reclaim for Christ a world which has come of age?"[27]

This brings us full circle. If Bonhoeffer was right, then we have before us not only the theologically ordered possibility, but also the theologically demanded necessity, that we address the problems arising out of the relations between church and state in the United States in such a way that the dominant secularism of our time is effectively confronted in the context of the modern world. The fact that the American political heritage includes the notion of the separation of church and state does indeed have a theological basis — in nothing less than the doctrine of the providence of God. The question before us is simply the question "How?" How shall we, in the midst of our given situation bear witness to our conviction that Jesus Christ is Lord over all? How shall we assert the Lordship of Jesus Christ with specific reference to the political problems of our time in such a way that our claim regarding His Lordship is clear, whether we are enthusiastically received or not? To return to Lehmann's way of putting it, what specifically shall we do regarding the question of church and state in the United States, in order "to live constructively in the gap between the will of God, theologically understood, and the concrete human situation, pragmatically understood"? In short, what are some of the steps *now* to be taken by way of discovering what it *now* means to reclaim for Christ a world which has come of age?

IV THE TASK OF DISESTABLISHMENT

Given the outlines of the problem at hand as we have now explored them, it should be self-evident that matters relating to the church-state question in this country cannot be dealt with effectively at the abstract level. Only by direct involvement in the political life of this nation can the church succeed in working its way toward the fulfillment of the tasks which its faith generates. At present this must take the form of a process of disestablishment for the sake of authentic encounter. That is, the church must succeed in disentangling itself from that comfortably innocuous religiosity which the nation as a whole seems to assume is its only basic concern. What in fact must occur is the development of a healthy tension between the church and the nation at large, which is all too lacking in contemporary life.

In this connection there is an exceedingly useful proposal which was first suggested by J. H. Oldham in a work which he wrote with W. A. Visser't Hooft in preparation for the Oxford Conference in 1937. This is the idea of the *middle axioms*. Oldham's proposal was as follows:

> . . . broad assertions as that Christians are bound to obey the law of love or to strive for social justice do not go far towards helping the individual to know what he ought to do in particular cases. . . . Hence between purely general statements of the ethical demands of the Gospel and the decisions that have to be made in concrete situations there is need for what may be described as middle axioms. It is these that give relevance and point to the Christian ethic. They are an attempt to define the directions in which, in a particular state of society, Christian faith must express itself. They are not binding for all time, but are provisional definitions of the type of behavior required of Christians at a given period and in given circumstances.[28]

Writing in 1946, John Bennett in his *Christian Ethics and Social Policy* picked up Oldham's concept and demonstrated its usefulness, commenting by way of introducing the concept as follows:

> The term may not be a good one but it points to something that is distinctive and I shall use it for convenience. A "middle axiom" is more concrete than a universal ethical principle and less specific than a program that includes legislation and political strategy. . . . To agree on these "middle axioms" will still leave many pressing problems unsolved, but clarity about them will give both the Church and the individual Christian a sense of direction.[29]

Now it is immediately self-evident that the concept is indeed nothing more than a helpful device, and a neutral one at that. Christians are not the only ones trying to define the next steps to be taken in the midst of the current political scene. Even so, there are marked advantages which are attendant upon its proper use. The concept cannot be used at all unless there is clear recognition that more than theological insight alone is needed before the concrete problems of the politico-social realm can be effectively handled, a view which Oldham elaborated in originally proposing the concept, and which Bennett reiterated in furthering it.

Theological insight must be blended with social-analytical knowledge if the church is to say and do anything meaningful on the issues at hand. Granted this, the role of the theological insight involved must be sharply clear itself if the concept is to live up to its promise. In the light of our discussion as a whole the matter may be put concisely:

(1) It is to Jesus Christ that the church must bear its witness — not to some prior social accomplishment, or some private political dream.

(2) The urgency to act on the matters at hand is rooted in the fact of Jesus Christ, and not in the facts which are to be discovered in the social-scientific examination of the political realm.[30]

For a comprehensive demonstration of the utilization of the concept of *middle axioms* explicitly under the control of the twofold theological formulation just noted, one may refer to the entire text of *Relations Between Church and State,* the report of the special committee on these problems submitted to the 174th General Assembly of the United Presbyterian Church, U.S.A. As an illustration of the concern which dominates this present discussion, a single example from this report will suffice. One of the issues to which the report speaks has to do with "The celebration of religious holidays, Bible reading and prayer in public schools." The committee has recommended to the church at large that its stance on these issues should be informed in general by the following conviction.

> Public schools are creations of the whole society operating through civil authority and justify their existence solely in terms of their usefulness to the society. Their role is to nurture the cultural, social, and material advancement of all citizens by a special system of instruction through intellectual and social disciplines and to stimulate a free search for truth within this discipline.
>
> In the fulfillment of this role, public schools should not ignore the personal beliefs in God which are a part of the life of its pupils, but should recognize and respect such beliefs. Public schools should neither be hostile to religious beliefs nor act in any manner which tends to favor one religion or church over another.

In the light of these broad and general assertions five specific recommendations are proposed. The second of these is as follows:

2. Religious observances [should] never be held in a public school or introduced into the program of the public school. Bible reading (except in connection with courses in literature, history, or related subjects) and public prayers tend toward indoctrination or meaningless ritual and should be omitted for both reasons. Ministers, priests, and rabbis should be free to speak in public schools, provided their speaking does not constitute religious indoctrination or their presence form a part of a religious observance.[31]

Diligent and comprehensive implementation of this tactical recommendation at the local level would serve the cause of that disestablishment for the sake of encounter for which we have called. It has become increasingly clear in the midst of our time that coercive methods are antithetical to the proclamation of the gospel. The freedom of God's redemptive self-disclosure in Jesus Christ evokes nothing less than a free response on the part of man. In this nation a realistic and aggressive dealing with the problem of church and state is by no means optional for the church. It is the *sine qua non* of its fulfillment of its sole and definitive task, the bearing of a living and relevant witness to its Lord.

NOTES

1. John Calvin, *Institutes of the Christian Religion,* IV, 20, 4. (McNeill-Battles edition: The Library of Christian Classics, Calvin: *Institutes of the Christian Religion,* Vol. XX–XXI, edited by John T. McNeill, translated by Ford Lewis Battles (Philadelphia: The Westminster Press, 1960).
2. Cf. Ernst Troeltsch, *The Social Teaching of the Christian Churches* (New York: Macmillan, 1931), and J. H. Nichols, *Democracy and the Churches* (Philadelphia: The Westminster Press, 1951).
3. Cf. Paul L. Lehmann, "The Foundation and Pattern of Christian Behavior" in *Christian Faith and Social Action,* edited by John A. Hutchison (New York: Scribner's, 1953), pp. 93–116.
4. Ibid. p. 105.
5. Ibid. p. 101.
6. Ibid. p. 112.
7. John C. Bennett, *Christians and the State* (New York: Scribner's, 1958), p. 205.
8. This receives exhaustive demonstration in Ernst Troeltsch's *The Social Teaching of the Christian Churches.*
9. The report of this committee was submitted to the United Presbyterian General Assembly in the spring of 1962, and is now before this church at large for its reflection and response. The report is entitled *Relations Between Church and State: A Report to the 174th General Assembly of the United Presbyterian Church in the United States of America, May 1962:* it is published by the Office of the General Assembly, Witherspoon Building, Philadelphia 7, Pennsylvania.
10. Bennett, op. cit. p. 97.
11. Cf. *The Church Speaks to the Modern World:* The Social Teachings of Leo XIII, edited with an introduction by Etienne Gilson, Image Books (New York: Doubleday, 1954), pp. 29–54.

12. Bennett, op. cit. p. 98.
13. Ibid. p. 98.
14. Ibid. p. 98.
15. Cf. Ernst Troeltsch, *Die Bedeutung des Protestantismus fur die Entstehung der modernen Welt* (1911), p. 25; *Protestantism and Progress,* translated by W. Montgomery (Boston: Beacon Press, p. 958), pp. 44–5. The words enclosed in quotation marks are a literal translation of Troeltsch's own title, *Die Bedeutung des Protestantismus fur die Entstehung der modernen Welt;* the title of the English translation, *Protestantism and Progress,* is most misleading.
16. It is a welter of discussion! The great giants of contemporary Protestant theology, all of whom are now in their years of retirement — Reinhold Niebuhr, Karl Barth, Emil Brunner, and Paul Tillich — present an astonishing panorama of alternative views. For a remarkably lucid discussion of this panorama see Charles C. West's *Communism and the Theologians* (Philadelphia: The Westminster Press, 1958).
17. Dietrich Bonhoeffer, *Creation and Fall:* A Theological Interpretation of Genesis 1–3 (New York: Macmillan, 1959). These were lectures delivered by Bonhoeffer at the University of Berlin during the winter semester of 1932–3; they were first published in 1937, and the English translation appeared in 1959.
18. Bonhoeffer, *Creation and Fall,* p. 91.
19. Bonhoeffer's *Ethics* exists only in fragmentary and unfinished form. It was postumously published, being edited by Bonhoeffer's close friend, Eberhard Bethge (*Ethik,* Chr. Kaiser Verlag Munchen, 1949); the English translation, by Neville Horton Smith, was publsihed by The Macmillan Company, New York, in 1955.
20. Bonhoeffer, *Ethics,* p. 73.
21. Ibid. pp. 73–4.
22. For Brunner's position see his *The Divine Imperative;* the point we are making here receives careful demonstration in Charles West's volume, cited above.
23. Bonhoeffer, *Ethik,* pp. 79ff. The translator's decision to render Bonhoeffer's juxtaposition by the terms "penultimate" and "ultimate" is not ideal, although it is both defensible and unavoidable, given the fact that the difference between the terms is simply the prefix. However, the thrust of Bonhoeffer's distinction is more clear if one knows that his own terms were *Vorletze* and *Letze* — the "things before the last," and "the last things."
24. Bonhoeffer, *Ethics,* p. 91.
25. For all of the citations in this paragraph, cf. Bonhoeffer, *Prisoner for God* (Letters and Papers from Prison), edited by Eberhard Bethge, translated by Reginald H. Fuller (New York: Macmillan, 1953), pp. 145–7.
26. Bonhoeffer, *Ethics,* p. 65.
27. Bonhoeffer, *Prisoner for God,* p. 157.
28. W. A. Visser't Hooft and J. H. Oldham, *The Church and its Function in Society* (London: George Allen and Unwin Ltd., 1937), pp. 209–10.
29. John C. Bennett, *Christian Ethics and Social Policy* (New York: Scribner's, 1946), p. 77.
30. The phraseology of this paragraph is drawn from a background study paper which the author prepared in connection with the work of the Special Committee on Relations Between Church and State, mentioned in this paper. The point at hand is elaborated in more detail on pp. 39–41 of the report of this committee.
31. *Relations Between Church and State,* pp. 10–11.

WILL HERBERG

Religious Group Conflict in America

Religious group conflict in contemporary America reflects the changing shape of American pluralism; and this pluralism is today essentially religious.

I THE SHAPE OF AMERICAN PLURALISM

In some sense, all societies, even the most monolithic, have been pluralistic, for there has never been a society without a wide diversity of interest, opinions, and conditions of life.

Yet, when we speak of a pluralistic society, we mean something more. We mean a society in which diversities not only exist as a matter of fact, but are recognized, accepted, perhaps even institutionalized into the structure and functioning of the social order. In this sense, American society is thoroughly pluralistic, but pluralistic in a very special way, with its own characteristic freedoms and restrictions. The shape of American pluralism helps define the underlying pattern of American life, within which emerge the so-called "intergroup" problems that confront us today in such a variety of shapes and forms.

The pluralism of American society is the product of its history, and therefore reflects its inmost being, for the inmost being of men and their societies is essentially historical. From the very beginning, America has been a land of diversity striving for unity. And from the very beginning, too, the diversities have been racial, ethnic, cultural, and religious, whereas the unity striven for has been that of a new "way of life" reflecting the "new order of the ages" established in the New World (*novus ordo seclorum,* the motto on the reverse of the Great Seal of the United States).

This was the vision that fired the imagination of Hector de Crèvecoeur, the author of the celebrated "letters from an American Farmer," who was so eager to interpret the new American reality to the New and Old World alike. "Here," Crèvecoeur proclaimed proudly in 1782, "individuals of all nations are melted into a new race of men, whose labors and posterity will one day cause great changes in the world." Thus early was the "melting pot" philosophy explicitly formulated, and thus early did the problem of unity amidst diversity, and diversity amidst unity, emerge as the perennial problem of American life.

The conception implied in the image of the "melting pot" (or the "transmuting pot," as George H. Stewart prefers to call it) [1] has always been subject to a misunderstanding that is itself not without significance. When, at least until recently, Americans spoke of the "melting pot" (the term as such did not come into use until the first decade of this century), they generally had in mind a process by which foreign "peculiarities" of language and culture which immigrants brought with them from the old country would be sloughed off in the course of Americanization, and a new homogeneous, undifferentiated type of American would come into being.

Against this, the apostles of "cultural pluralism" protested; they stressed the richness of the immigrant cultures, deplored their threatening dissolution, and advocated a multicultural, even a multinational society, along familiar European lines. Both groups — the theorists of the "melting pot" and the "cultural pluralists" — gravely misunderstood the emerging patterns of American pluralism.

American pluralism, through all its changes and mutations, has remained characteristically American, quite unlike the pluralistic patterns prevailing in other parts of the world. The sources of diversity have been different, and the expressions of it even more so. By and large, we may say that, since the latter part of the nineteenth century, the sources of American pluralism have been mainly race, ethnicity, and religion, with sectionalism or regionalism playing a diminishing, though in some cases still not insignificant, role. It is in terms of these that Americans have tended, and still tend, to define their identities amidst the totality of American life.

The process of enculturation perpetuates the pattern. When asked the simple question, "What are you?", Gordon W. Allport has noted, referring to certain recent researches, only 10 per cent of four-year-olds answer in terms of racial, ethnic, or religious membership, whereas 75 per cent of nine-year-olds do so. "Race" in America today means color, white versus non-white; and racial stigmatization has introduced an element of caste-like stratification into American life.

For white Americans, ethnicity and religion have been, and still remain, the major source of pluralistic diversity, although the relation between them has changed drastically in the course of the past generation. It is this change that provides a clue to an understanding of the shape of present-day American pluralism, and of the nature and sources of religious group conflict in present-day America.

As long as large-scale immigration continued, and America was predominantly a land of immigrants, in the days when "the immigrants *were* American history," as Oscar Handlin puts it, the dominant form of self-identification, and therefore the dominant form of pluralistic diversity, was immigrant ethnicity. Religion was felt to be part of the ethnic heritage, recent or remote. The enthusiasts of the "melting pot" were eager to eliminate this diversity as quickly as possible; the "cultural pluralists" were determined to perpetuate it; but both alike moved within a framework of a pluralism based substantially on ethnicity, ethnic culture, and ethnic religion.

Within the past generation, the picture has changed radically. The stoppage of mass immigration during World War I, followed by the anti-immigration legislation of the 1920's, undermined the foundations of the immigrant ethnic group with amazing rapidity. What it did was to facilitate the emergence of the third and post-third American generations, with their characteristic responses and attitudes, as a decisive influence in American life, no longer threatened with submergence by the next wave of immigration. This far-reaching structural change has, of course, been reflected in the shape and form of American pluralism.

Specifically, within the threefold American scheme of race, ethnicity, and religion, a shift has taken place from ethnicity to religion as the dominant form of self-identification, and therefore also in the dominant form of pluralistic diversity.[2] Ethnic identifications and traditions have not altogether disappeared. On the contrary, with the third generation, as Marcus Lee Hanson has cogently shown, they enjoy a lively popularity as symbols of "heritage."

But the relation of ethnicity and religion has been reversed: religion is no longer taken as an aspect of ethnicity; it is ethnicity, or rather what remains of it, that is taken up, redefined, and expressed through religious identifications and institutions. Religion — or, at least, the tripartite differentiation of Protestant, Catholic, Jew — has (aside from race) become the characteristic form of pluralistic diversity in American life. American pluralism is today (again aside from race) characteristically *religious* pluralism, and all problems of American unity and diversity, cooperation and conflict, have to be interpreted in the light of this great fact.

This shift from ethnicity to religion is well documented in the recent and most impressive of community surveys particularly concerned with religion — the Detroit metropolitan area survey of 1958, reported and interpreted by Gerhard Lenski in *The Religious Factor:*

> Among the possible trends cited above [Lenski states in his concluding chapter], one deserves special comment both because of its far-reaching implications and because many of these implications have received so little attention from the general public. This is the possible trend toward increased socio-religious communalism. As we noted, . . . communalism along socio-religious group lines seems to have been gaining in strength in recent years, and promises to continue to gain in the foreseeable future.
>
> This development is one which has been greatly hastened by the rapid decline of the older ethnic subcommunities in recent years. . . . Until about a generation ago, the American population was sharply divided into a rather large number of relatively small ethnic subcommunities. . . . These groups, however, were unable to preserve their organizational integrity in the face of the powerful and pervasive pressures to Americanize the immigrant, and intermarriage across ethnic group lines has now become quite common. . . . *The successor of the ethnic subcommunity is the socio-religious subcommunity. . . . There seems to be little doubt that socio-religious groups are rapidly replacing ethnic groups as the basic units in the system of status groups in American society.*[3]

Such is the emerging shape of American pluralism, within which intergroup conflicts today arise and take their course: it is a religious pluralism, a pluralism defined in terms of religious identification and belonging.

But American pluralism, it has often been noted, is not simply plurality; it is also unity: it is, in fact, best designated by the term *pluriunity* — a unity in plurality as well as a plurality in unity. *E pluribus unum:* this phrase, which was originally employed to celebrate the unification of thirteen colonies into the new nation, serves very well as the formula for American pluralism as that has developed through the decades since the Civil War.

What is this unity that supplies the centripetal force in American life, or (to change the image) the common framework within which the pluralistic allegiances find both their freedom and their limits? This unity is the unity of the *American way of life.*

It is not easy to put into words just what the American way of life is, or how it functions to provide the over-all unity for the pluralistic diversity of American society. Perhaps the most important thing to say about it is that, for the American, the American way of life is that by virtue of which he is an American. Americans, with their incredible diversity of race, culture, and national origin, find their unity, their common "Americanness," in their adherence to, and participation in, the American way of life. This provides them their common allegiance and their common faith: it provides them, to use the words of the sociologist Robin M. Williams, Jr., with "the common set of ideas, rituals and symbols" by which an "overarching sense of unity" is achieved amidst diversity and conflict. If the pluralism of contemporary American society is primarily a religious pluralism, the unity within which this pluralism is expressed and contained is a unity of the American way of life. Religious group conflict in contemporary America is conflict within this overarching unity.

II PROTESTANT-CATHOLIC TENSIONS: SOME FACTS AND FACTORS

Because American pluralism today is basically a religious pluralism, the tensions that affect the religious communities would seem to be of special importance for the future of America and the unity of its people. It is these tensions I should like to discuss — particularly, the Protestant-Catholic tensions, which concern us most immediately; but also Jewish-gentile tensions, which, though at the moment not very prominent, we cannot altogether ignore.

When I say I am going to discuss Protestant-Catholic tensions, I do not mean that I am going to take up all the various matters that are alleged to be at issue between Protestants and Catholics in this country. Not that these matters are not real and important; they are. But there are two considerations we should bear in mind.

1. These questions at issue, however real and important, do not seem to me to be so much the cause of the tensions as their expression. They are not merely questions under discussion; they are what we call issues. They become issues precisely because they arise in an already established context of tension, and become vehicles of this tension and conflict.

2. These controverted questions, even though they become issues between Protestants and Catholics, and Jews too for that matter, are rarely if ever questions on which one group is aligned all on one side and the other group all on the other. On the contrary, on every one of these questions, there are differences and divisions in each of the three religious communities, with sizable minorities in each group crossing

the lines. Only in a very limited sense can it be said that the three religious groups have their special social and cultural outlooks, conflict over which is engendering the group tensions we are concerned with.

The real sources of religious group tensions in the America of today seem to me to be emphatically pre-ideological, although no doubt they are quickly rationalized and ideologized. The tensions we are concerned with, particularly the Protestant-Catholic tensions, seem to me to emerge from a number of closely related social changes under way in this country today, with far-reaching repercussions upon the religious situation.

The first of these basic social changes directly affecting religious group relations is the transformation of America, within this present generation, from a "Protestant nation" to a "three-religion country."

Writing just about thirty-five years ago, André Siegfried, the French observer, described Protestantism as America's "national religion," and he was largely right despite the ban on religious establishment in the Constitution. Normally, to be born an American in those days meant to be a Protestant; this was the religious identification that quite naturally and appropriately went along with being an American. Non-Protestants felt the force of this conviction almost as strongly as did the Protestants; Catholics and Jews, despite their greatly increasing numbers, experienced their non-Protestant religion as a problem, even as an obstacle to their becoming full-fledged Americans: it was a mark of their foreignness. Protestantism — not any of the multiplying denominations, but Protestantism as a whole — was America's "established church"; the others, the non-Protestants, were to some degree, and in varying measure, outsiders. America was a Protestant nation.

This is no longer the case. Today, unlike fifty years ago, the natural and appropriate religious belonging that goes along with being an American is not simply being a Protestant; it is (as the evidence amply shows) being a Protestant, being a Catholic, or being a Jew. These have become the three ways of being an American. Today, Catholics and Jews, as well as Protestants, feel themselves to be Americans not apart from, or in spite of, their religion, but because of it.

If America today possesses an "established church" in Siegfried's sense, it is the emerging tripartite system of Protestant-Catholic-Jew. Whereas Justice Sutherland, in the 1920's, could still speak of America as a "Christian nation," Justice Douglas, in the 1950's, spoke of Americans as a "religious people, whose institutions presuppose a Supreme Being." From a Protestant nation, we have become a three-religion country. This transformation is the consequence not of any marked increase of Catholics or Jews in the population, but an accompaniment of the shift we have been discussing in the pattern of self-identification, and therefore also in the source of pluralistic diversity, from ethnicity to religion.

The second factor I should like to mention is closely related to the first. It is the transformation of American Catholics, again largely within our generation, from a peripheral, foreign, lower-class group into a nuclear, middle-class American community.

The remarkable upward mobility of the Catholic groups in the course of the past generation has been well presented and documented in Father Andrew M. Greeley's report to the International Conference of Religious Sociology, held in Brussels.

Now what have been, what are, the consequences of these two interconnected processes for the religious situation, especially in terms of Protestant-Catholic tensions? I think it must be said that these two major social developments are having a discernible double effect, making at one and the same time for an exacerbation and a mitigation of these tensions, though at different range. In brief, it seems to me that their effect has been, in the short run, to aggravate the tensions, but, in the long run, to reduce and alleviate them.

Let us consider the latter effect first. Through the concomitant operation of both of the tendencies I have mentioned, Catholicism has become a legitimate part of American religion, one of the "three great faiths," with an assured place in the American scheme of things; and Catholics have become—perhaps I should say, are becoming — middle-class Americans, a recognized part of the American people. To increasing numbers of Protestants, especially younger Protestants, Catholics have become, are becoming, "our kind of people," embraced in that potent formula of American comprehension: "After all, we're all Americans!" I shall have occasion to develop this point a little later; for the present, it is enough to bring it to the fore, and to emphasize how strongly it makes for the mitigation of Protestant-Catholic strains and tensions in the long run.

But the very same process that promises, in the long run, to mitigate these strains and tensions, would seem very much to exacerbate them in the short run. Why this double and contradictory effect?

Consider the position of the Protestant, particularly of the middle-aged or older Protestant, in present-day America. His whole outlook was shaped, his mind was formed, his feelings were articulated, in an America that was a Protestant nation; and he was America. Now he finds himself propelled into a post-Protestant America, into a three-religion country, where he is not the nation, but merely one of three.

Suddenly he finds himself faced with the threat of a loss of accustomed status; a privileged status long enjoyed and taken for granted is being subverted before his very eyes. He feels himself dispossessed; the Catholics — and Jews too — have moved in on him, and taken over what was once his. He feels himself threatened: Catholics are multiplying prodigiously, and are about to take over the country!

This nightmare of "Catholic domination" is not in the least warranted by the facts, but it has its own significant logic. Whereas Roman Catholic growth in the country as a whole has been relatively moderate, what one may call the Roman Catholic "presence" has grown prodigiously. There was a time when the mass of Catholics were of the lower classes, at the margin of society — laborers and servant girls, hewers of wood and drawers of water. The middle-class Protestant, resting securely in a middle-class Protestant nation, did not, generally, see them as a threat; indeed, in good times, he hardly noticed their existence, for they were not present in the nuclear institutions of the community.

Within the past generation, however, the extraordinary upward mobility of American Catholics have converted large numbers of these Catholics into solid middle-class Americans, and have brought them in mounting proportions into these very nuclear institutions. No wonder the old-line Protestant, with his older attitudes, feels himself surrounded and threatened: wherever he turns, in those very places he had been accustomed to regard as his own — the nuclear middle-class institutions and organizations of the community — he finds more and more of these Catholics, who, for him, remember, are still outsiders and interlopers. No wonder he finds himself terrified at the specter of "Catholic domination"!

He also resents what he thinks of as Catholic "divisiveness." As a minority group, Catholics were early constrained to build up separate Catholic community organizations to protect themselves and to advance their interests in the fierce group competition always so characteristic of American life. And so we have the vast proliferation of Catholic "separatist" organizations from the early Irish-Catholic Protective Society to the associations of Catholic lawyers and firemen and policemen and veterans and educators, and so on and on, today.

In this respect, Catholics have behaved very much as did the other minority groups in this country —— Jews, Negroes (after emancipation), and first- and second-generation immigrants, who all felt the need for separate community organizations and quickly developed them. But, of course, in the older days, Protestants felt no such need, and took no such action. Until well into this generation, the general community institutions and organizations were, in fact, Protestant institutions and organizations, because this was a Protestant nation and a Protestant culture.

In the course of the past generation, the situation has been changing drastically: this is no longer a Protestant nation, and Protestants are today only one of three. Protestants can no longer count on the general community institutions and organizations as theirs; so that, in effect, they find themselves organizationally and institutionally disarmed in the face of the tightening Jewish and Catholic communities. The natural, one might almost say the normal, response of most Protestants has been to denounce the whole system of separate community institutions as "divisive" and "un-American," despite the fact that it fits in very well with the emerging pattern of American religious communalism, and actually operates as an integrative factor in American life. A growing number of Protestants, however, are coming to recognize the hard facts of the situation, and are proceeding, though haltingly, to build up their own Protestant communal institutions in the new three-religion America. In this, they are being prompted by the Negro Protestants, who, though Protestants, have never had America as their own, and have therefore been forced from the very beginning to elaborate a system of separate Negro institutions and organizations.

It is not necessary to extend this argument. It seems to me very clear that the rapid shift in social structure involved in the emergence of a three-religion America has imposed heavy strains on the Protestant mind and on Protestant attitudes, and has resulted — among large numbers of the older Protestants — in a feverish anti-Catholicism. This has been clearly recognized by many Protestant leaders themselves.

Some years ago, the editor of the *Christian Century* referred to this problem in a powerful editorial entitled, "Protestant, Be Yourself" in which he characterized this frenetic attitude as "Protestant paranoia." [4] Lest this characterization seem to be outrageously extreme, permit me to quote a passage in an editorial from the very same *Christian Century* three years before when the publication was under different editorship. "The worst mistake the new [Eisenhower] administration could make, short of plunging the world into atomic war," the *Christian Century* pronounced editorially, "would be to attempt to send an ambassador to the Vatican." [5] When sending an ambassador to the Vatican can be regarded as the Number Two Calamity to the Universe, it would seem that "Protestant paranoia" is not too strong a term.

But if we can speak of "Protestant paranoia," we must not forget the corresponding affliction of Catholics, which the *Christian Century* editorialist very aptly calls "Catholic claustrophobia." If many Protestants reveal the effects of a desperate anxiety over a threat of loss to their accustomed status, Catholics are status-anxious in another sense, in the sense of being anxious over the preservation of their newly acquired status.

They feel hampered, closed in; they are suspicious and touchy, discovering everywhere evidence that their highly prized, newly achieved status is not being properly or adequately acknowledged by the "others"; in this, curiously enough, they are very much like the famous "Texas millionaires," who too feel that their newly achieved status is not being adequately recognized by "intellectuals" and "society snobs." Catholics still uneasy in the new tripartite scheme of American life are easily tempted to self-assertiveness and to assuming postures of uneasy superiority. All along the line, they tend to overcompensate.

Here again it is not necessary to extend the argument. If we take these phrases, "Protestant paranoia" and "Catholic claustrophobia," as no more than figures of speech, we must recognize how apt they are in describing the attitudes of large numbers of Protestants and Catholics in the present changing religio-social situation. It is out of these attitudes that the strains and tensions emerge which characterize religious group relations in this country today. In this supercharged emotional atmosphere, almost any question of social policy may easily become a matter of bitter conflict and hostility.

But within this situation of strain and tension, there are profound differences of attitude, almost as profound as the over-all situation itself. The first, and perhaps the most significant, kind of difference is the difference of generation. It is widely known that the younger people of all religious groups show a far less hostile attitude, a far less rigid attitude, than do the older people of their communities. This is often set down to their youth, which is supposed to keep the young people more "flexible," or to their education, which is supposed to render them more "tolerant." Whatever truth there may be in these allegations, they cannot point to the main factor. For if it were only youth, there would be no long-range shift, what with the younger people becoming older and therefore allegedly assuming less "flexible" attitudes; but there definitely is a long-range shift. Nor, if it were simply education, would there be any difference between the younger people and their elders of the same educational background; but there is a difference. The explanation must be sought somewhat deeper.

Every election year since 1940 (as well as at points in between), the American Institute of Public Opinion (Gallup Poll) has asked the same question: "If your party nominated a qualified man for the presidency this year, and he happened to be a Catholic, would you vote for him?" Here is a breakdown by age groups of the 1956 returns:

	21–29	*30–49*	*50 and over*
Yes	83	79	62
No	14	17	31
No opinion	3	4	7

At the same time, let us examine the long-range trend:

	1940	*1956*
Yes	62	73
No	31	22
No opinion	7	5

Anti-Catholic bias has been, and is, considerably lower in the youngest age group than in the oldest. At the same time, too, such anti-Catholic bias was considerably lower among the people as a whole in 1956 than it was in 1940. And, in 1960, a Catholic President was elected, for the first time in our history.

It seems to me evident that the younger people see these things in a rather different way from the older; and this less biased attitude, if we can call it that, persists after they become older. It appears to be not so much a matter of age as of the religio-social climate of opinion in which the mind had been formed: the older generation came out of a Protestant America, where Catholics were largely regarded as foreigners and outsiders; the younger people have come out of a three-religion America, where Catholics are "our kind of people" and are Americans like us.

On the issue of federal aid to parochial schools, a Gallup poll conducted in 1949 indicated that "the greatest acceptance of the Catholic argument . . . was to be found among young voters of all religions." Very much the same was revealed in a survey (as yet unpublished) of public opinion in a New England town, which had become more than half Catholic in the course of less than thirty years. There was a great hue and cry about the "Catholic menace" in that town, but the survey indicated that it was largely limited to Protestants, and Jews, over 45 years of age. Very few of the younger people saw any menace; they were well aware that Catholics were multiplying in the town, but they refused to be thrown into a panic by that. Their characteristic response was: "So what? we're all Americans, aren't we?"

Martin Marty found something very similar among Lutheran groups in the Midwest. Here is how he is quoted in *The New York Times:*

The Rev. Dr. Martin Marty, a noted Lutheran pastor, author, and editor, made an observation that had cropped up in other interviews in the south and midwest in the last month. It was that in the churches themselves, it was primarily the older generation of Protestants who were raising cries against a Catholic for President. The younger generation, he said, is not so dead set on preserving the old Protestant domination. . . .[6]

In other words, the older Protestant America is passing; but it is naturally only the younger generation which is having much success in adjusting itself to a post-Protestant three-religion country. This is one of the chief reasons for the present exacerbation of tensions; but it is also a very good reason for expecting a considerable alleviation of these tensions in the coming years. For, as the younger generation, formed in a three-religion America, comes to constitute the mass of the nation, those attitudes that are now the special attitudes of the younger generation are bound to become the dominant attitudes of the American people. In this lies our best hope; but it is still a hope for the future.

Generational differences are not the only differences worth noting. It is a familiar fact that Protestant-Catholic relations are best and most amicable on the highest theological levels, where a genuine religious dialogue is beginning to emerge. Anti-Catholic bias among Protestants, and anti-Protestant bias among Catholics, would seem to be worst among those whose religious life is most primitive, and is most indiscriminately identified with the local culture. Or perhaps a qualification ought to be made; the most virulent anti-Catholicism is to be found among secularistic-minded "liberals," for whom Catholicism still represents Voltaire's l'Infâme, the quintessence of "dogmatic," "institutional" religion to be fought in the name of Enlightenment.

As Peter Viereck has well put it, "Catholic-baiting is the antisemitism of the liberals." The Kennedy campaign, for a time, disrupted this syndrome; but recently it has been showing signs of recovering its old vigor, easily fusing with the more common anti-Catholicism long endemic in this country.

III JEWISH-GENTILE RELATIONS

A word now about Jewish-gentile relations, before I attempt to bring these various threads together to a conclusion. Although there are a number of communities, particularly in suburbia, where gentile-Jewish relations exhibit the same kinds of tensions as characterize Protestant-Catholic relations elsewhere, it seems to be generally agreed that what is usually, though I think inaccurately, called "anti-Semitism" is today at the lowest ebb in our history. It is hard to explain just why this should be so, but I will venture a guess or two.

It seems to me that something happened during the last World War that produced a sharp change in the American mind. In that war, we faced Hitler not only as the national enemy, but as the incarnation of evil, and the name of that evil was "anti-Semitism" or "racialism." Since the war, Americans, especially younger Americans, have been very uneasy about anything that smacks of race or ethnicity; gone is the minstrel show that had become so much a part of American entertainment; gone, too, are the lusty old ethnic jokes — what survives, at least in public, is a pale and genteel imitation of the genuine article.

Anti-Semitism has come to be regarded not merely as unenlightened, but as positively indecent, and, what is more, un-American, as well. Even those who harbor anti-Semitic feelings — and there are, of course, many millions of such people in our country — find it difficult to acknowledge it even to themselves, let alone to others. As I say, anti-Semitism — at least, overt anti-Semitism — has become un-American. This development has been considerably aided by the fact that, in the course of the past generation American Jews, even more than Catholics, have, in increasing numbers, become solid, well-educated, American-minded Americans.

Jews, on their part, especially the older generation, still retain something of the older attitudes, expressed in an almost neurotic defensiveness. Jews still see themselves, in fact, most threatened by Roman Catholics, though recent political and social causes have thrown them together quite closely. And Jews, particularly the spokesmen of Jewish institutions and organizations, seem to insist on thoroughgoing separation of church and state, that is, on the thoroughgoing secularization of public life. This attitude is shared even by Jews who are themselves deeply religious in their private lives.

This curious duality, which has brought Jewish organizations in repeated conflict with Roman Catholic and much of the Protestant opinion, seems to be due to the conviction, widely held though not often articulated, that because the western Jew achieved emancipation with the secularization of society, he can preserve his free and equal status only so long as culture and society remain thoroughly secular. It is easy to understand these fears; and it is easy to see how they engender that curious "Jewish schizophrenia," which has puzzled many observers — Jews, religious, even orthodox in their private life, yet radically secularistic in their public activity. This duality is bound to become more and more difficult to maintain in present-day America, with its very high valuation of religion; indeed, considerable sections of the newer generation of American Jews are beginning to find the negativism of this attitude unreasonable and unviable, and are searching for new approaches that will bring them closer to the main body of the other two religious communities in the United States.

I have said that anti-Semitism, at least overt anti-Semitism, is today at an all-time low; and that perhaps the major factor in bringing this about is the deep moral impact of the war against Hitler. However much we may welcome this development, there is one aspect that might give us pause. The extraordinary prudishness of Americans today on matters of race and ethnicity would suggest that there is involved a very considerable repression of quite contrary impulses. If such is the case, there may be storing up now great quantities of resentment, which, though for the time being repressed, may someday break through again in more virulent form. It might perhaps be better for the American Jew if all remarks about Jews were not so nervously taboo in decent American society. The repression is too close to the surface to be comfortable.

I know that these scattered remarks about Jewish-gentile tensions are inadequate; but actually we know very little about the situation, except one or two large-scale generalizations. In any case, I think it can be taken as a fact that when we speak of religious group conflict in this country today, we speak primarily of Protestant-Catholic conflict.

IV SOME CONCLUSIONS

What do these remarks add up to? To me, it seems that they add up to the conclusion that sociologically what we have in this country today are really three religious minorities linked in a trifaith system. I know that, according to the 1957 Census survey, Protestants constitute over 66 per cent of the population, Catholics nearly 26 per cent, and Jews only 3.2 per cent; other estimates put the Protestant proportion even higher, nearly 70 per cent.

Yet, by and large, American Protestants feel and act as though they were a minority, just as Jews, with only 3.2 per cent, feel and act as though they were one of three. This formula, one of three, is precisely what I have in mind. When I say that all three are minority groups, despite statistics, I mean that all three — Protestants as well as Catholics and Jews — are coming to see themselves as involved in a continuing interplay of group interests, aspirations, and pressures in a situation where no single one of the groups can any longer hope to dominate the other two, and in which each group recognizes itself as inextricably linked with the others, for better or for worse.

Each group develops its characteristic form of minority-group defensiveness; each has its own image of itself, and correspondingly, its own stereotyped caricature of the others; each has its own notion of its particular virtues, and each has its own tale of grievances about bias and discrimination. Each sees itself as the best expression of American ideals and values, but each is ready to acknowledge the existence, and even the legitimacy, of the other two in the totality of American life.

The tensions and conflicts we are concerned with emerge out of this triple minority system, which falls in so well with the socio-religious communalism we have seen arising in this country today. In the context of a never sleeping minority-group defensiveness, every question of religious or social policy is transformed into an "issue" of group conflict, and thereby removed from the realm of serious, judicious discussion. Such is the case with the so-called "school question," with the birth-control question, with the question of the proper use of ecclesiastical power in politics, and with a score of other questions where religion so obviously impinges upon social policy.

It can only be hoped that the disturbing emotive factors, so powerful today, will diminish with the fuller development of current trends; and that a time will soon come when "Protestant paranoia," "Catholic claustrophobia," and "Jewish schizophrenia" will no longer be the apt characterizations of the minority-group attitudes they are now.

In that happy day, perhaps, the religious and social questions that now serve merely as battle-cries in religious group conflict, will receive the attention they deserve. For they *are* serious and important questions, touching on a variety of moral and social concerns and interests. They involve the religious communities, but do not necessarily set one against the other; in short, though they are religious questions, they do not necessarily have to become questions of religious conflict.

For, basically, the trifaith religious pluralism that characterizes mid-century America makes for national unity and cohesiveness rather than for division and disruption. All of the three groups are now American groups, committed to essentially the same American values, seeing things in essentially the same American way.

Group diversity and group interplay are of the very essence of our kind of democratic society, which (in principle, at least) abhors every form of uniformitarianism and totalitarianism. And it certainly augurs better for our national unity to have three American groups, all at the center of American life, than to have one group claiming to be the nation, with two other large groups relegated to an "outsider" position of foreignness and inferiority.

Despite the frequent bitterness and extravagance of our religious group conflict, it still remains a fact that the strength of our system resides in its pluriunity, in its capacity to comprehend diversity in unity, and to preserve unity in diversity. And in the America of today, this means a pluriunity of religious communities.

NOTES

1. George R. Stewart, *American Ways of Life* (New York: Doubleday, 1954).
2. For a fuller discussion, see my *Protestant, Catholic, Jew* (New York: Doubleday-Anchor Books, 1955).
3. Gerhard Lenski, *The Religious Factor* (New York: Doubleday, 1961), pp. 326–7 (emphasis mine).
4. Editorial, *The Christian Century* (October 19, 1955).
5. Editorial, *The Christian Century* (December 31, 1952).
6. *The New York Times* (September 19, 1960).

JOHN R. BODO

The Pastor and Social Conflict

What is a pastor's responsibility in the presence of social conflict?

The goodly fellowship of the prophets "bids him speak" a word from the Lord. He remembers the Beatitude, "Blessed are you when men revile you and persecute you and utter all kinds of evil against you falsely for my sake. Rejoice and be glad, for your reward is great in heaven; for so men persecuted the prophets who are before you" (Matt. 5:12).

On the other hand, the expectations and beliefs of the congregation may be radically different. A prominent citizen of Georgia stated recently:

> If their advocacy from their pulpits (in which they are, in the last analysis, the paid guest speakers) becomes sufficiently obnoxious to their listeners to cause a substantial decline in attendance and gross receipts . . . the clergyman mustn't be too surprised when the church fathers arrange for his transfer to more favorable climes.[1]

These, then, are the two poles between which our exploration must range: the pastor as a prophet of the living God, prepared to suffer, if necessary, for proclaiming and doing the will of God as he perceives it; and the pastor as "paid guest speaker," employed by the congregation to preach the Gospel as they understand it.

This tension between prophetic integrity and popular expectancy is always present, at least latently. For instance, racial conflict may be absent in an all-white church in an all-white suburb. However, the tension is there because the pastor knows that this condition is unjust and that he should speak to it. On the other hand, the members of the congregation know that he knows and either fear or desire that he might say and do something about it.

Our task, then, is threefold: first, to examine the pastor's role conflict as a prophet on the payroll; second, to point out certain strictures in his situation which prevent him from exercising truly prophetic leadership; and, finally to suggest ways to set him free from these strictures so that he may be able to function as a prophet even while on the payroll. It is our conviction that the pastor must participate in social conflict, both as the leader of his congregation and as a citizen of his community.

I THE PASTOR'S ROLE CONFLICT

If the pastor's role were defined only by such historic exemplars as the prophets or by the formal statements of pastoral responsibility which may be found in the constitutions of the various denominations, there would be no role conflict. However, the pastor's role is also defined by the culture, insofar as the Christian community and the secular community intermingle and overlap to a degree which makes it indeed justifiable to talk about a "religious establishment" in America [2] or about an "American religion" vaguely resembling the Christian faith.[3]

The pastor's role, then, is defined by a variety of factors in the culture. For one thing, it is defined by the prevailing image of the minister. This may range from Peter Marshall to Oral Roberts, from the Rev. Mr. Mackerel of *Mackerel Plaza* to Billy Graham.

It is defined also by his predecessors and by the other pastors serving churches of the same denomination and/or in the same community.[4] From these varied derivations we have the paradox of a ministry garlanded with prestige but significantly lacking in influence upon the great social issues of the day.

The prestige of ministers was graphically demonstrated by at least one nationwide survey of the post-war era which revealed that "forty per cent of the American people regard religious leaders as the group "doing the most good" and most to be trusted.[5] On the other hand, the pastor's lack of social influence has been amply documented. An important study of ministerial roles does not even refer directly or indirectly to the prophetic or "social change agent" function of the minister. Floyd Hunter's *Community Power Structure* includes a spontaneous listing of "influentials" by a systematic sample of the white population of Atlanta which failed to yield the name of a single clergyman; even in the Negro sub-community just one pastor was named.[6]

Gerhard Lenski does, indeed, find that religion is more of an influence in the shaping of people's familial, economic, and political decisions than might have been expected; this does not clearly relate to the pastor's leadership, however. In fact, Lenski concludes that the influence of religious leaders has been greatly over-rated. The rank and file of church members are not significantly influenced in their social thinking by their ministers, although they are still profoundly influenced by the "tribal" or class mores of their religious sub-communities.[7]

Whose fault is it that the Protestant clergy by and large do not exert social influence? It is not altogether the fault of the congregations, whose members, we may assume, want only "safe" pastors, good "chaplains to the *status quo*." The fault lies, in large part, with the churches and with the ministers themselves.

For one thing, from the standpoint of legitimizing social concern in the churches, doctrine has been miles ahead of practice for the last fifty to seventy-five years — and practice does not seem to have gained much on doctrine. Washington Gladden, writing in 1898,[8] and Robert Clyde Johnson, writing in 1961,[9] pleaded in almost the same words for an "instrumental" view of the Church. They plead that the church's chief business is to serve the world, that is, to lead the members in service to God and man in the world, and that all the internal program of the church must be justified with reference to this primary goal. One may ask, however, how closely the average member today accepts and practices this view of the church. Does he not rather conceive of the church as one of the institutions in the community to which he pays dues in exchange for certain services? And if the members do not know any better, someone has surely failed to inform them!

In the second place, the churches have failed to exorcise from their thinking and operation two images of the minister which get in the way of his doing his proper job as a prophet of God. One is the "exemplary image," the image of the pastor as a "full-time Christian," setting a moral example for his people which will relieve them of their equal responsibility for the outreach of the church, whether in personal evangelism or in social action. The other blocking factor is the "representative image" which stresses the pastor's role as the people's representative before God. Thus a Southern Baptist seminary professor writes:

> A mixed emotion comes over most ministers when they realize that they symbolize and represent a *specific congregation of people*. The definite form of a pastor's ministry is greatly affected by the history, traditions, the personal opinions, even the passing whims of this group of people . . . Therefore a Christian pastor . . . must have confidence in his congregation; he must believe in their essential integrity. He must be committed with a clear con-

science to the major objectives, principal teachings and operational strategy of the church to which he accepts a call. The time to clarify this loyalty is *before* he agrees to become their leader.[10]

Some prophet indeed! One recalls the seminary senior who went to be interviewed by the pulpit committee of a church which he wanted and which wanted him. All went well until one of the members of the committee asked for his views on a recent strike in the city. He offered his views with evangelical candor, and the interview was promptly terminated with a cordial, "Don't call us, we'll call you" sign-off. Needless to say the present pastor is one hundred per cent "representative" of his congregation!

We conclude, then, that any role conflict which the pastor feels and suffers with respect to his responsibility for prophetic leadership cannot be blamed solely on the laymen. They have not been tutored in the prophetic dimension of the gospel but have been allowed rather to confront its demands for social justice only occasionally and then largely in generalities. They have also been left undisturbed in their faulty imagery of minister and ministry. On both counts the clergy are at fault.

The pastor as a rule does not even know how to evaluate his prophetic witness or lack of witness, because:

> The institutional structure of the Church, within which ministerial role obligations are determined, specifies a set of evaluative criteria to which he may compare his performance as manager of the religious enterprise. It does not so specify comparable criteria by which to evaluate himself as an agent of community reform and change on controversial issues.[11]

This is a crucial distinction. We can *count* members, dollars and buildings. We have not learned to weigh or to evaluate influence for social justice. Thus the Protestant Churches of America, or, rather their ministerial leaders, continue to acquiesce without protest in a number of inherited strictures. If these were understood and removed, pastors might be released for effective participation in social conflict. They might serve as prophets of the Lord rather than as muzzled employees of the congregation.

II STRICTURES UPON THE PASTOR

In describing the strictures which limit the pastor in the fulfillment of his prophetic function, we will use, as an informal frame of reference, the three vows of the Roman Catholic religious: obedience, chastity, and poverty. The intention is not to suggest that we imitate the Catholic system, in whole or in part. It is rather to discover whether the "secular" freedom which has long been claimed by the Protestant ministry may not be, in effect, nearly as restrictive as the avowedly rigorous discipline of the Catholic religious.

1. *Chastity.* What does the Catholic vow of chastity — or the celibate state without a vow — suggest? It suggests that for the sake of his calling to the "higher order" of Christian life, the priest must be willing to do without a wife. *How medieval!* we exclaim. But wait a moment! The following paragraph is by a Protestant about Protestant pastors:

> Social pressures among Protestant churches today almost demand of a minister that he be married. So universal is this demand that occasionally theological students depend upon this external motivation for the selection of a mate rather than upon inner devotion to the woman they marry.[12]

And further:

> The divorcee (whether he is remarried or not does not seem to matter) is so consumed by his inner fears that he cannot do the work of a pastor . . . Furthermore, it is next to impossible for a divorcee to be called by a congregation when there are so many happily married pastors available.[13]

Whatever we may think of these comments, one thing is sure: we have made our own bed — the marriage bed has become a kind of prison from the standpoint of prophetic leadership. For a married minister is simply not as free to participate in social conflict as a single minister is. The whole *Gestalt* of the parsonage presided over by the minister's wife militates against a prophetic ministry. It stands for domestication — in every sense of the word.

Professor William Douglass' nationwide study of the minister's wife cites one "first lady of the parsonage" as saying:

> A minister's wife has a whole congregation to love and call hers. And she is also blessed with the services of the best doctors, dentists, and other professional men in the community and often free of charge.[14]

It is not hard to see why the husband of this "first lady" might be more vulnerable to pressure from his influential members than an unmarried fellow-minister.

Another example: when unknown members of a far right organization in Southern California recently decided to persecute a Lutheran pastor for participating in anti-rightest meetings, they did not ambush him in a dark alley. They preferred to bomb his home — and narrowly missed injuring his wife and children.

We may conclude, then, that the Protestant clergy are almost as much "under oath" to marry as the Catholic clergy are pledged to chastity, and that, if this stricture — or stereotype — were removed, many pastors might be saved from the burden of semi-compulsory marriage and be set free for a more boldly prophetic ministry.

2. *Poverty*. The resignation of private property and income makes the Catholic religious leader wholly dependent upon the hierarchy for his support. Even the "secular" parish priest must live in the rectory where all his living is provided for him. While he does receive a token allowance to spend as he sees fit, he is not permitted to engage in any remunerative outside activities.

This dependence of the Catholic religious leader upon the hierarchy has its compensations, however. Being economically secure, he is immune to economic pressure from his congregation. It is at this point that his Protestant counterpart is most vulnerable, and his vulnerability increases with the number of his children.

Ministerial discounts constitute only the mildest threat of pressure. A greater threat resides in the acceptance of fees or gifts for "special services." The dilemma of the underpaid pastor is delightfully illustrated by an entry in the diary of Reinhold Niebuhr, written at the age of twenty-six:

> I'd better get started on this whole fee question, and make an announcement that I won't accept fees for anything. I think I'll except weddings, however. It will just make a scene when the groom or best man shyly crosses your palm with a bill and you make a righteous refusal. They will never understand. Marriage is not a sacrament, anyway. Then, too, it's fun getting a little extra money once in a while. But isn't marriage a sacrament? [15]

The extent of the sacrifice which any pastor would have to make if he adopted a strict no-fee policy is almost beside the point. What matters is the effect of the practice on the image of the pastor. It is difficult to "prophesy" while receiving tips from one's clientele!

A far more severe stricture on the pastor's freedom to exercise prophetic leadership is involved in his living in a house owned by the congregation. Beyond the obvious disadvantages of the parsonage "goldfish bowl," there is the plain social fact that any citizen who is not a home owner does not have as much of a voice in public life as a home owner does. Any pastor engaged in the struggle for equal access to housing for Negroes knows that hardly a day will pass without some attack upon him on this score. "It's easy for you to talk," he will be told. "You have nothing to lose. You don't own your home!"

The conclusion is obvious: the Protestant pastor is on the payroll of his congregation which is likely to be governed by socially conservative businessmen. He is largely independent of the hierarchy of his church, although the hierarchy may retain a degree of control over the economic arrangements affecting his employment. On the other hand, the hierarchy is generally helpless to sustain him against economic pressure from his congregation — or even to remove the strictures placed upon him by such symbols of his "employee" status as we have been discussing.

It may be worthwhile to note that at least one denomination of mainstream Protestants — the Quakers — manage not only to survive institutionally but to offer an impressive example of prophetic witness without a paid clergy. This amazing anomaly, which harks back quite literally to the apostolic church, may have far-reaching implications for our problem.

3. *Obedience.* The Catholic religious leader is wholly subject to his "ordinary," i.e. the bishop of his diocese. So is the "secular" parish priest. This, of course, goes very much against our Protestant grain.

Two things must be noted here. First, in any organization there must be leadership, a system of authority and power to carry out the purposes of the organization. The alternative to such a system of formal authority is not freedom but unrecognized power wielded irresponsibly.[16] In other words, a tighter hierarchical structure, with larger powers vested in superior officers and a clearer chain of command, does not necessarily impair freedom. On the contrary, it may enable both freedom and organizational effectiveness, provided there is a constitutional framework with democratic processes of election and safeguards against arbitrary exercise of office. Thus the symbol of "obedience" need not mean more than effective discipline in a system of visible authority and appropriate power.

Second, when there is little or no discipline, obedience will be given to the person or group with the heaviest artillery. In the case of the Protestant pastor, this means the congregation — focused in the Board of Trustees. As for the hierarchy, it can be counted on to administer *punitive* discipline to pastors guilty of conventional moral transgression, but its administration of *supportive* discipline is, as a rule, pitifully weak. The "peace of the church," interpreted in terms of increase of membership and a smooth flow of money into both congregational and denominational treasuries, generally overrules considerations of prophetic witness or even ordinary justice to the prophetically oriented pastor.

There are exceptions, of course. Funds set up by several denominations for the relief of pastors for compliance with the Supreme Court decree in the South have been significant, though minimal, symbols of the rewards of the right kind of "obedience." The rule, however, is a safely institutional orientation rather than a boldly prophetic one, because not only the pastor but the program of the denomination itself is at the mercy of the ultimate "employer," the layman, according to whose age-long expectations religion is "mainly a matter of social establishment, of the taken-for-granted order of society." [17]

III WAYS AND MEANS

Against the background of the pastor's role conflict and the specific strictures which inhibit his functioning as an agent of social change, we must raise the question, "What can be done?"

Ways and means to attack the problem appear on two levels: a denomination may make changes in its polity; or other possibilities may be implemented by the pastor or a local group of pastors of the same or of different denominations.

To be sure, responsibility for action on these two levels overlaps. Any denomination depends for legislative proposals and policy formation largely upon its clergy leadership. Any pastor is defeated from the start without at least the approval of his denomination. Recognition of this also helps to answer the question whether prophets are born or made. The answer is "both-and." Some pastors with a great prophetic gift will break through the inadequacies of their training, conquer their role conflict and overcome the strictures inherent in their situation — all by themselves. However, for every one so gifted and so courageous, there are probably forty-nine whose more modest gifts of social awareness and courage could be developed — and institutionalized — if today's prophetic "remnant" in the ranks of the clergy were to initiate the structural and ideological reforms necessary for the encouragement of responsible prophecy.

1. *What the Denominations Could Do.* To this end, there are a number of things which the denominations can do.

(a) For one thing, the barrage of denominational pronouncements on public issues can be kept up. A survey by Glock and Ringer has shown that while such pronouncements do not materially affect the laity, they do significantly encourage and support the clergy. They note:

> Ministers' attitudes clearly tend to reflect church policy. Where the Church has elected to compromise on an issue, the minister has also compromised with the views of his parishioners. However, where the Church has taken a partisan point of view, the minister generally identifies with this view, *despite the opposition of a substantial segment of his parishioners.*[18]

(b) Second, denominations must learn to select and treat public issues on the basis of objective concern for the whole body politic, with the least possible admixture of churchly self-interest.

Protestants tend to criticize the Catholic church for showing undue concern for issues in which the self-interest of the church is clearly at stake, as in government aid to parochial schools. However, the Protestant denominations have been similarly tainted. Kenneth Underwood points out that the difference is not so much in the presence or absence of self-interest as in the degree of political effectiveness. For instance, the Catholic clergy justify and promote charity gambling because it builds Catholic schools and hospitals. The Protestant clergy oppose charity gambling because its proceeds strengthen the competitor. In the conflict which ensues, charity gambling carries the day, thanks to the superior organization and realism of the Catholic clergy.[19]

In order to counteract this legacy of self-interest and the skepticism which it has bred, we would propose that the denominations take two steps, one of a short-range, the other of a long-range nature.

We would propose a network television series, sponsored by the National Council of Churches, showing facets of the checkered record of the churches with respect to social justice: the churches divided over the slavery issue; the original hostility of the churches to organized labor and their gradual, belated endorsement of the labor movement; the largely uncritical — though increasingly critical — endorsement by the churches of all the wars our nation has fought thus far. There must be no breastbeating, nor any pretence that all is well now since we are confessing our past sins. This should be an historically honest, artistically persuasive, and theologically solid documentary series!

We would propose, further, that the denominations begin to take steps toward ending the tax-exempt status of the church. If this step proved too drastic, somewhat the same effect could be obtained by a voluntary levy of "taxes" on church property — in the form of donations to at least the local governing body. Such action would speak to the world about the meaning of the Incarnation as a ton of sermons could not.

(c) Third, the denominations can greatly strengthen the position of the local ministerial organization or ecclesiastical judicatory. We need some effective equivalent of the Catholic *diocese,* in which

> . . . the diocesan priest is a sharer in an apostolic ministry and in the apostolic responsibility of the bishop, not merely by reason of the fact that he is placed in charge of some individual congregation or parish within a diocese but primarily by reason of his membership in the bishop's own *presbyterium.*[20]

This vesting of effective power close to the point where power must be exercised is something for Protestants to ponder. Local area organizations should have more power and exercise it more frequently. They should also have their boundaries redrawn so as to correspond as far as possible to political communities. Thus revitalized, they would be more effective in assisting pastors in prophetic witness.

(d) Finally, since economic pressure on the pastor is probably the greatest deterrent to his exercising prophetic leadership, the denominations can initiate changes to mitigate the pastor's economic dependence on his congregation. To this end we would propose that all contributions by members be given to the local area organization (e.g. the presbytery, the district, the classis) and that the budget of each local church be determined, upon proper consultation and concerted planning, by this organization. This is not as un-Protestant as it may seem; the Swiss Reformed Church, for instance, operates on this basis.

Upon this change in the system of church support hinge three further suggestions: first, that all pastors should be paid a *gross salary,* from which they would then secure and pay for their own housing, travel, books, etc., subject to adjustment on the basis of expenses occurred in the line of duty; second, that over a period of, let us say, five years, the salaries of all pastors should be *equalized* at some appropriate level to be subsequently modified in relation to the current cost of living; and, third, that the denomination should levy upon all its pastors a special tax — say two per cent — graduated at first, then, after a salary equalization, uniform. Revenue from this special tax should establish: (1) *a permanent "defense fund"* for the assistance of pastors who are facing economic reprisals from their congregations for taking a stand on any issue on which the denomination has officially committed itself; and, (2) *a permanent "frontier fund"* to help train both pastors and key laymen for experimental social action ministries in support of positions officially adopted by the denomination.

2. *What Pastors Can Do.* Beyond these things which denominations can do to strengthen the position of the prophetically oriented pastor, there are certain ways in which a pastor can equip himself for vigorous leadership in social conflict.

(a) In the first place, a twofold change in the pastor's thinking is needed. For one thing, he will have to make his peace with the fact that the will of God cannot be fully known in relation to any specific problem, social or personal. He will never be absolutely certain that he is not being at least somewhat mistaken in the name of God; and, theologically speaking, this is only right and proper! Reinhold Niebuhr observes:

> It is not because we are Protestants rather than Catholics that we must dispense with moral norms which rely on deductions and assume fixed forms and "essences" to guide us in our responsibilities in the varied configurations of history, but because the circumstances of a technical age shift the essential conditions of life so rapidly that we must determine the right action in unprecendented situations by a true analysis of the factors and interests involved in our choices. In short, we are forced as never before to be thoroughly pragmatic in our *proximate norms,* holding still to the general standard of the love commandment for our *ultimate norm.*[21]

Again, the pastor will have to make his peace with the presence of antagonism in his own heart, especially with respect to members of his own church. He will have to dispose of the cliché about "hating the sin and loving the sinner" and instead so saturate himself with the Biblical meaning of the love of God that he will not feel guilty about honestly hating the member who uses the church to support the John Birch Society or who threatens to stop his pledge when his pastor takes a stand favoring racially integrated housing. To admit the existence of "holy hatred" while seeking genuine reconciliation without surrender in the name of a false peace is an art which, with God's help, can be learned — and must be learned — for the sake of truly prophetic leadership.

(b) In the second place, any pastor who wishes to exercise effective leadership in social conflict will have to face some unwelcome facts about the alleged influence of preaching. Peter Berger's caustic comment, "The most common delusion (of pastors) is that what they preach on Sunday has a direct influence on what their listeners do on Monday," [22] jibes only too well with the growing number of tests to which preaching is being submitted.[23] But Berger goes one step further by pointing out that "the person listening to the minister is a radically different one from the person who makes his economic decisions the next day. . . . What the church has said to him might conceivably have a bearing on his private life. But it is quite irrelevant to his involvement in public life."[24]

We do not advocate the discontinuance of preaching, though much can be said for fewer, shorter, and better sermons. From the standpoint of social influence, however, at least two questions must be raised. First, to what extent must a pastor be prepared to offer a solution to the controversial problem with which he would deal in the pulpit? Traditionally he would hardly dare raise the issue unless he thought he had an answer. However, we would agree with William Lee Miller that "fewer answers and more of the right questions" would be far more effective.[25] Second, how should a sermon on a controversial public issue be timed? Generally, pastors have waited for the crisis to break — at the sacrifice of any chance of real effectiveness. We would offer the advice of Walter Rauschenbusch:

> The best time to preach on political questions is *before* they have become political questions . . . Jesus said, 'If your righteousness exceed not the righteousness of the Scribes and Pharisees, you are not fit for the Kingdom of God.' In the same way, I say, unless you see righteousness before the world sees it, you are not fit for the kingdom of God.[26]

In the third place, there is no substitute for the pastor's personal participation in secular organizations, which serve either as barometers or as thermostats of the socio-political climate. At the very least, his active membership in such organizations will be an effective supplement to his preaching and teaching ministry. Insofar as his time is limited, however, he will do well to choose wisely. For instance, if he can make room for only two such organizations, he may deliberately select the local service club, to which most of his businessmen officers and members belong, and a social action organization like the ACLU or the NAACP or the AAUN, which most of the businessmen are likely to "view with alarm." By securing their friendship through the former and rattling their complacency through the latter, he can develop a bifocal ministry of truly 20/20 vision!

Finally, any pastor who hopes to exercise prophetic leadership in the midst of social change and conflict, will have to learn to keep his expectations realistically humble. For one thing, the whole "instrumental" view of the church as primarily the servant of God's purpose of righteousness in the world is so grossly misunderstood — and so hotly opposed when set forth in specific terms — that it is irresponsible to expect too much of any congregation, especially in the mainstream Protestant denominations where the doctrine of "self-service" rather than of "world service" has been so long and so deeply entrenched. As a matter of fact, unless the renewal of congregations is assisted and stimulated by experimental ministries beyond the level of the congregation — or even of any single denomination — the outlook is dim indeed. Fortunately, such ministries, whether patterned after the Laymen's Academies of Germany, or taking their cue from the French "worker priest" movement, are slowly multiplying.

Again, humble expectations are in order because of the very "religiousness" of our culture in which "martyrdom is much more likely to come with a shrug of indifference than with a cry of hatred." Therefore, Peter Berger adds,

> We must dismiss heroic fantasies of either variety — both of that which imagines the glory of victory and of that which eagerly expects to be crucified. Our contemporary society is unlikely to give us either satisfaction.[27]

In closing, let us suggest that the thesis of this chapter and the propositions which it sets forth do not necessarily negate present attempts to bridge the gap between clergy and laity. It is true that in the New Testament KLEROS and LAOS referred to the same group of Christians and that we should work for the day when, as H. Richard Niebuhr put it, the congregation becomes the minister while the minister, as "pastoral director," directs them in service to the world.[28]

NOTES

1. Quoted in Franklin H. Littell, *From State Church to Pluralism* (New York: Doubleday, 1961).
2. Peter Berger, *The Noise of Solemn Assemblies* (New York: Doubleday, 1961).
3. Martin E. Marty, *The New Shape of American Religion* (New York: Harper, 1959).
4. Samuel W. Blizzard, "The Parish Minister's Self-Image of His Master Role," in *The Minister's Own Mental Health,* edited by Wayne E. Oates (Channel Press, 1961), pp. 112–4.
5. Quoted in Will Herberg, *Protestant, Catholic, Jew* (New York: Doubleday, 1955), p. 64.
6. Floyd Hunter, *Community Power Structure* (Durham: University of North Carolina Press, 1953).
7. Gerhard Lenski, *The Religious Factor* (New York: Doubleday, 1961), pp. 309–10.
8. Washington Gladden, *The Christian Pastor and the Working Church* (New York: Scribner's, 1898), pp. 45–6.
9. Robert Clyde Johnson, in *The Church and Its Changing Ministry* (Philadelphia, Office of the General Assembly, United Presbyterian Church in the U.S.A., 1961), p. 40.

10. Wayne E. Oates, *The Christian Pastor* (Philadelphia: The Westminster Press, 1951), p. 40.
11. E. Q. Campbell and T. F. Pettigrew, *Christians in Racial Crisis* (Washington, D.C.: Public Affairs Press, 1959), p. 92.
12. Wayne E. Oates, *The Christian Pastor* (Philadelphia: The Westminster Press, 1951), p. 47.
13. Ibid. p. 48.
14. Quoted in *Time,* April 26, 1960.
15. Reinhold Niebuhr, *Leaves from the Notebook of a Tamed Cynic* (New York: Meridian Press, 1957), p. 25. The date of the entry is 1916.
16. This is the thesis of Paul B. Harrison, *Authority and Power in the Free Church Tradition* (Princton: Princeton University Press, 1959).
17. Berger, op. cit. pp. 11–12.
18. Charles Y. Glock and Benjamin B. Ringer, "Church Policy and the Attitudes of Ministers and Parishioners on Social Issues," privately circulated, 1961, p. 16.
19. Kenneth W. Underwood, *Protestant and Catholic* (Boston: Beacon Press, 1957), pp. 130–33.
20. Joseph C. Fenton, *The Concept of the Diocesan Priesthood* (Milwaukee: Bruce Publishing Company, 1951), pp. 13–14.
21. Reinhold Niebuhr, "The Christian Moral Witness and Some Disciplines of Modern Culture," in *Making the Ministry Relevant,* edited by Hans Hofmann (New York: Scribner's, 1960), pp. 49–50.
22. Berger, op. cit. p. 37.
23. For instance, at the Institute of Pastoral Care at Cranbrook, Michigan, directed by Reuel Howe.
24. Berger, op. cit. p. 57.
25. William Lee Miller, "On Meddling," in *The Churches and the Public* (Santa Barbara: Center for the Study of Democratic Institutions, 1960), p. 40.
26. Quoted in a *Rauschenbusch Reader,* edited by Benson Y. Landis (New York: Harper, 1957), p. 146.
27. Berger, op. cit. p. 139.
28. H. Richard Niebuhr, *The Purpose of the Church and Its Ministry* (New York: Harper, 1956), p. 82.

MARTIN E. MARTY

Epilogue: The Nature and Consequences of Social Conflict for Religious Groups

"Man is a wolf to man." Certainly this dour comment on human nature, borrowed from the title of an engraving by Georges Rouault, seems to apply in this study of "Religion and Social Conflict." Whoever reads the preceding chapters cannot but be impressed by the ways in which religion often brings not peace but a sword in society.

He who takes seriously the surveys of the various authors must be bewildered. Where are the consolations of religion? Where is the comfort it promises; the peace that passes understanding—what has happened to it? Does religion exist only to dislocate man from his environment, to pit him against his brother, to make him so uneasy with human life that he indulges in unsettling protest? Conflict often grows out of selfishness: is the presence of conflict in religious elements in society a witness to the fact that we have learned little from our religions?

These valid questions can be blunted or softened somewhat by recalling that these authors were assigned a study of but one aspect of religious life. A symposium could be gathered, for example, to discuss what religion has to offer to the peacemaking elements in society. One could be devoted to a theological statement on peace with God or to a social statement on peace among men. These authors were asked to isolate one element, and to survey the whole religious enterprise in society from the viewpoint of conflict. Inevitably, therefore, conflict will assume a larger-than-life place in their views. A laboratory worker who is assigned the task of studying only tissues in which malignancies are present would be ill-advised to believe that malignancy is the only reality. So, too, the contributors to this volume know that one could select other aspects of religious experience, and conflict would take a quieter or more secondary role among these aspects.

However, a still more disturbing strand may have disquieted the reader. He may approach this volume expecting the authors to detect signs of conflict associated with religion. That was their assignment. But he would hardly be prepared to see so many of them ready to live with conflict or, even more, to say some good things about it. Where they are not speaking well of conflict they seem to be still less satisfying in that they cannot make up their minds.

Is conflict good or bad, in the religious realm? Should men work to eliminate it or to incite it? What would society look like if religious groups eliminated conflict between themselves and came to nearly perfect adjustment in relation to their environment? Or, on the other hand, what would religion and society look like if the highest premium were set upon the values of competition and creative conflict?

These disturbing questions are raised on page after page of apparent ambivalence and ambiguity. The reader grows restless; he wishes someone could enter the symposium and with one emphatic decision and one great shout sweep away the hesitancies of the writers and give religious people a clue as to what they should do about the future of conflict. Sebastian de Grazia has portrayed how psychologically detrimental it is for the maturing person to be torn between the co-operative and competitive directives of society. Eventually the person chooses *anomie,* the rejection of standards and norms of conduct. It would be psychologically detrimental if all sermons sounded like this symposium; if they were devoted chiefly to analysis of positive *and* negative factors in both conflict and its minimization. What is the use of such a survey? What, after the sermon, are we to do with it?

Almost all of the authors have explained why comment on these questions in this last chapter is so difficult. A doctrinaire or an absolute answer which would suggest how all values and energies shall be directed is obviously impossible. Perhaps that has been the main point of the implied "sermon" in this book. The authors seem to be telling us this: if conflict disappears there will be no reform and revolution, no self-purification and examination of motives, no progress or setting of new goals; there will be only a shallow and untested tolerance which holds everything to be true because nothing is true. Men in society will grow bored and apathetic. They will yawn and despair and die. On the other hand, if conflict is enhanced and uncontrolled, a beast will be turned loose in the streets. Men wear the stitch of horror on their hearts in the twentieth century; violence, unchecked, bears new weapons in our age. The people who live in the decades which produce Nazis and Communists, Black Muslims and White Citizens' Councils, concentration camps and atomic weapons, do not often need reminders of the dangers of conflict. Each author in this volume, whether he deals with a case study (race, political extremism) or with theoretical issues and social methods, stands between these two alternatives.

We might reflect for a moment on some of the alternatives in the light of the various presentations.

After reading Robert A. Nisbet we can ask: without conflict, would technology produce those factors which enlarge the scope of human activity? Yet there must be some control on the competition of technology: complete automation or total nuclear destruction are the generation's final parables in this respect.

Charles Y. Glock causes us to ponder: if no one felt deprived, if no one felt motivated to form religious groups to meet the problems of deprivation, what check on complacent and settled religious groups would there be? How would religion reform itself? Yet, if one were to agitate and stimulate people into a sense of their deprivation, their own self-devised sects would exist mainly to divide men and to keep conflict alive.

Charles S. McCoy has eloquently depicted leadership in a time of racial change. If these leaders abolish conflict will there be advance or progress for the Negro, or will he be consigned to a sort of slavery for another one hundred years? On the other hand, conflict turned loose to eliminate racial evil brings with it the unlovely face of violence and all of its problems.

One can see benefits in the conflict brought by the right- and left-wing extremists of Ralph Lord Roy's description. They can, in some limited way, stimulate political debate and make more feasible and attractive a range of possibilities between them. But should either group prevail and should they be permitted to introduce their own kind of conflict, the civil dialogue as such would be cut off and civil society could be cut down.

Seymour M. Lipset produces almost a book in itself in the chapter on religion and politics. The telling conclusion to be drawn from his interpretation of historical and sociological evidence is this: men live in two realms; the two are often in conflict. Men band together in churches and political parties to provide social integration. Religion serves to adjust people to the complexities of political life. On the other hand, the religious record in politics has enlarged conflict there and the political issue in religious groups has ordinarily been disruptive.

Benjamin A. Reist would bring us to the same conclusions on a completely different set of grounds. What has happened in Lipset's America was predestined to happen, Reist implies, because Americans even in their most unreflective moments, have been bringing certain theological issues to bear in their political decision. Reist also makes clear that America has been best served when that contribution has been reflective, drawing on resources in the Protestant Reformation. These resources work, on the one hand, for the good of the commonwealth; on the other they forbid men from letting either realm prevail — so conflict of sorts is inevitable and creative.

Will Herberg deals directly with the theme of the book when he discusses the peculiar configuration of religions in American society. If conflict between them disappeared, people would lose their identities and be blurred into a vague "Americanistic" understanding of life. On the other hand, in order to build up loyalties within pluralism, competition and conflict are often so valued as to create meaningless and self-defeating pluralism.

Finally, John R. Bodo poses the religious professional in this setting. The minister of the gospel is called to work to eliminate conflict between men and yet he cannot be obedient to the heavenly vision without introducing conflict, for human affairs stand in need of judgment from without. Through the frail instrument of words and action, the minister is to represent a community which bears witness that it listens to a Word which serves to judge and to redeem a community from without.

Including the introducer of the theme, Robert Lee, we have then nine (and now ten) authors, working from a variety of disciplines and in a variety of styles; men who did not meet each other in working on this project and who in many instances have never met each other. They were not asked to edit or tailor their materials to suit the conclusions of other contributors. Yet there is considerable homogeneity of viewpoint, almost as if our times (modernity) and our place (a pluralistic, free society), imposed a kind of logic on thoughtful people who must deal with co-operation and competition/conflict as elements in society. We detect the emphatic importance of this kind of logic when we contrast the observations or conclusions of these authors with those of people who are impatient with ambiguity, who are obsessed with the idea of cutting through complexity.

Thus the cult of toleration and brotherhoodism, the genial pacifiers and single-minded reconcilers, would come to an entirely different conclusion from that of these ten contributors about the inevitable and even creative aspects of conflict. Members of this cult — we may surmise — would no doubt stimulate conflict with the members of this symposium, in the interest of removing conflict! But from the other side, picture the reaction of the fanatic or those of prophetic temperament; picture the deprived, as they set out to form new political or religious mass movements. What would they make of men who see benefit in political decision and in compromise or conciliation? Does not compromise mean denial of a heavenly truth?

I have tried in what follows to sketch what I believe to be some of the lessons to be derived from the "middle way" between the tolerationist and the fanatic particularist. No doubt every individual carries away different directives from a sermon, and so no one else's list would be the same as mine. If my conclusions are wide of the mark I can further plead that the professional reputations of most participants in this symposium depend upon the degree to which they can refrain from sermonizing, so I have had to dig into their presuppositions, their tentative conclusions, their hints, their implicit instruction. I shall risk all by being explicit as possible and numbering my conclusions so that they can become propositions for debate; then I shall take new refuge in reflection upon some of them — where I can again be properly distant and ambiguous!

1. *A free society cannot exist without the element of conflict;* in fact, it is free because there is freedom for conflicting viewpoints and forces — including religious ones. James Madison's comfort in the "multiplicity of sects" still holds good.

2. Since conflict always is based in part in the quest of men to see their own selves and their own interests protected, it has *an unlovely and uncreative side*. This must be recognized and the "tragic sense of life" which learns to cope with this inevitability is an asset in a society which, being free, does not admit facile solutions.

3. It is the task of reflective people in a society to see *creative elements in both co-operation and conflict;* to listen to the inherited intuitive wisdom and "common sense" of the people as they face the alternatives; to learn particularly from the humane and religious tradition how to isolate and relate these elements; to attempt to communicate a way of life that lives with both.

4. In a free society, *the liberty which allows for competition shall not be permitted to become a license for unrestricted conflict.* To keep it from becoming so is primarily the task of those custodians of civil society in the political and religious order who bear responsibility for large groups of people. For example, in educating the young, it is important to depict reasons for choice between competitive and cooperative directives. One must not confuse maturing people with meaningless alternatives in order to stimulate jungle-type business competition, intentionally divisive religious sectarianism, or artificially exaggerated political

extremes. In other words, the arts of legitimate compromise must be learned early.

5. Those bearing some responsibility for groups of people and those who help form opinion in a free society do well not only to learn to *analyze* the competitive and cooperative alternatives; they must *move to therapy*. But therapy also must be patient. The social scientist is not to be the manipulator of people; he does not come with "Plan D" from the Pentagon or "Answer 73-B" from the sacred Scriptures. When in doubt he may do well to do what a physician does: help a patient learn to live with an ailment that cannot be cured; wait and watch and see; experiment; let things get worse so that they can get better. The attempt to pacify every kind of minor conflict may abort society's "natural" ways of healing and can often stimulate major conflicts.

6. In times of quiet, however, political and religious leaders may do some anticipating. They can *educate*. They set up "hot lines" of communication should conflict develop; they can *establish patterns of trust*. The arts of compromise and the attempts to consolidate gains in human relations are not incompatible with loyalties to their own groups or obedience to higher visions.

7. Reflective and responsible people in religious and secular realms can work, in season and out of season, to *seek new levels of human relations*. There is no good reason why groups of the deprived must always wait for situations to grow so bad that they must revolt in violence. Our societies have indeed developed extensive patterns of institutional life which work constantly and creatively to help eliminate the causes of unnecessary human conflict. The religious institutions which are looking for new mission can find almost unlimited work in this field!

8. Since competition and cooperation have been "in conflict" before our time and in places other than our own, religious people can *learn from those elements in their past which promote creative civil life*. At the same time, they do well, in a society of many sources, not to impoverish their own generation by isolating but one element of the past and making unreasonable claims for the religious monopoly in human solution. Not only "The Judeo-Christian" tradition is theirs — whatever it may be, and whatever it is, it has many sources and founts. Egypt is also theirs, as are Greece and Rome, Renaissance and Enlightenment, and today's para-Christian resources.

9. Conflict *of some sort* or other is inevitable when the faithfully religious person is confronted with the need "to obey God rather than men" in a concrete area of human choice. It is the task of religious leaders not only to develop this sense of faithfulness but also to depict legitimate

"sorts" of conflict and to help develop the wisdom which discriminates between what it is to which God calls man and what it is that man defends in the name of God, though it is only his own pretense at stake.

10. Some sort of *"communion of saints" consciousness* can develop in political and religious groups. In such a collective life there can be a sense in which people who must work for conflict (the prophet, the reformer, the revolutionary) can be supported by those who share many of his goals (obedience to a divine vision) but not his immediate social situation. We think, for instance, of the Christian in a placid northern suburb who by seeking identity with and being patient with the southern Christian Negro leader can help him achieve his goals with less stridency and agitation than if he must also "fight" many who ostensibly share his goals. Conversely in the matter of cooperation and minimizing conflict. The militant Catholic or Protestant, interested in one area of self-protection (e.g., the pocketbook in church-state affairs) can learn from the irenic and ecumenical leaders in each community who work for inclusive harmonious goals for the good of civil society and in response to religious motivation.

None of these ten points have shown a way to eliminate the elements of conflict in society. To do so would be untrue to the nature of the problem and certainly untrue to the intention of the authors of this book. I should like to join them, having summarized their positions, with my own independent reflections which relate to the ten suggestions.

Social conflict, in Max Weber's definition, implies a relation in which activity is "oriented intentionally to carrying out the actor's own will against the resistance of the other party or parties." [1] The "actors" in this book have been Mr. Glock's "deprived" or Mr. McCoy's racial leaders; Mr. Roy's political extremes fighting against moderation and Mr. Lipset's and Mr. Reist's citizens of two kingdoms; Mr. Nisbet's technologically oriented men or Mr. Herberg's religiously oriented ones; Mr. Bodo's clergymen who may be fighting for Divine Truth or denominational statements or against an element in the Ladies' Aid. In every instance we have seen that *conflict emerges when an individual or a group acts against resistors.*

In the instance of religious conflict we may observe, along the lines of the proportion of this book, that most of it may not originate with two religious parties or "actors." One of the parties may be non-religious, as in the instance of technology, race, etc. But in a society where religious goals are consolidated in large institutions and organizations, one cannot go far without coming into conflict with some goal or ideal of one or another. If most conflict in our society is of other than religious origin as it "acts," this is not necessarily a compliment to religious groups. It may mean that they are not necessarily adept at working concordantly — they are not stimulants in society at all; their idea-patterns simply need not be reckoned with so much as their vested interests.

In the eyes of many, except when seen in its vested-interest form, the vitality of religion has been so dissipated that it could not be the agent of social change or of conflict if it desired to. Religion, to be the "actor," must have some of the energy of a young, generative social movement. The fanatic Ivanov depicts such an energy in first-generation Marxism in Arthur Koestler's *Darkness at Noon:* "How anything more wonderful ever happened in history? We are tearing the old skin off mankind and giving it a new one. That is not an occupation for people with weak nerves." [2]

Rather than serving as the *actors,* religious groups in our current society ordinarily serve as the *reactors.* They may hitchhike on secular elements of change (e.g., the 1954 Supreme Court decision on racial equality) or ride the bandwagon of secular appeal (in much religious public relations). Thus assigned and assenting to an ordinarily passive and quiescently conservative role, they may assume that they are thus established and stable in character in the midst of change and conflict. Chesterton's warning applies to those thus seduced: it is a mistake to think that "if you leave things alone, you leave them as they are. But you do not. If you leave a thing alone you leave it to a torrent of change." [3]

The consequence of social conflict *for* religious groups is change *in* religious groups: whether by torrent or trickle, the change is real and inevitable. Now we can look summarily at current cultural expectations which relate to religion and social conflict.

MINIMIZING CONFLICT IN THE RELIGIOUS SETTING

1. It is a legitimate task of religion, viewed from one aspect, to *minimize conflict* for the individual and the group. There is an assigned therapeutic intention of all "long-pull" (church-type?) religion which serves to aid the individual in organizing his reactions and responses. As such, the *religious warrant* may serve as an insulator, as a buffer, or as a separator in the face of diffuse and chaotic social change.

In this sense religion may be thought of as providing a kind of cuticle (not a cocoon or a callus, let us hope) which gathers, covers, and protects nerve endings so that not all stimuli must be dealt with in equal proportion. This function can contribute to the sanity, strength, and wisdom of man. It can be the function of religion in its organic, familial, primary, and automatic clusters, its *Gemeinschaften,* or in its *Gesellschaften,* with their more specific and pointed, if not pragmatic intentions. The family *exists* to provide a resource for identity, nurture, protection; the association can be *formed* to provide one. In many contexts, these are legitimate.

2. Today there is a *societal expectation* extended to the religious group. It is, in the public majority's eyes, to be established and conservative, a protector of existing values, and hardly responsive to (and certainly not responsible for!) social conflict. This is the theology of common-sense America, heard delineated in subway and taxicab and barber shop. The religious groups exist only to bring peace. They are dismissed if they introduce or respond to elements of social conflict.

In a sense this is a paradoxical expectation. Americans want both nonconformity and absence of conflict; they want the excitement of the mistresses of change without surrendering the sameness and security of the double standard that demands one wife. When churches are in conflict they are seen to be contradicting their own highest ideals — and these are usually reduced by the public to superficial categories of harmony and love. When they are agents of religio-secular conflict they are criticized for meddling in the non-religious.

3. If there is a religious warrant and a societal expectation, an *historical achievement* must also be cited as an occasion of interest in minimizing social conflict and its impact on religious groups. The long memory of man, whether from an African Genesis or from the pre-Cain and Abel generation, through inquisitions and intolerances, is too full of bloodshed and inhumanity for us to set up past models of conflict as examples for our age. The relative quiescence of American life is a *concordia* that can be seen as a divine gift or a beneficial human achievement. One does not lightly ridicule the groups which absolutize the movements toward minimization of conflict through brotherhood, reconciliation, or blurring of distinction.

4. Seen against this, however, is a less flattering view of religion which, as implied in the introduction, sees it to be *quiescent* because it is unexciting and possibly belief-less. It is necessary to ask whether there would be absence of conflict if America were a revolutionary society, if the nation produced ideologies and aggressive stances and if its religions were to take on intense character. The total absence of competition and conflict may mean the ultimate stage of ennui, or the end of man and his aspirations.

5. There may be a religio-political aspect to the hopes for minimiza-

tion of conflict. The quiet state can be the result of a quasi-official *establishment* of religion as part of the security of national life.

Gerhard Lenski, in *The Religious Factor,* surprised many sociologists by reverting to Weber instead of Marx to report on religious response in a large American metropolis. He found that religion *does* have a large influence on economic, political, and racial decisions in American life. However, it is ordinarily so safely located that its influence is "grooved" and predictable. It echoes in the main the safer national aspirations; it is in its consensual forms part of the glue that holds together American life; it is the lubrication of the national process. Such a location has many advantages, and religious groups will not lightly forego them by adopting prophetic stances in the face of social conflict.

We may quote the too-familiar words of the late C. Wright Mills:

> If there is one safe prediction about religion in this society, it would seem to be that if tomorrow official spokesmen were to proclaim XYZ-ism, next week 90 per cent of religious declaration would be XYZ-ist. At least in their conforming rhetoric, religious spokesmen would reveal that the new doctrine did not violate those of the church. As a social and as a personal force, religion has become a dependent variable. It does not originate; it reacts. It does not denounce; it adapts. It does not set forth new models of conduct and sensibility; it imitates. Its rhetoric is without deep appeal; the worship it organizes is without piety. It has become less a revitalization of the spirit in permanent tension with the world than respectable distraction from the sourness of life. In a quiet direct sense, religion has generally become part of the false consciousness of the world and the self.[4]

These words would strike Christians in some parts of the world as strange. Iron Curtain, Bamboo Curtain, new nationalisms, anti-colonialism, competing ideologies: these have dislocated the church in social conflict and rapid social change. Yet other critics, taking a cosmic if over-simplified view, would say that even these reactions of religious groups are limited, last-ditch efforts in a mature secular world. This leads to a final observation:

6. Also contributing to the minimization of social conflict (though it may serve to heighten intra-religious competition) is a self-serving *institutionalism,* an introverted ecclesiological obsession in Christian circles. This self-concern is usually seen as the result of illusions about the world and a cover-up for unbelief. Karl Heim notes:

> The Church is like a ship on whose deck festivities are still kept up and glorious music is heard, while deep below the water line a leak has been sprung and masses of water are pouring in, so that the vessel is settling hourly, though the pumps are manned day and night.

In such a view, social conflict rarely relates to religious groups because they are dismissed as irrelevant. What enemy of the good must reckon with them? There may be furious but meaningless activity within religious groups, but this may belie the total lack of impact they make on the realm of potential social conflict. Religious groups may produce, to the eye of the potential "actor" in conflict with their historic goals, merely the agencies of boredom, the *daemon meridianus,* the *acedia* that anticipates the end. (We are told that some Melanesian tribes died out solely because of boredom.)

If one clusters together the bowling leagues, the fish-fries, the bazaars, the building campaigns, the denominational claims, the charts and graphs and preoccupations of any group beyond his own, and then asks what aspect of it must excite, challenge, antagonize, or counter the "actor" in today's dramas of social conflict, it is possible to empathize with critics in this camp.

SOCIAL CONFLICT: MOSAIC AND PALIMPSEST

Despite these pressures for or tendencies toward the minimizing of conflict, evidences of conflict are apparent and the potential for future conflict is present and must be dealt with. Even groups that move with a minimum of belief and clarified intention may crowd each other, causing conflict. This is true when the multidimensional aspects of our concerns are kept in mind: religious, racial, technological, class, and political groups overlap and counteract. Each seeks its place.

The airplane passenger is aware of the essentially mosaic character of the earth's land use: forest, pasture, tilled field, city. But the human element in today's world changes that essentially static, spatial, diagrammatic picture. It is *interactive* and *intersectional,* if not authentically *interpersonal;* it is *pluralistic,* and the pluralistic elements come into conflict with each other.

To change the picture: there may be social representations of the human mosaic but these are translucent. They are superimposed as in the fashion of the palimpsest. The outlines of the layers do not perfectly coincide and are not exactly congruous. There are different stresses on different layers; this causes expansion or contraction in erratic patterns; it pushes new elements into contact. The Dutch sociologists have begun to speak of their compartmentalized society in an ostensibly intersectioned world as *Verzuiling,* "columnization," organized in parallels of pillars or columns (J. A. A. Van Doorn, I. Schöffer, and others). There is not merely a homogenizing, a blurring of modern life. Separate, superimposed, conflicting groups remain in ever more complex relation.

Many of these groups may be quiescent and atrophied (the *Turnverein,* the Grange, the Socialist party). Others may suddenly erupt (the Radical Right, a World Order Study Commission). Sometimes out of new ideas or new starts, sometimes out of insecurities and boredom, reformers, traitors, activators, strangers, "actors" reappear as mutations or transformations. "If anything ail a man so that he does not perform his functions, if he have a pain in his bowels even . . . he forthwith sets about reforming — the world." [5] Such new action is a stress, a disruption, with new potential for social conflict.

Missionary activity, propaganda, legislation, war are characteristic patterns of social change which induce conflict; they are intersectional occasions in a complex-sectioned modern world. Very often some of the mosaic character remains apparent. The new action or idea seeks a place. This can be seen in most eras of human or religious change. It is most apparent when change occurs among the nearly-like. Notes Heini P. Hediger: "The further apart two species are in the zoological system, the less is one a threat to the territory of the other. Every species occupies its own mosaic system, with units of specific size." [6]

Social conflict is most potent in civil war, between brothers, or between emerging groups of once shared but now competitive orientations. Each such move or stress occasions some sort of territorial demarcation. In the time of prehistoric man the pattern of demarcation was presumed to follow first optical lines, then second, acoustical lines, then third, olfactory lines, and fourth, a combination of lines. One "camped on" his new territory and occasioned new conflict. The German word for "possess," *besitzen,* implies this "sitting on."

Is one cynical if he observes that intra-religious competition (such as between Catholic and Protestant for a place in the American tax structure, or between Protestant and Protestant as each shoe-horns into the new housing developments) is not a significantly different pattern from the most primitive competition? To the outsider, in the latter instance, the olfactory may appear to predominate as the pattern for territorial demarcation! Again, the stench and potency may be most violent between the species that are nearer each other.

What was true of the pre-historic mythos is apparently true of existing primitives or simple societies. The researches of Clyde Kluckholn bore this out.[7] Now one sophistication is observable. When certain biological and social processes were universally human and conflict came about through differences in refined cultural traditions, Kluckholn observed that antagonisms between culturally differentiated units were almost always based upon "one or more 'realistic' conflicts of interest and upon 'unrealistic' dislike." Tensions over realistic conflicts are often insoluble except at the price of deprivations to members of one group or by unsatisfactory compromises (compensation, shifting of group goals, or extinction and absorption).

The "realistic" demand for place belongs to the tragic sense of history; the "unrealistic" is the proper domain for real gain by the social scientist or human engineer. But Kluckholn had modest expectations for the minimization of conflict:

> When it comes to large canvases, the social scientist would still do well to abide by what has proved a helpful rule in many medical cases: "do nothing. Sit tight. Watch. Prepare for probable developments but do not interfere with natural forces making for recuperation until you are sure that action will be helpful or, as an absolute minimum, do no harm." [8]

What such a view would do to Brotherhood Week it is hard to guess.

In the forms of Biblical religion the "actor" is disruptive, causing realistic stress. The Children of Israel in bondage, because they had no hope, were quiescent, established, located. A Mosaic interruption of this mosaic pattern is symbolized in the Exodus and the conquest of a Promised Land. Social conflict is characteristic of the unfolding of the history of salvation among the People of God in the Old Testament. Exile has as disruptive a character as exodus, and the prophetic word in its vital stage is a dialogical interruption of the securities of diagrammed, mosaic patterns: people gathered at solemn assemblies or worse, in the groves of Baal.

In the new covenant an even more disruptive element is seen to be creative. There is little minimization of necessary or "realistic" conflict in the word, "I did not come to bring peace but a sword." Had Jesus been content to call disciples out of the world to form conventicles or religious enclaves social conflict could have minimized. He sought no "place" to lay his head. But he sent them back into the world as a salt, a ferment, a leaven, as moving lights. The stresses of such inter-sectionality led to his being edged out of the world in the suburbs of Jerusalem and eventually to the charge that these disciples had indeed "turned the world upside down."

As Christians found their place under the imperial sword they became actors in the arena of social conflict on a new set of terms. "However incompatible the spirit of Jesus and armed force may be, and however unpleasant it may be to acknowledge the fact, as a matter of plain history the latter has often made it possible for the former to survive."[9] The conversion of the barbarians, the reversal of the Muslim invaders, the suppression of the sects such as the Cathari and Waldensians, the Inquisition — all these illustrate the potency of "unrealistic" combined with "realistic" factors in social change and conflict.

The Reformation settlements were also based on the quest for place in the mosaic of the West. Neither Luther nor Calvin wholly renounced the use of force to gain sway. This is important here only for its background as an original intention for American Protestant life. Nathaniel Ward wrote in 1647:

> I dare take upon me, to be the Herald of New England so far, as to proclaim to the world, in the name of our Colony that all Familists, Antinomians, Anabaptists, and other Enthusiasts shall have free liberty to keep away from us, and such as will come to be gone as fast as they can, the sooner the better. . . . He that is willing to tolerate any religion . . . either doubts of his own, or is not sincere in it. . . .

But the New World produced a New Thing: It produced a formal political resolution which served to minimize the impact of social or religious conflict on religious groups. This is not the place to assign credit for the happy achievement: to dissenters, to the practical situation, to the Enlightenment, etc. Instead, one may observe that in Kluckholn's terms "unrealistic" conflict was minimized through political structures and "realistic" conflict had less impact on religious groups because of it. All in all, religious groups have been largely protected by the mores of national life and their own pluralistic situation.

It is assumed in American life that the residue of social conflict as it affects religious life will be creative. Thus Justice Oliver Wendell Holmes: "the best test of truth is the power of the thought to get itself accepted in the competition of the free market." The real patron saint of the settlement was James Madison. Security "consists . . . in a multiplicity of interests and . . . in a multiplicity of sects."

Those who seek only reconciliation or reduction of competition and conflict, and those who press for concord and harmony on any terms may do well, but they at least must be constantly informed of the price they pay for the absence of conflict or for the realistic dealing with realistic *and* unrealistic causes. Some of the earlier stages of the ecumenical movement seemed to work merely for this kind of reductionism. The earlier version of the National Conference of Christians and Jews, with its avowed disinterest in anything controversial or the genteel aspects of the "pluralistic dialogue," may serve to reinforce the sacred notions of our national Shinto by covering up realistic points of potential conflict on larger scales.

The Herbergian Protestant-Catholic-Jew triple-melting-pot inside a hospitable national attitude (not the entity but the observation is Herberg's responsibility!) is not necessarily the final way-station toward complete removal of conflict. The impending years of battle over federal aid to parochial schools, the religious aspects of Radical Rightism, the pockets of anti-Semitism illustrate this. Reinhold Niebuhr points out in *Moral Man and Immoral Society:*

> The extension of human sympathies (toward ever-larger communities) has resulted in the creation of larger units of conflict without abolishing conflict. So civilization has become a device for delegating the vices of individuals to larger and larger communities.[10]

I am just enough of an "early Niebuhrian" not to share too much of the expectations of the minimizers of conflict depicted earlier in this chapter.

In the face of the dangers of future social conflict, many turn with expectation to the social engineers. It is hoped that they can provide the laboratory for experiment: how much competition and conflict is necessary to keep pluralism healthy and dialogue alive and truth open? How much is necessary to tip the balance to barbarism and the destruction of pluralism and concord? Unfortunately the universe does not hold still for observation and the new societies do not provide petri dishes for growing cultures that will interest the academies. Decisions must be made *in via.*

We have to this point shown several naïve and sophisticated types of pressures to minimize social conflict in relation to religious groups and then looked at some historic manifestations of conflicting realities.

CONFLICT: PLUS AND MINUS

Since we live our lives in the dialectic of quiescence and conflict and shall have to make the best of each along the way, it is now valid to summarize by pointing to some *assets and liabilities of conflict.*

1. Conflict was seen to be a *tribute to the youth and vitality of a religious group.* It welcomed social conflict from without and was the occasion from within. This was characteristic of the sect, if by sect we are not content to speak only of the withdrawn but also of the missionary, the propagandizer, the aggressive.

2. Conflict was a *tribute to the intensity of conviction of a group* as it set out to seek a place in the territories of earth and mind. The end of

ideology, the rise of unbelief, however was not seen automatically as the assurance of the absence of future conflict. When the unclean spirit has gone out of a man, he passes through waterless places seeking rest; and finding none he says, "I will return to my house from which I came." And when he comes he finds it swept and put in order. Then he goes and brings seven other spirits more evil than himself, and they enter and dwell there; and the last state of that man becomes worse than the first. Modern totalitarianisms and post-ideological fanaticisms illustrate this.

3. A third asset of conflict is the *contribution to nurture and definition.* Karl Löwith has observed the clarity of Christian definition and motive for discipline and strengthening in those periods when the Church faced heresy, heterodoxy, or formal challenge. Absence of conflict leads to apathy, ataraxia, acedia.

4. Finally, conflict provides opportunities for creative realignments that provide *protection against worse conflict.* An illustration: the American Jew is better off in ripely pluralistic America than he was in Protestant or would be in Protestant-Catholic America. In many instances he will ally with the avowedly secular, for good reason. He will share needs, instrumental actions, and goals with such orientations and will ally his own with them, thus gaining protection. He may in the process be contributing to one more new "bloc" seeking place, but the alliance is pragmatic and fluid, not ordinarily ideological.

Conflict has liabilities. *Annihilation, bloodshed, insecurity, anxiety, hunger* may be among them. Again, the history of man points to more reasons for allying with the reconcilers than stimulating the competitors. But conflict also produces subtler liabilities. It may prolong the illusion of realistic reasons for difference between groups. American denominationalism is often theologically irrelevant, prolonged because of competitive loyalties and conflicts. This may do a disservice to truth. Peter Abelard had to flee secretly from the Abbey of Denis one night when he told the monks in passing that the abbey had not been founded by St. Dionysius Areopagitica. The monks felt he would "take away the honor which was their greatest glory," their claim for superiority and the basis for their competition in the religious world. Or social conflict may affect one aspect of a religious group and destroy its reality, create illusions about its purpose. Consider the bees:

When a honeybee is collecting honey from a flower its abdomen can be removed and the forward end of the bee will go on drawing honey, only to have it discharged into the open air. This is a failure on one part of an animal to take into account what the condition of another part is. The illustration is not a perfect one because, even if the forward end had wind of what had happened to the rear, it is possible that there would still be nothing better to do in the circumstances. But at least the unfortunate bee will serve to illustrate a failure of communications which interferes with the coordination of action. The interaction of the parts of an organism so as to conserve the identity of the whole we may call integration.[11]

Purposeless activity in one part of the religious organism may render absurd the rest of the organism. Conflict can serve as the stimulus. The agent or "actor" outside the group is thus an unnecessary but vivid threat. Henry Sidgwick in the *Ethics* describes this: "The denial by another of what I hold true, impairs my confidence in it." This issues in erratic action. Finally, it may cut off the main purpose of the religious group. Necessity to compete or stave off conflict may reduce witness and service. The war dance, "emotional reinforcement of action" supplants the purposeful walk.

MEANS OF MINIMIZING

On balance, conflict based on "unrealistic" interests and unlimited conflict based on "realistic" interests can be described as more harmful than creative. A number of means for minimizing or ending conflict present themselves. Behind the decision it is necessary to take a theological attitude toward the presence of conflicting elements in society and religion. As a Protestant I do not find it necessary to disagree with Father John Courtney Murray's summary: "Religious pluralism is against the will of God. But it is the human condition; it is written into the script of history. It will not somehow marvelously cease to trouble the City." [12]

Some would have it that pluralism (religious and ideological) *is* the will of God because it is the human condition. Others argue that the human condition is the will of God as we find it, and that one cannot speak critically of pluralism at all. Others theologically criticize any version of defense of pluralism. We are given only the choice to deal theologically with the human condition — this is how the cards of history are dealt. Pluralism — and hence potential conflict — will not disappear in the City of Man.

Specific conflicts between specific political, racial, class, social, economic, technical *and* religious groups can be ended or minimized in many ways if this is the desired goal. First is *annihilation*. One alternate capitulates to the other, to contribute to the ending of pluralism. The second is *conditional surrender*. Social conflict represents overpowering forces; religious groups surrender to the extent that they are not really any longer free, but they retain an identity. Complex forms of *compromise* are another alternative. The danger here in the American Religious Establishment is mediocrity.

Tacitus writes of Tiberius: *ex optimis periculum sibi a pessimis dedecus publicum metuebat;* "he feared the best, was ashamed of the worst and chose the innocuous middle." This was the source of an imminent if not a wholly idolatrous popular religion that was impotent to judge or to save; its dimensions were cut too small. But at least there was no conflict!

The fourth pattern of changing or ending conflict is *coexistence,* hopefully of a creative type. This means more, ordinarily, than placing cushions, buffers, or neutral zones between the layers of the palimpsest or failing to have to do with others.

Members of religious groups are also members of races, classes, states and nations, clubs, organizations, interest groups; they will come into at least some forms of contact — even in the situation of *Verzuiling* — with others. They can work to find modes of coexistence. First among these is the recognition of the human condition. Many "hate" groups in America have not yet recognized the basis of pluralism. They work on the assumption that the old mosaic can be restored through static solutions: diagram, emigration, exodus, exile, segregation, curtaining off the conflicting voice. Once this possibility is denied, once it is observed that Democrats, Catholics, Kiwanians, and Jews are here to stay, coexistence (not "total victory") becomes a possibility.

A fifth form is the quest for *consensus.* Members of religious groups may explore what in the ground rules of national life, what in the shared values of various religious impulses serves to provide a common basis of life in the presence of social conflict. It is important to see that this consensus is not manufactured to serve as an ideology; it must pre-exist.

The most productive form has been the promotion of information and understanding between religious and other conflicting groups. Such an affirmation need not betray an absolute faith in the educative process as the final solution to the clash of wills. Yet, much intergroup misunderstanding and erratic response to social change has grown out of misinformation and absence of face-to-face relations. Information is a step in rendering conflict productive. Thus Don J. Hager writes:

> Social science seems to have forgotten that conflict is a form of social interaction. It relieves tensions. It forces the contending groups to modify their claims. It is often the only way that groups may express opposition to ideas and practices they abhor. Uncontrolled conflict (and violence) can be destructive, but the important task of creating and maintaining a productive social system is subverted by denying the efficacy of conflict in stabilizing the social order and advancing the commonwealth . . . The important task

is not, therefore, the indiscriminate and undisciplined elimination of conflict but, rather, the creation and preservation of devices whereby conflict can be made socially productive.[13]

The nerve cells in the human cortex, we were told long ago, number 9200 million — I am sure they have found more since. The numbers of interconnected possibilities between them are too manifold to make the mathematical statement of them meaningful. Multiply these times the numbers of minds involved in religious groups and then ask: does one know all that he is ever going to know? Are the current two choices in social conflict the only two that can present themselves? Intergroup information has been one productive means of keeping alive competition while minimizing violent conflict in the face of social change.

Finally, *fulfillment.* To some social engineers, ideologues, and brotherhood advocates the ideal earthly city is the *acedian* removal of conflict. Most religious groups hold that this occurs only eschatologically. Some (one thinks of Julian Huxley or the Christian Teilhard de Chardin) have a sufficient cosmic-reaching evolutionary vision that foresees fulfillment at an "Omega" point of social development. Huxley looks toward the development of mankind into a single psycho-social unit with a common pool of thought; the evolutionary process is provided, then, with the lineaments of a rudimentary head. Teilhard finds his Omega point in a this-worldly socio-human fulfillment in Christ. Most Christians would move with Father Murray or with St. Augustine who says "this world will never be reconciled fully with Christ within history" (and thus will not see the removal of all social conflict.)

GOD MAY WORK THROUGH CONFLICT

Where "realistic" conflict cannot be further minimized, there is the place for the birth of the tragic sense of life. Certain religious groups would, if they prevailed, usher in a kind of absolute social conflict which would disrupt the pluralistic pattern seen to be so productive. (Jehovah's Witnesses profess such a this-worldly eschatology.) Current threats more likely come from the social engineers who are unwilling to recognize the limits of the finite and are unwilling to let the religious person ultimately place his tomorrow in the hands of the deity. It is "the black envy of philosophy to be like the physical sciences" (Berdyaev) and of the social expert to be like the technologist. Georges Bernanos warns us:

Watch out! Among all the techniques there is a technique of discipline for which the mere obedience of the past is not satisfactory. Obedience used to be obtained by all kinds of empirical methods, so that we may say it was less a discipline than a moderate disorder. Technique, on the other hand, will sooner or later insist on forming its own collaborators who will belong to it body and soul, who will accept without discussion the technical concept of order, life and the reason for living. In a world entirely devoted to Efficiency and Production, it is imperative that each citizen, from his birth, should be consecrated to the same gods. Technique cannot be called into question since the solutions it imposes are by definition the most practical.[14]

Unbelief is not the protection against either future social conflict with a religious context or technological disappearance of apparent conflict; these would be alternatives within the terms of *1984*. Unbelief and technique secrete their own ideologies. They also take on a religious guise. Remember, the name of God is invoked at White Citizens' Council rallies and Christian Anti-Communism Crusades. More profound alternatives must serve as safeguards for the possibilities of creative conflict and, one hopes, limitations on its potency of violence. Practical outlets are present. Association of conflicting groups with the other's goals have been cited. But the treasury of theological resources must be explored in the new setting.

Here numbers of possibilities present themselves. The world of rapid social change and racial, political, and economic conflict is not to be written off and abandoned. It is in part a product or by-product of Christian thought and action (witness both the pseudo-Christian character of modern anti-Christian ideologies and the new nationalisms of the once-missionized colonies). It may carry possibilities for the life of God in the City of Man. God may work here, and the Lordship of Christ be asserted in unexpected places.

Theological resource minimizes conflict yet maximizes faithfulness among Christians when there is no longer an interest in apologizing for Christianity in terms of its superiority. To be a Christian is to accept what God gives in Jesus Christ; it is to seek to share this through means consistent with His servanthood. This view does away with the arguments over superiority that were born in the religious thought of the Enlightenment. It undercuts the competition and complication of witness within Christian groups. It aborts crusades and other fanaticisms.

Christians do well again to look at the dialectic of holding to the truth and yet not failing to see the partiality of the hold (I Corinthians 13: *Unser Wissen ist Stückwerk*). Then one seeks means congruent with the affirmation. Most of all, social conflict is appropriated and faced in the Christian groups with some of the basic form of God's action in the world, in the servant Jesus Christ.

One may say from the viewpoint of social science and history that ordinarily institutions do not act that way; ordinarily they do not face social conflict in the name of belief by surrendering status and prerogatives and self-seeking. This may be true: but they must at least be judged in the light of their stated intentions, in the shape of One who came not to seek His own; who came not to be ministered unto but to minister.

NOTES

1. Max Weber, *The Theory of Social and Economic Organization* (Glencoe: Free Press, 1947).
2. Arthur Koestler, *Darkness at Noon* (New York: Signet Edition, 1946), p. 116.
3. G. K. Chesterton, *Orthodoxy* (New York: John Lane, 1909), p. 212.
4. C. Wright Mills, *The Nation* (March 8, 1958), 200.
5. Henry David Thoreau, *Walden* (New York: Modern Library Edition, 1937), p. 69.
6. "The Evolution of Territorial Behavior," in *The Social Life of Early Man,* edited by Sherwood L. Washburn (Chicago: Aldine, 1962).
7. Clyde Kluckholn, "Group Tensions: Analysis of a Case History," in *Culture and Behavior* (New York: Free Press, 1962), pp. 301ff.
8. Ibid. p. 322.
9. Kenneth Scott Latourette, *A History of the Expansion of Christianity* (New York: Harper, 1937), Vol. I, p. 164.
10. Reinhold Niebuhr, *Moral Man and Immoral Society* (New York: Scribner's, 1932), p. 49.
11. Edwin L. Guthrie, *The Psychology of Human Conflict* (Boston: Beacon, 1962), p. 20.
12. John Cogley, ed., *Religion in America* (New York: Meridian, 1958), p. 40.
13. Don Hager, "Religious Conflict in the United States," *The Journal of Social Issues,* XII (1956), p. 7.
14. Quoted by Thomas Molnar, *The Decline of the Intellectual* (New York: Meridian, 1962), p. 300.